PEACEFUL PEOPLES
An Annotated Bibliography

by
BRUCE D. BONTA

The Scarecrow Press, Inc.
Metuchen, N.J., & London
1993

British Library Cataloguing-in-Publication data available

Library of Congress Cataloging-in-Publication Data

Bonta, Bruce.
　Peaceful peoples : an annotated bibliography / by Bruce D.
Bonta.
　　p. cm.
　Includes bibliographical references (p.　) and index.
　ISBN 0-8108-2785-9 (acid-free paper)
　　1. Ethnology – Bibliography. 2. Peace (Philosophy) – Cross-
cultural studies – Bibliography. 3. Aggressiveness (Psychol-
ogy) – Cross-cultural studies – Bibliography. I. Title.
Z5118.P33B66　1993
[GN378]
016.30336'6–dc20　　　　　　　　　　　　　　　93-41560

To my wife Marcia . . .
the most peaceful person I know.

CONTENTS

PREFACE

This book had its beginnings about a decade ago in Powell's Bookstore, on East 57th Street in Chicago. The semi-annual meetings of the American Library Association are often held in that city, and one year I took the No. 6 Jeffery bus from the Loop down to 57th and walked the couple blocks to the bookstore that someone had recommended. It was a perfect match of second-hand books and a tired reference librarian, a delightful afternoon escape from the flurry of meetings, exhibits, and socializing. Among the many bags of books I dragged home from that conference, and successive meetings in Chicago, I discovered some treasures: *Never in Anger*, by Jean Briggs, *The Semai: A Nonviolent People of Malaya*, by Robert Dentan, *Village Without Violence*, by Mary Buffwack, *The Forest People*, by Colin Turnbull, and *A People among Peoples*, by Sydney James. Each was an excellent read. But beyond the fun of good reading, I began to see a pattern--there are a small number of societies scattered around the globe that have achieved a substantial measure of peacefulness.

Then I found Ashley Montagu's book, *Learning Non-Aggression*, a collection of essays by anthropologists on the ways different peoples teach their children to be peaceful. Not only were there a number of additional peaceful peoples, there were other individuals who were aware of this collective phenomenon. I began a search for books describing other societies that might fairly be described as peaceful, and for additional works on the ones I already knew about.

I soon broke from the limits of my personal collection and started pursuing references in the stacks of the Penn State University Libraries, where I work. With annotated citations to books, articles, and chapters from edited volumes slowly sifting into the database I had designed, the work started growing from a pleasant hobby to a full-scale publication project. But after a few years I realized that finding and evaluating literature, carefully reading hundreds of works, taking copious notes, and writing up annotations would require years. The only way to really cover the literature of peaceful peoples was to take a sabbatical year off. Fortunately, all of my administrators up the line at the Penn State University Libraries strongly encouraged me to pursue the project. I really appreciate the supportive attitude of Jack Sulzer, Head of the General Reference Section, Diane Smith, Chief of the Reference and Instructional Services Department, Torre Meringolo, Associate Dean for Collections and Reference Services, and Nancy Cline, Dean of Libraries.

Also, the work could not have progressed beyond the bumblings of a book lover without the resources of a large research library, and throughout the preparation of this work the collections at Penn State have been a key resource. Particularly in anthropology, sociology, and psychology, I have found that an amazingly high percentage of the references I needed were already in our library, a tribute to my colleagues Helen Sheehy and Diane Zabel, and their predecessors, who have wisely and carefully developed the subject collections in those fields over the years.

No single research library collection could possibly contain everything needed for a compilation such as this. As I began my sabbatical year, Dean Meringolo suggested I should consider travel to other libraries to pursue leads and seek added inspiration. I very much appreciate his advice, and the financial support he provided, which led to productive visits to the libraries of the University of Wisconsin and the University of Illinois in the summer of 1992. Throughout the course of this work I have relied on the efficiency of the Penn State Interlibrary Loan staff, especially the borrowing unit supervised by Ruth Senior, without whom dozens of references would not have made it into this bibliography. Their work is invaluable.

Support for publication projects comes from people in many areas of a research library. The clerical staff in the General Reference Section has provided invaluable support for this work: Nancy Struble, who has a Midas touch on any computer keyboard, has turned a bunch of bytes on a little blue disc into a presentable book. We'll let others decide how golden it is. Patricia Olsen, in the midst of preparing for her own comprehensive exams, did a thorough job of editing the citations in the work. And Gwenda Lougy, the supervisor of the reference support operations, has lent her assistance on numerous occasions. They are all great people to work with and I thank them for their help.

Most of all, though, I need to acknowledge the assistance of my family, who have endured years of conversations about peacefulness and peaceful societies. How often we have discussed issues intensely, and suddenly someone asks rhetorically, "I wonder if those peaceful peoples would be discussing these points so heatedly?" (Most wouldn't!) Our son David Bonta has lived at home with us this past year while I've been on sabbatical, and he has helped me on a number of occasions with his incisive thinking about issues. Above everyone, though, I am grateful to my wife, Marcia Bonta, for her unfailing support. Without her willingness, we could not have drawn in our belts and survived on the reduced sabbatical salary; without her example, the concept of peaceful peoples probably would not have taken root and grown into this book.

Bruce D. Bonta
July 1993

INTRODUCTION

Numerous societies have developed strong traditions of peacefulness. In southern Mexico, for instance, several communities experience very little fighting, in contrast to nearby towns which have much greater amounts of violence. Anthropologists have studied these peaceful (and violent) Zapotec communities, examined their comparable histories and economic patterns, and probed for the causes of the peacefulness in some towns but not in others. Likewise, several anthropologists have examined the peacefulness of some communities in rural Northern Ireland to try to determine why they differ from nearby areas where the culture of hostility, strife, and violence is engrained.

Some peoples in all parts of the earth have developed peaceful social structures. The residents of Tristan da Cunha island, a British dependency in the South Atlantic, cherish their tradition of anarchism, reciprocal relationships, and peace. The Fipa of southwestern Tanzania now have a peaceful society, though it was highly warlike and violent shortly before the colonial period began. In India, the Yanadi people not only have no history of warfare, their mythology includes no wars. In North America, the Amish cherish their traditions of gentleness toward one another and they refuse to fight with anyone.

What forces prompted 80,000 Fipa people to completely abandon their former violence and adopt peaceful social structures? How can people like the Amish live peacefully in the heart of American and Canadian societies? What are the psychological, sociological, and religious characteristics that foster peacefulness among the Yanadi, the Tristan Islanders, some of the Zapotec, some of the rural Northern Irish, and scores of other peoples around the world? How have the histories of these peaceful peoples affected the development of their ideals? In fact, exactly what are peaceful peoples?

Peaceful peoples are societies that have managed to develop harmonious social structures which allow them to get along with each other and with outsiders without violence. Contrary to many Westerners who believe, based on their own cultures, that such societies are impossible, these peoples demonstrate that peacefulness is indeed feasible.

Many social scientists and popular writers argue that humanity is intrinsically aggressive and competitive, a condition which is reflected by the apparently warlike, destructive nature of societies. Those arguments are challenged by much of the literature on peaceful peoples. These peoples use a variety of strategies to effectively control and dissipate hostilities. Most (though not all) of them foster a spirit of cooperation rather than competition, promote sharing rather than glorifying greed, and live in harmony with the earth as well as with other people. They differ enormously from one another, and their approaches to peacefulness are a study in contrasts. Perhaps most importantly, virtually all of them believe that peacefulness is the defining characteristic of humanity.

This bibliography includes selected references to books, articles, essays within edited volumes, and dissertations in the English language that provide significant information about peaceful societies. The literature of fields such as anthropology, psychology, sociology, history, and religious studies has been combed for appropriate works. The cutoff date for inclusion of references is 1992.

Purposes of the Bibliography

Scholars and peace activists who are interested in societies that foster peacefulness have difficulty finding references to appropriate literature. Researchers investigating the peacefulness of the Quakers would probably be familiar with works on the Mennonites and other Anabaptist groups, but they might not be as acquainted with the other peaceful Western peoples, such as the Tristan Islanders. Similarly, the student of cooperation and peacefulness among the traditional, pre-literate peoples of the earth might not be aware of the peaceful societies within the Western tradition. One of the major reasons is that standard indexes and abstracts do not provide access to literature on these societies via usable subject approaches, such as PEACEFUL PEOPLES.

For example, *Peace Research Abstracts* includes extensive references on arms limitation, diplomacy, international alliances, international law, and so on, but nothing on peaceful peoples. A cross-cultural search on peaceful peoples cannot be done easily in the Human Relations Area Files (HRAF), a large collection of extracts from anthropological publications.

While HRAF includes writings about several peaceful peoples, the reference manual for the system[1] provides numerous subject headings for violence and aggressive categories but none for nonviolence or peacefulness. Thus, the user of the files can find a lot of cross-cultural materials under antisocial subject headings but none under prosocial terms.

Likewise, *Anthropological Subject Headings* includes the heading SOCIOLOGY--CONFLICT and a number of cross references from WARFARE to related headings and subheadings, but nothing for peace, peacefulness, or nonviolence. Therefore, since that work is the authority for the subject headings used in the published catalogs and indexes compiled at Harvard University's Tozzer Library--bibliographic gold mines of information about peoples worldwide--users can easily find works on conflict but not on peace, aggressiveness but not peacefulness.

Therefore, one of the major purposes of this bibliography is to serve as a source of information about the literature on peaceful peoples and the strategies they use which successfully build group harmony and ameliorate violence. A related purpose is to foster peace research on the intriguing social, psychological, and cultural similarities and differences that exist among peaceful peoples. Furthermore, the author hopes that the bibliography will promote an awareness among anthropologists and other social scientists who investigate peaceful societies of the peacefulness of peoples within the Western tradition, such as the Quakers and Anabaptist groups; correspondingly, perhaps this work will alert the students of Western pacifism and peace history about the peacefulness of the traditional, non-literate societies. Such a broadening of focus by both of these interest groups should strengthen the study of peacefulness in today's world.

Background

In 1966 the English translation of Konrad Lorenz's exceedingly influential book *On Aggression* was published in New York by Harcourt, Brace and World. Based on his own ethological research and selections from sociological, anthropological, psychological, and historical literature, he described the nature of aggression in animals and argued persuasively that humanity is innately aggressive also.

While many scholars have accepted and added to Lorenz's basic ideas, others have challenged them. Ashley Montagu, an early leader of the challengers, wrote *Man and Aggression* in 1968 (New York: Oxford University Press) which contested the points made by members of the Lorenz school. In 1976 his *The Nature of Human Aggression* (New York:

Oxford University Press) pointed to the peaceful behavior of many animals. It argued for the cooperative nature of much of human behavior and concluded that people learn either aggressive or nonaggressive behavior patterns in their societies--those are not instinctive tendencies. These debates have continued among social scientists, who have raised far more ideas and complexities than can be reviewed here.

The important point for this bibliography is that Lorenz and his followers cited aggressive, warlike peoples from the ethnographic literature in attempting to support their points, while Montagu and others refuted the arguments by citing the existence of peaceful peoples. Writers on both sides of the issue have frequently cited the *numbers* of peaceful peoples, past and present, to indicate how few there are or how many there are. Otterbein[2] did a cross-cultural study of warfare and found, out of a sample of 50 peoples, only 5 that had an infrequent level of war in the three different categories he established. Another scholar writing about aggressiveness a few years later needed to identify additional peaceful and warlike societies, and as he examined the literature on 130 more peoples, he found that 11 were peaceful.[3]

Recently J. M. G. Van der Dennen provided a list of over 150 peaceful peoples, gleaned from an exhaustive search of European and American ethnographic and travel literature, to support his rejection of the "central dogma," as he calls it, that "man is considered to be universally belligerent, and he is supposed to have been so from the very first beginning of hominid evolution." He calculates, on the basis of his literature search, that "we are left with more peaceful than warlike peoples" among the traditional societies of the earth.[4] While the existence of peaceful peoples and their numbers have been disputed among scholars, another major issue has been the problem of defining terms.

Definitions

Peacefulness, for the purposes of this bibliography, is defined as a condition whereby people live with a relatively high degree of interpersonal harmony; experience little physical violence among adults, between adults and children, and between the sexes; have developed workable strategies for resolving conflicts and averting violence; are committed to avoiding violence (such as warfare) with other peoples; raise their children to adopt their peaceful ways; and have a strong consciousness of themselves as peaceable.

A *people* is defined as a group of human beings who live in the same area, who have common beliefs and value systems, who share basically the same culture, and among whom there are substantial kinship ties. Adoption of some new members into the "people" and departure of others born from within does not affect the status of being a people for purposes of this bibliography. A "people" can number in the scores or in the millions. A commune, where most of the members are immigrants from the larger society, is not a "people" for the purposes of this work. Religious groups such as the Quakers, however, have been accepted as "peoples," even though they are now spread out worldwide. The Quakers lived in the same area during their formative years in England, southeastern Pennsylvania, and a few other locations, and their subsequent expansion has been matched by a very strong consciousness of their common beliefs and value systems.

Criteria for Inclusion of Peoples

The criteria for inclusion of peoples in this bibliography, therefore, is that they must be a people and they must meet most, if not all, of the criteria in the definition of peacefulness. This is not always as simple as it may sound. As far as evaluating whether a group fits the definition of a "people," there have been only a few problems. For instance, the Bruderhof religious communes are not included, even though their beliefs are very similar to the Hutterites, who are represented here: according to the definitive sociological work on them,[5] a substantial number of individuals and families steadily join and leave this group, so they do not really appear to fit the above definition of a people.

The problem of deciding whether a people meets the definition of "peacefulness" is not as straightforward. Anthropologists debate at length about whether or not peoples can be accepted as "peaceful." Some of these debates are the focus of works included in this bibliography, such as the ones in which Dentan and Robarchek rebut the arguments of their detractors that the Semai are not really all that peaceful.[6]

In general, if a scholar considers a people to be peaceful and provides substantial data to support that contention--and presuming that the society appears to match most of the characteristics of the definition above--then the group has been included.[7] However, peoples are not included solely on the basis of popular accounts of their "peacefulness," since the American press frequently romanticizes as "peaceful" indigenous peoples who are confronted by destruction from the larger societies that surround them.[8]

Works that discredit the peacefulness of these peoples are included in the bibliography also, as long as they provide reasonably substantial information about them. For instance, the Fore people of New Guinea are included because one anthropologist--E. Richard Sorenson--argues for the peacefulness of the South Fore until they became too crowded to move away from people with whom they had problems. However, a representation of other anthropologists' works, who describe the Fore as highly violent people, is also included.[9] Several other peoples represented in the bibliography who are, or were, considered highly peaceful by some scholars--the !Kung, the Mbuti, the Inuit, the Balinese, the Toraja, and the Zuni--have been described as violent by other writers. In some cases, such as the Ifaluk and the Semai, the arguments of the doubters do not appear to this author to be very persuasive, though these are issues that should be evaluated by readers after careful study of the literature.[10]

There is no reason to propose an absolute scale of peacefulness at one end of the spectrum and of violence at the other. The social structures among human societies are far too complicated and varied to permit such a simplification. The problems of providing acceptable definitions of "peaceful" and of related concepts such as "aggression" are very real ones that many authors address.[11] But even though defining terms is critically important, continuing, healthy debate about definitions should not stop the search for peacefulness or retard the production of a bibliography on the very significant literature related to peaceful peoples.

This bibliography is thus not intended as an authoritative listing of peoples who are certified as 100 percent PEACEFUL, though some of them appear to be extremely close to meeting that definition, if they aren't absolutely so. Most of them have some social patterns that would be considered as violent, or aggressive, or at least distasteful to those of us who are not part of their cultures. These are not utopian societies where everyone is always happy with their perfect styles of life.

For example, a number of these peaceful peoples use sorcery in different ways to harm their perceived enemies. Others treat animals quite violently. Some of the societies are highly atomistic--everyone is considered as an autonomous being--while others are tightly controlled by social hierarchies. Women have equal rights with men in some, and are completely subject to the rule of men in others. The methods used by some groups, such as the Utku Inuit (see the works by Jean Briggs), to instill in their children an aversion for selfishness and interpersonal violence may repel some outsiders. Some of the peoples practice methods of population control, such as abortion and infanticide, that are morally repugnant to many Christians. In summary, the common theme for all of the peoples included in this bibliography is their strong consciousness of the importance of maintaining peacefulness, their commonly felt responsibility to preserving it, and their (mostly) successful strategies for carrying out that commitment.

Scope and Description of the Bibliography

Scope

If the peoples who have developed peaceful societies are extremely varied, the literature about them is equally diverse and fascinating. The aim of this bibliography is to include works that in some way provide a *significant* contribution to the literature about peaceful peoples. Works that analyze the historical reasons for a people becoming peaceful, or the effects of their peacefulness on their development, are included; psychological analyses of peaceful peoples are equally valuable; sociological or anthropological studies of peoples who are or were peaceful form important components of this book. Works that analyze or describe the religious structures of peaceful peoples, as long as they relate in some way to their peacefulness, are included. Popular works such as travel writings are included if they provide significant information about the peacefulness of a people.

Many works about peacefulness are not included. Works about individual peacemakers, inspiring though they may be, are excluded along with fictional works such as utopian literature.[12] Also, this bibliography ignores the large body of literature which deals with the amelioration of interpersonal strife, whether from the perspective of anthropology, psychology, or sociology. In order to be included, a work must deal in some way with a specific people or group of peoples and it must provide a significant contribution to the literature about the peacefulness of the people. Works about pacifism in general are not included unless they are primarily about the contributions of specific peoples such as the Quakers. If the peacefulness of a people is only mentioned briefly in a work, then normally it has not been included.

Quaker/Mennonite Literature

For peoples about whom there is a vast amount of literature, particularly the Quakers and the Mennonites, this bibliography is, of necessity, somewhat selective. It includes only selections of the literature on the peacefulness of the Friends and Mennonites. Many important works have not been included in order to keep the work balanced--to allow space for the inclusion of publications about the other peaceful peoples. Many types of works about their pacifism, such as study guides, sermons, personal testimonials, and educational materials, are not included. The bibliography only includes a sample of the works that describe the commitment among the Quakers and Mennonites to the social processes which foster peacefulness--their outreach services for social justice, economic development, minority advancement, human rights, and personal integrity. Likewise, the history of the pacifism of these two peoples is not fully represented here.

Annotations

The purpose of the annotations is to convey the importance of the works for understanding the peacefulness of the peoples. They attempt to describe the research, summarize the arguments, and communicate the conclusions of the work. Phrases such as "the author argues" are not normally used, since the style of the annotations is to convey the point of view, the research, and the conclusions of the authors.

The annotations often do not attempt to capture the whole context of the works listed in the citations. The discussion about the peacefulness of the people may be, in fact, a relatively minor aspect of the publication. The facts, arguments, and interpretations about peacefulness are emphasized in the annotations since that is the thrust of this bibliography. In many cases, of course, the central arguments of the works listed relate very directly to the peacefulness of the people. In some of those cases, when the works are lengthy, and numerous interesting, relevant facts and arguments are presented, instead of preparing lengthy annotations only a few of the salient points have been included in order to present a flavor of the works. The annotations are often written in an appreciative rather than an analytical style.

Some of the works included in the bibliography are written in a profoundly beautiful style, and contain eloquent descriptions of peoples and their ways; others are thoroughly scholarly and reward careful reading with significant insights into the nature of peacefulness; still others, unfortunately, are insufferably dull, pedantic, or poorly written. The latter are included, the same as the rest, if they appear to include something that contributes to the information about peaceful peoples. While it would be tempting to include comments such as these in the annotations of specific works, the temptation has been resisted since the important issue is to stick to the criteria already described for inclusion and allow students of peacefulness to study the literature of their own choice.

Arrangement

The book is arranged alphabetically according to the names of the peoples. The names chosen were based primarily on the forms authorized in the *Library of Congress Subject Headings*, 15th edition. Peoples who are not in *LCSH* were listed as they are entered in the *Tozzer Library Index to Anthropological Subject Headings*, 2nd revised edition (Boston: G.K. Hall, 1981).[13] Each section has a brief introduction to the people, including information such as their location, population, and economic livelihood. The introductions are based primarily on the works included in the sections; other reference sources used for introductory information are noted at the end of the bibliography.

Throughout the book, numbers in brackets provide cross references to entries in the bibliography.

Since many libraries may lack some of the works listed in this bibliography, interested readers may want to request publications via interlibrary loan. While standard bibliographic practice for citing journal articles is to include volume, year, and pages, in deference to the possible needs of the interlibrary loan process the issue dates have been included also.

Index

The index combines subject, title, and name entries. The subject entries may be used to trace cross-cultural features of peacefulness, such as Anger, control of, or Conflict-avoiding strategies, or perhaps Women's roles. These headings were taken from the language used by the authors of the works. Titles of books have also been included, though not the titles of articles or chapters. Personal and geographical names, historic events, and peoples have been included. References to important concepts of the peoples which are referred to in the annotations are included in the index: for example, *Song* (Ifaluk concept). All references are to the entry numbers of the works.

Notes to the Introduction

1. Murdock, George P., et al. *Outline of Cultural Materials*, 5th edition. (New Haven: HRAF, 1982).

2. Otterbein, Keith F. "Internal War: A Cross-Cultural Study." *American Anthropologist* 70 (1968): 277-289.

3. Sipes, Richard G. "War, Sports and Aggression: An Empirical Test of Two Rival Theories." *American Anthropologist* 75 (1973): 64-86.

4. Van der Dennen, J. M. G. "Primitive War and the Ethnological Inventory Project." In *Sociobiology and Conflict: Evolutionary Perspectives on Competition, Cooperation, Violence and Warfare*, edited by J. Van Der Dennen and V. Falger (London: Chapman and Hall, 1990) p.247-269. The author lists 152 peaceful peoples from his Ethnological Inventory Project, with the reference sources that evidently indicated the peacefulness of the peoples. However, for each reference he provides only an author's last name and a date, and the book lacks a more complete bibliography. Some of the references that could be found, after many hours of hunting in the reference resources and collections at Penn State, turned out to be only mentions--the named people was simply referred to in the source work as "peaceful."

5. Zablocki, Benjamin David. *The Joyful Community: An Account of the Bruderhof Movement Now in Its Third Generation* (Chicago: University of Chicago Press, 1971).

6. Dentan, Robert Knox. "[Response to Knauft and Otterbein]." *Current Anthropology* 29(1988): 625-629 [371]; Robarchek, Clayton A. and Robert Knox Dentan. "Blood Drunkenness and the Bloodthirsty Semai: Unmaking Another Anthropological Myth." *American Anthropologist* 89(1987): 356-365 [382].

7. But judgments have been made in all cases. For instance, Thomas Gregor wrote *Mehinaku: The Drama of Daily Life in a Brazilian Indian Village* (Chicago: University of Chicago Press, 1977) describing the regular pattern of violence toward women and the witchcraft slayings of a Brazilian Indian people, the Mehinaku. Subsequently, he wrote the chapter "Uneasy Peace: Intertribal Relations in Brazil's Upper Xingu" that appeared in *The Anthropology of War*, edited by Jonathan Haas (New York: Cambridge University Press, 1990, p.105-124). The recent work describes the role that witchcraft plays in maintaining peacefulness among these people, and emphasizes the peaceful nature of their culture. However, it would be unreasonable to ignore the evidence he provided about the violence of those people in his earlier book, so the Mehinaku were left out. Conversely, the Waura were described by Emilienne Ireland in a couple of articles as highly peaceful [413 and 414] so they were included, even though she and Gregor both indicate that their culture and that of the Mehinaku are closely connected.

8. After the Yanomamo were described by Chagnon as fierce, aggressive, and warlike in his popular book *Yanomamo: The Fierce People*

(New York: Holt, Rinehart and Winston, 1968) they became the epitome of peoples who like to fight and do so constantly. (This characterization has been challenged by other writers, however.) When the Yanomamo were struggling with the government of Brazil to gain their rights to control their traditional territory, they were described in a very reputable newspaper (Michaels, Julia, "Brazil Creates Homeland for Yanomamis." *Christian Science Monitor*, November 19, 1991: p.4) thus: "The largest indigenous group in the Americas still living in a primitive state, the Yanomami lived peacefully in the Amazon for thousands of years."

9. One scholar (Ross, Marc Howard. "A Cross-Cultural Theory of Political Conflict and Violence." *Political Psychology* 7 (1986): p. 428) cited the Fore as an example of a people "where open physical expression of differences is rare and strongly discouraged," basing his comments on Sorenson. Either this author was unaware of the contrary literature about the Fore, or he decided that Sorenson's work was the most convincing.

10. Works such as Bruce M. Knauft's "Reconsidering Violence in Simple Human Societies: Homicide Among the Gebusi of New Guinea." *Current Anthropology* 28 (August-October 1987): 457-500 and Robert B. Edgerton's *Sick Societies: Challenging the Myth of Primitive Harmony* (New York: Free Press, 1992) that debunk the supposed peacefulness of a number of peoples are not included in the bibliography when the amount of significant information provided about each people in question is minimal.

11. See, for instance, many of the contributors to *Societies at Peace: Anthropological Perspectives*, edited by Signe Howell and Roy Willis (London: Routledge, 1989) [1], who wrestle with definitions of aggression and peace.

12. Note, however, that several works have been included in the Mennonites section that analyze fiction dealing with the peace commitment of those people. See index heading "Literature and fiction."

13. In some cases this proved to be a bit strange. For instance, the only author cited for the Malapandaram, Brian Morris, rejects that term and prefers to call them the "Hill Pandaram," though other writers have used the term Malapandaram. Briggs referred to the people she writes about as "Eskimos" in her earlier writings, and "Inuit" in the more recent ones. "Dukhobors" is the heading used by the Library of Congress, but since the literature seems to prefer the spelling "Doukhobors," that form was chosen.

PEACEFUL PEOPLES

General Works

1 Howell, Signe and Roy Willis, editors. *Societies at Peace: Anthropological Perspectives*. London: Routledge, 1989.

While a majority of social scientists believe that aggression is an innate aspect of human nature, the basic assumption of the editors is that humans are inherently social beings, and that cooperativeness is essential for their survival. The editors indicate in the introduction that humans have the potential for both violence and peacefulness, but social anthropology has been focused on explaining violent societies more than on understanding peaceful ones. This book provides a collection of papers about societies that have achieved a measure of peacefulness. The introduction sums up some of the pertinent arguments in the debate about the nature of human aggression, and it describes the similarities and differences among the societies described in the individual chapters: many of the societies see themselves as peaceful, while others envision themselves as dangerously violent; several prefer to avoid rather than confront threatening situations; many, but not all, emphasize personal autonomy over instituted authority; and several accept female and male natures as equal. See separate entries for the chapters on the Balinese [23], Buid [48], Chewong [53], Fipa [60], Piaroa [280], Rural Northern Irish [342], Semai [377], and Zapotec [425].

2 Montagu, Ashley, editor. *Learning Non-Aggression: The Experience of Non-Literate Societies*. New York: Oxford University Press, 1978.

In his introduction the editor strongly contradicts the school of thought that argues for humanity's basic aggressiveness. His evidence consists, in part, of this collection of essays by anthropologists who have observed peaceful peoples in their traditional social environments. See individual entries for articles about the Fore [64], Inuit [104], !Kung [131], Mbuti [177], and Tahitians [386].

Amish

Roughly 130,000 Amish lived in the United States and Canada in 1990, about 70 percent of whom lived in Pennsylvania, Ohio and Indiana. An

Anabaptist people along with the Mennonites and Hutterites, about half of the Amish continue to run small, traditional family farms although they are increasingly involved in small-scale business enterprises. They are probably best known for their reluctance to adopt many of the prominent technologies of modern North American society, such as electricity and automobiles. They are uncompromising pacifists regarding military service, and they are highly non-confrontational with one another and with the outsiders that they encounter in social or business dealings.[1]

3   Cong, Dachang. "Amish Factionalism and Technological Change: A Case Study of Kerosene Refrigerators and Conservatism." *Ethnology: An International Journal of Cultural and Social Anthropology* 31(July 1992): 205-218.

While the Amish try to live in harmony, peace, and unity, their communities are nonetheless bothered by conflicts, particularly over issues such as whether or not to adopt new technologies. Visible technologies such as the buggy serve to define their separation from the dominant culture and are not questioned, but controversial decisions about acceptance of other devices are made by the leaders of a church district with the support of the members. In 1987 a bishop in one Indiana district refused to allow his congregation to purchase kerosene refrigerators, despite their need, and acted inconsistently with some of the families. An informal group of protesters met with him and he agreed to begin a formal process of inquiry from outside bishops. Ultimately he refused all efforts at suggested reform and was removed from his lifetime office. A bishop in another district solved the kerosene-refrigerator crisis by avoiding a divisive vote and reluctantly announcing that the devices would now be permitted, though he counseled against them and built a prominent new icehouse on his own front lawn to signify his continued resistance to change.

4   Engle, T. L. "Attitudes Toward War as Expressed by Amish and Non-Amish Children." *Journal of Educational Psychology* 35(April 1944): 211-219.

A study in 1943 compared the attitudes toward war of 294 rural seventh- and eighth-grade youngsters, of whom 47 percent were Amish. The children were asked to write theme papers on how war affects them. Then five separate graduate-student judges evaluated the attitudes toward war shown in each theme on a scale of 1 (most opposed to war) to 7 (most in favor). The results showed a statistically significant difference in the attitudes between the two groups of children: the Amish supported war much less than the non-Amish. In both groups, the boys were more favorable toward war than the girls, though the differences were not statistically significant. The children were also asked to react to a series of questions about war. The Amish and non-Amish agreed that international issues should not be settled by wars and that war exacts a high price, but the Amish children rejected more than the non-Amish did statements approving war, such as the idea that it brings out men's best qualities, or that it has value in certain circumstances, or that at times justice warrants it.

5   Engle, T. L. "Attitudes Toward War as Expressed by Amish and Non-Amish Children: A Follow-Up Study." *Elementary School Journal* 53(February 1953): 345-351.

A study of 443 rural children in the seventh and eighth grades in 1952, one-third of whom (150) were Amish, was designed to see how children reacted to war in a time of relative peace. Using the same questions that were asked of other children in the same schools nine years earlier [4], the author elicited responses from both the Amish and non-Amish children that were slightly more favorable toward war than those from the earlier study, though they would still be classified as "moderately opposed to war." Differences between the Amish and non-Amish were not as pronounced as before, though the former, because of their backgrounds, did not think about war nearly as much as the non-Amish. The Amish children also had less tendency than the non-Amish to think of war as important for maintaining justice, and they less frequently believed that the results of war are desirable. Both groups were much less inclined than their predecessors during World War II to agree with the statement, "war brings out the best qualities in men."

6   Foster, Thomas W. "Separation and Survival in Amish Society." *Sociological Focus* 17(January 1984): 1-15.

Due to the changing economy of farming and high birth rates the Amish increasingly have to work for non-Amish employers, which challenges traditional values that were sustained in an isolated farming society. In a study of the Amish in northeastern Ohio, the author found few differences between the lifestyles of Amish on farms and those living in settlements and working in factories. Their leaders insisted that they were still one people with one religion, able to resolve issues through consensus among all of the congregations. As another way of gaining supplemental income without too much interaction with outsiders, a substantial number of Amish households generated income through cottage industries. Despite the pressures that are bringing them closer to modern society, they still successfully maintain their traditional values through psychosocial strategies that prevent the development of an appetite for consumer goods, such as continuing to use their German dialect, so-called "Pennsylvania Dutch," as their first language, forbidding exposure to the mass media, and insisting that their children only attend their parochial schools through the eighth grade.

7   Gruter, Margaret. "Ostracism on Trial: The Limits of Individual Rights." *Social Science Information* 24(March 1985): 101-111.

The Amish enforce their discipline through "shunning," a procedure which compels conformity and prevents the spread of individual decision making which might conflict with the judgments of the group. In 1947, an Ohio Amish man willfully violated the rules of his church because of a family emergency; he withdrew his membership in the church, which responded by instituting the shunning procedure, thus prohibiting any member, including his family, from interacting with him lest they also be shunned. While the man and the church acted without violence or aggressiveness, the consequences, as intended, were devastating to the man--none of the reciprocal services so important to farm life were available to him. He brought a civil suit in court for monetary damages and an injunction against the ban. The jury decided in the man's favor and the judge ordered an end to the ostracism; however, no one resumed dealing with him. In this case, the jury accepted the ideas of individual freedom and the process of decision making via reason above the Amish values of group conformity and unquestioning acceptance of God's ordinances.

8   Hostetler, John A. *Amish Society*, 3d edition. Baltimore: Johns Hopkins University Press, 1980.

The Amish view themselves as separate people, who live in a broader society but are not part of it. They believe Christ has forbidden them from becoming involved in any warfare or violence. They do not defend themselves against hostility, and if they are attacked by hostile neighbors or governments they have to abandon their farms and move. They cannot bring suits in courts. They marry for life and form close, cooperative unions in which the man is the head of the family and the woman follows his leadership. Amish children learn when they are quite young that they must obey their parents or they will be soundly punished. Obedience to higher authority is one of the foremost principles of their church. Old people are respected as the preservers of Amish culture and tradition: they have considerable influence in the home and the church, and the oldest members of the clergy carry the most authority. Grandparents normally turn their farms over to their sons but continue to live there, in separate houses, during their retirement years. A lengthy, thorough book on the Amish community, family, relations with outsiders, stability, change and rigidity.

9   Kidder, Robert L. and John A. Hostetler. "Managing Ideologies: Harmony as Ideology in Amish and Japanese Societies." *Law & Society Review* 24(1990): 895-922.

The Amish have two major beliefs: living separately from the rest of American society, and nonresistance--settling conflicts peacefully without contesting the will of outsiders. Much as they profess that they do not deal with the outside society, in fact a national Amish leadership has developed relationships with a wide range of outsiders in positions of power and influence, whose actions often help protect Amish lives and communities from harm by the larger society. While these Amish leaders are not referred to as lawyers, lobbyists, or politicians, their effectiveness in resolving problems is comparable to them. For instance these leaders, expert in the laws, friendly with highly placed officials, and resourceful in finding compromises, helped Amish families nationwide with draft problems during the Vietnam War era. A number of other examples of effective problem solving are given, in which the informal Amish leaders, supported by networks of outsiders sympathetic to their cause, find creative solutions to bureaucratic regulations that appear to threaten the Amish. The work of these leaders is not subject to local discussions or consensus approval.

10   Kraybill, Donald B. *The Riddle of Amish Culture*. Baltimore: Johns Hopkins University Press, 1989.

The Amish occasionally punish their children by spanking, and their young people sometimes get into trouble with the law, but otherwise they live almost entirely without violence or crime. The key to understanding their culture is the German word *Gelassenheit*, which translates roughly as "submission." It implies acquiescing to the will of higher authorities and accepting a life of simplicity, humility, thrift, and obedience.

While the goal of modern society is aggressiveness, individualism, and personal fulfillment, the Amish ideal is humility and satisfaction in the ways of the community. They talk, act, and dress modestly, serve others, and yield to the will of God, as they perceive Christ to have done. Their belief in nonresistance prevents employing force in human relationships: they cannot file lawsuits, serve on police forces, hold political offices, or engage in competition. They handle conflicts with silence and avoidance. Kraybill's focus is to explain to "moderns" the apparent contradictions within the Amish culture of Lancaster County, Pennsylvania. He analyzes the nature of their society, worship, and education, and he describes the ways they adapt modern technologies to their own system of values.

11   Savells, Jerry. "Economic and Social Acculturation among the Old Order Amish in Select Communities: Surviving in a High-Tech Society." *Journal of Comparative Family Studies* 19(Spring 1988): 123-135.

The results of a research project involving Amish families in five states indicate that their values and practices permit them to control the very slow rate of change in their society. One of the factors that strengthens the Amish social system is their ability to adapt to the surrounding non-Amish environment. Their distinctiveness as a separate group gives them some social distance, which minimizes confrontation and conflict with the larger society, and they define themselves as a devout, peaceful people who try to maintain harmony with others. Their system is strengthened by their success in attaining their social goals--service to God and living a life of humility--which alienates them from the materialistic, leisure-seeking, mass-consuming goals of American society. The Amish emphasize the security of the group above the desires of the individual in a manner which integrates their faith with their family, school, community and economic systems. Children learn their value patterns at an early age, and since the whole community lives by these values the individual has a security system that encourages control of tensions.

Anabaptists

A Protestant sect that originated in the early 16th century in Switzerland and rapidly spread to the Netherlands and the rest of Western Europe. The Anabaptists rejected infant baptism in favor of baptism of adults, hence the name, and they believed that true Christians should follow the directives of the Sermon on the Mount. They adopted the concept of nonresistance, patterned after the nonresisting way Jesus suffered and died. They believed it was contradictory to the teachings of Christ to engage in warfare, to assume government offices which might require force, or to defend against any kind of aggression. Since they sought to establish a new social order based on what they perceived to be true Christian principles, for several hundred years government officials and church authorities tried to terminate the movement by torturing and killing members. The major branches of Anabaptism to grow out of the early period of trials are the Mennonites, Amish, and Hutterites (see those separate sections). References included in this section were too general to be included in the sections for the three branches of the Anabaptist movement.

12   Bender, Harold S. "The Pacifism of the Sixteenth Century Anabaptists." *Church History* 24(June 1955): 119-131.

The earliest Swiss Anabaptists, Andreas Castelberger and Conrad Grebel, rejected violence during the early 1520s while they were still followers of the militaristic Zwingli. Most of the later Anabaptist leaders were similarly uncompromising in their beliefs in peaceful nonresistance: Michael Sattler testified at his trial in 1527 that even war against the Turks, if they should invade, was not justifiable; Peter Riedemann stated in 1545 "that Christians can neither go to war nor practice vengeance. Whosoever doeth this hath forsaken and denied Christ and Christ's nature." Menno Simons, leader of the Dutch Anabaptists, was equally uncompromising. The 16th-century Anabaptists, basing their nonresistance on the New Testament, rejected a dualism that would allow them to follow Christ in peace, but serve their prince in war. They viewed nonresistance not as weakness, a retreat from the stronger force of government, but as the way Christ is reestablishing his church. Their thinking differed from the pacifism of Erasmus because he based his conclusions partly on humanistic principles, and he could accept arguments for defensive and just wars. Article also appeared in *Mennonite Quarterly Review* 30(January 1956): 5-18.

13   Bender, Wilbur J. "Pacificism among the Mennonites, Amish Mennonites and Schwenkfelders of Pennsylvania to 1783." *Mennonite Quarterly Review* 1(July 1927): 23-40.

The Mennonites and Amish were pacifists because they accepted literally the biblical account of Christ's teachings

about peace. For similar reasons, they refused to resist governmental authority in courts of law, even if their cases seemed just.
When they settled in Pennsylvania, they paid their taxes and
tried to live separately from the rest of society. The agents of the
Pennsylvania proprietors directed the Scotch-Irish Presbyterian
immigrants to settle on the frontier areas of Dauphin and
Cumberland Counties, areas more exposed to Indian attack,
while they settled the Anabaptists away from the frontier in
southern York and Lancaster counties. The frontiersmen were
hostile to the pacifists because of their many differences; the
Anabaptists, to protect their interests, gave up their insularity
and started voting in favor of Pennsylvania's Quaker party. The
Anabaptists felt that the pacifism of the Quakers was similar to
theirs, and they wanted to keep them in control over the colonial
legislature. Anabaptist votes helped maintain Quaker power
until 1756 when they finally resigned under pressure. The Amish
and Mennonites then retreated once again from further involvement in voting.

14   Bender, Wilbur J. "Pacifism among the Mennonites, Amish
      Mennonites and Schwenkfelders of Pennsylvania to 1783, II."
      Mennonite Quarterly Review 1(October 1927): 21-48, 76.
      Several factors separated the Mennonites, Amish Menno-
nites, and Schwenkfelders from the patriot cause and prevented
them from getting involved in the American Revolution: their
pacifism required them to be strictly neutralist; they were
constantly told by their leaders not to become involved in
outside affairs; they were alienated by the radical frontier
patriots; they had already promised their allegiance to the
crown; and they felt they owed their peace and prosperity to the
British, which might be lost during a revolution. During the early
period of the war the patriots repeatedly tried to increase the
punishments and fines against the pacifist peoples, who responded with numerous petitions arguing their peaceful principles. When taxes were required in lieu of military service,
many Quakers resisted, Schwenkfelders paid, and Mennonites
varied depending on where they lived. Mennonites objected to
selling their farm surplus to the government, not for pacifist
reasons but because of a desire for hard currency rather than
paper money. They did not suffer as much hostility and oppression during the Revolution as they did during World War I from
neighbors.

15   Homan, Gerlof D. "Post-Armistice Courts-Martial of Consci-
      entious Objectors in Camp Funston, 1918-1919." *Mennonite
      Life* 44(December 1989): 4-9.

      During World War I many Mennonite, Amish, and Hutterite
conscientious objectors (C.O.s) refused to perform any work
under the direction of the military which they felt would support
the army. On November 19, 1918, a week after the armistice,
army officers at Camp Funston, Kansas, decided to test the C.O.s
there by ordering them to pave a road across the camp. The
officers wanted either to expose the C.O.s as hypocrites if they
compromised their ideals by performing the work, or to have a
case for court-martialing them if they refused. Eight of the men--
Hutterites and Mennonites--refused the order because of their
consciences, which prompted an officer to respond, "to hell
with your conscience." The eight were charged with willfully
disobeying a lawful order and tried in a military court. The
officers who served as judges asked few questions about their
beliefs, though when one man was reminded that Christ drove
the money changers out of the temple, he answered he had
"never heard that He had hurt anybody." All were found guilty
and sentenced harshly, though they were all soon released.

Balinese

Approximately 2.5 million people live on Bali, an island of 2,000 square
miles in Indonesia immediately to the east of Java. Bali is a very popular
tourist destination because of its scenic beauty and the highly colorful
nature of the festivals and rituals of the people. While the majority of the
people are Hindu, there are minority populations of Muslims and others.
Anthropologists have been fascinated by the way the Balinese maintain
their poise and control. For the Balinese, the paramount virtue is mastery
of their emotions at all times, which includes suppressing any manifestations of hostility or anger. Literature about their poise, grace, beauty,
and peacefulness is complemented by works about their mental illnesses,
produced by the stresses of their emotional control system, and the folk
healing practices which cure those illnesses.

16   Bateson, Gregory. "Bali: The Value System of a Steady State."
      In *Social Structure: Studies Presented to A. R. Radcliffe-Brown*,
      edited by Meyer Fortes, 35-53. New York: Russell & Russell,
      1963.

      Bateson shows how Balinese culture modifies an earlier
hypothesis of his about culturally standardized systems of

emotions. He describes the ways Balinese mothers dull signs of strong emotions in their children by exciting them and then ignoring their affectionate responses, or by showing pleasure if their children throw temper tantrums because of being ignored. A mother will tease her own child by giving her breast to another child and then show enjoyment when hers attempts to push away the intruder: an effective way of diminishing tendencies toward competitiveness and rivalry in children. Their culture avoids fostering climaxes. One way they achieve this is to formally register their quarrels at the local government office. Though the formal contracts will later be nullified when and if the quarrels are terminated, the process of formalizing them in that fashion serves to stabilize them rather than end them.

17   Belo, Jane. "The Balinese Temper." *Character and Personality* 4(December 1935): 120-146.

The Balinese social structure requires poise, careful bearing, measured gait, dignity, excellent manners, and great care to avoid anger or fighting. When boys quarrel and the weaker one is struck, he utters a brief cry and passively submits to the stronger, which always stops the aggression. The author, in four years of life on Bali, never witnessed a case of a boy beating up another. They are highly conscious of social status, but in formal situations everyone speaks with great care to preserve equanimity and to avoid any appearance of someone having authority over others. There are occasions when they break their codes of conduct, such as when a person will "run amok" in the same manner as the Malays. At funerals and ceremonies they frequently burst out in great storms of anger, joy, and exaltation. These two phases of Balinese culture--a normal, daily life of peace and tranquility broken on special occasions by stimulation and tensions--contrast with Western urban life, where people live with daily tensions and take periodic vacations to escape briefly to a life of peacefulness.

18   Connor, Linda. "Corpse Abuse and Trance in Bali: The Cultural Mediation of Aggression." *Mankind* 12(December 1979): 104-118.

The Balinese, often celebrated for their peaceful ways, socialize their children during their early years to inhibit aggression and anger. When children are about three years old they sometimes display violent tantrums as they learn to cope with frustration, but everyone close to them simply ignores the displays. Connor argues that this process of inhibition leads to psychological dissociation and the substitution of mediated emotions, such as those associated with corpse abuse during funeral ceremonies and the stylized violence that is part of the trance that people go into after certain festivals. Conflicts in social roles also help produce withdrawal mechanisms and the culturally mediated distancing that result in the normally controlled, ritualized violence associated with funerals and ceremonies.

19   Dean, Stanley R. and Denny Thong. "Shamanism Versus Psychiatry in Bali, 'Isle of the Gods': Some Modern Implications." *American Journal of Psychiatry* 129(July 1972): 59-62.

The Balinese are willing to let modern medical doctors handle major mental illnesses such as schizophrenia and brain diseases. *Bebainan* on the other hand, mental illnesses caused by evil spirits, are handled by the community *balians*, shamans who function in a sense as doctors' helpers. As respected men in their communities with noticeable therapeutic personalities, the *balians* frequently are able to cure the culturally associated mental problems. Since these healers are so effective in the sharing environment of Bali, their practices may offer lessons appropriate for Western societies as well: the use of the healer carries no social stigma, since the mental problem is identified with the evil spirit rather than the victim; the illness is a routine part of community life, much as any other physical illness; the healer is a peer who also may suffer from *bebainan*-- hallucinations, trances, supernatural experiences--so it is easy to identify with him; the *balian* heals in a supportive, community environment so there is little disruption of normal social ties.

20   Geertz, Clifford. "Deep Play: Notes on the Balinese Cockfight." In *Rethinking Popular Culture: Contemporary Perspectives in Cultural Studies*, edited by Chandra Mukerji and Michael Schudson, 239-277. Berkeley: University of California Press, 1991.

Balinese men take a very serious interest in cockfighting. The spurs on the cocks are fitted with deadly sharp, steel swords so the fights frequently result in quick slashing and death to one, or perhaps both, of the birds. In contrast to normal Balinese reserve, the cockfight is a chaotic mob scene of shouting, waving, pushing and clamoring men. In substantial contests, the owners of the two cocks represent intergroup or intervillage alliances which pool resources to place large bets on their birds. The significance of the fights is their affirmation, defence, justification and celebration of prestige through a rooster bloodbath. They dramatize alliances and allow people to safely express the opposition between two individuals or groups. The Balinese are aware of the complex social forces at work during the cockfight: the activation of intergroup and intervillage hostilities and rivalries, the close brush with open expressions of aggression. The Balinese rarely confront trouble, they avoid conflicts obsessively, and they interact through indirection, dissimulation, and obliqueness. Thus, the slaughter of cocks is an imaginative representation of how things might get out of control among men. Reprinted from *Daedalus* 101(1), Winter 1972, p.1-37.

21   Geertz, Clifford. "Person, Time, and Conduct in Bali." In *The Interpretation of Cultures: Selected Essays*, edited by Clifford Geertz, 360-411. New York: Basic Books, 1973.

Balinese concepts of personal identity and time are closely linked with their conceptions of ideal conduct. They have personal names but rarely use them, preferring in various contexts to use birth-order names, kinship terms, teknonyms, status names, and public titles. Their uses of these terms symbolize the fact that interpersonal relationships are abstract, stereotyped, generalized and standardized--they may share a period of time with others but they try not to become involved. Their conception of time is based on two calendar systems and cycles within cycles, and is more oriented to determining what kind of time it is rather than how much time has accumulated. As with personal naming, it serves to detach individuals from others and to foster the view of other people as impersonal others. Social intercourse with (relatively speaking) anonymous individuals is viewed as ceremony, with the creative aspects of human relations--emotionality, spontaneity, vulnerability, individuality--controlled in favor of relationships based on aesthetics and theatrical postures. Their etiquette is appearances, the social act is designed to please the audience, the act of courtesy is a work of art.

22   Hobart, Mark. "Is God Evil?" In *The Anthropology of Evil*, edited by David Parkin, 165-193. Oxford, UK: Basil Blackwell, 1985.

A wide-ranging discussion of evil in Western and Classical

thought, with a particular focus on the concepts of good and evil in Bali. The major value for the Balinese, order, depends on situation, occasion, and place, with circumstance varying from village to village or one time to the next. Order is the state of things here and now, and while everything has its code--the crow to warn of impending doom, the tiger to eat humans, the witch to harm people--somehow order and harmony result. The Balinese do not have neatly ordered ideas of good and evil, preferring instead a pragmatic approach--the Western notion that God is exclusively good is funny to them. To them, God is good and evil: pragmatically, He is the one who wins, an inspiration for the Balinese who value pragmatism and order.

23   Howe, L. E. A. "Peace and Violence in Bali: Culture and Social Organization." In *Societies at Peace: Anthropological Perspectives*, edited by Signe Howell and Roy Willis, 100-116. London: Routledge, 1989.

The Balinese ideology of equilibrium, order, and balance dampens manifestations of aggression, quarreling, and confrontations. They have a variety of mechanisms to resolve conflicts over property or boundaries, and individuals will avoid one another if they have personal disputes. But even though peaceful values are espoused on Bali, open conflicts have occurred in the past and they still do. Balinese lords fought violent wars and at times treated their slaves very harshly. The author argues that the hierarchical differentiation of individuals, which allows some people to exploit, dominate, and have power over others, weakens the connection between the emotional state of a people, such as the Balinese, and their actions. Frequent causes of contemporary disputes are the problems of women getting along with their son's wives when both families live in the same family compound and the two women share the same kitchen. Disputes also arise between adult brothers about their respective agricultural work on the family farm. In these family-compound situations, outside sources of conflict resolution cannot be brought to bear and the conflicts can become intolerable.

24   Suryani, L. K. "Culture and Mental Disorder: The Case of Bebainan in Bali." *Culture, Medicine and Psychiatry* 8(March 1984): 95-113.

The Balinese conceive of *bebainan* as an illness caused by the soul being possessed by an evil spirit. The attack comes on suddenly: the victim feels intense pain and cold, loses complete control, cries and screams, and frequently gains sufficient strength to resist the restraining efforts of numerous men. The symptoms are almost always cured by the work of a traditional healer, a *balian*. The results of a study conducted in the compound of a former king of Bali show that the victims are overwhelmingly young women who had pampered childhoods that did not prepare them for the stresses and frustrations of their roles in the confining life of the compound. They are generally lacking in confidence and tense about their marriages or prospects for marriage. The author concludes that attacks of *bebainan* allow the victims to release their conflicts, frustrations and feelings of anger about the confining social environment which they are powerless to modify, to gain briefly some attention, and to suffer no negative responses or stigmas as a result.

25   Thong, Denny. "Psychiatry in Bali." *Australian and New Zealand Journal of Psychiatry* 10(March 1976): 95-97.

Balinese society requires people to remain in harmony with their gods, their environment, and their community. Violators might suffer a misfortune, be temporarily possessed by a spirit, or even suffer a mental disorder. Religious taboos generally guarantee this harmony, but when occasional conflicts arise traditional psychiatric methods are used to relieve tensions. People can go into *bengong*, a state where almost all mental activity ceases, though they retain awareness and can continue with routine physical activities such as walking. Cultural mediums relieve tensions: examples include the performances of folk dramas in which actors vividly express their inner emotions, the works of artists who transpose emotions onto their art works, and mass trance dances. A 1973 survey of one village found that out of a population of 1,774 people, 15 admitted that they habitually went into trances; most of them were men. In some cases Balinese appeal to their *balians* (traditional healers) for help in dealing with their frustrations. They rarely turn to suicide. Modern psychiatric care has been brought to Bali, but many people still rely on the traditional psychiatry.

26   Tugby, Donald, Elise Tugby, and H. G. Law. "The Attribution of Mental Illness by Rural Balinese." *Australian and New Zealand Journal of Psychiatry* 10(March 1976): 99-104.

When a rural Balinese person is committed to the mental hospital on the island, relatives and friends fill out a form which asks for a description of the behavior characteristics of the patient's illness. The behavior "confused talk" was reported in 50 percent of the 208 cases analyzed, the most common one by far. A cluster analysis of all the behavior signs reported on the forms indicates that inabilities to relate to others in public are the primary causes of incapacitating behavior for both sexes: the mentally ill people cannot hide symptoms of aggression, handle the language appropriately, and respect the independence of others. The patients have invaded the individuality of others, acted in hostile fashions, and communicated in culturally inappropriate ways. This clustering shows that many of the rural people with mental illnesses have failed to meet the Balinese expectations that adults take increasing social responsibilities in the different planes of rural life.

27   Wikan, Unni. "Illness from Fright or Soul Loss: A North Balinese Culture-Bound Syndrome?" *Culture, Medicine and Psychiatry* 13(March 1989): 25-50.

In northern Bali, *kesambet* is a serious illness among nursing children. It is caused by fright, shock, or loss of soul by the mother, which harms her milk enough to hurt the child. When children die of unknown causes, the Balinese ascribe their deaths to *kesambet*. Other strong, hot emotions such as envy, jealousy, sadness and anger also may affect mothers and cause the death of their children. Thus, nursing mothers must always preserve their composure and never become emotional; this attitude magnifies the normal equanimity and peace that Balinese maintain toward each other. Adults also experience *kesambet*, which is caused by sudden or shocking events such as receiving sudden bad news, hearing a loud noise suddenly, or seeing an accident. Since quarrels are avoided in Balinese society, just witnessing an open disagreement can cause the illness. One woman became ill with *kesambet* as a result of being publicly teased about giving the author some honey. The cures for *kesambet* are carried out by *balians*, healers who treat patients with complex rituals.

28   Wikan, Unni. "Managing the Heart to Brighten Face and Soul: Emotions in Balinese Morality and Health Care." *American Ethnologist* 16(May 1989): 294-312.

The Balinese are constantly concerned about morality and proper actions, which are essential to good health. They believe the epitome of poise--a bright, clear face--is essential to health since it conveys a positive, cheerful, reinforcing social message. Behind the face is the heart, a force for good or evil--source of compassion, regeneration, and therapy, or origin of misfortune, illness and evil. Calmness is highly desirable; it involves the ability to adjust to circumstances, forget misfortunes, relax inside, combat anger, live in harmony with good feelings toward others, and give without any expectation of receiving. Anger, they feel, is dangerous in an individual because it erodes their *bayu*--inner spiritual force and physical energy--and it is dangerous if provoked in others because of the possibility of retaliation through sorcery. Health care for the Balinese is an integral part of their daily experience, focusing on a healthy body, emotions and thoughts; laughter celebrates life, benefits their well-being, and enables them to cope with distress and even tragedy by forcing a cheerful face.

29   Wikan, Unni. *Managing Turbulent Hearts: A Balinese Formula for Living.* Chicago: University of Chicago Press, 1990.

The portrait of the Balinese drawn by several earlier anthropologists--that their culture must be viewed as an aesthetic performance--is challenged by this book. The Balinese struggle with difficulties and dangers but try to maintain good hearts and pleasant fronts for society. Two of their compelling social values are to refrain from arrogance and to strive for *polos*--being companionable or smooth. A person with *polos* treats others well and has a patient, calm, quiet, and uncritical manner. The Balinese feel that, in ordinary society, people must maintain a friendly, polite, accommodating, self-effacing demeanor no matter how they feel since the moral fabric of society is based on it. They fear black magic as much as Westerners fear violence in their cities, which prompts them to be cautious with others in order to protect themselves against covert violence. They judge their society to be extremely violent: deaths, injuries, and illnesses are blamed on the black magic of their opponents.

30   Wikan, Unni. "Public Grace and Private Fears: Gaiety, Offense, and Sorcery in Northern Bali." *Ethos* 15(December 1987): 337-365.

The Balinese display an outward poise, calmness, politeness, cheerfulness, and grace which hide inner fears about the possible evil intentions of others, including friends and relatives, who might hold grudges about unintended offenses and try to retaliate via black magic. Their strong sanctions against showing anger, grief, displeasure, or any behavior that might offend others serve to guard against the possibility of retaliation: virtue is essential for self-protection. Composure and smoothness are prized, while disruption, unhappiness and negative emotions are to be avoided. Individuals handle their emotions and fears in different ways, however, depending on their life situations, sex, age, and relative social positions. For example, a very cultivated woman, combing her hair in the bathroom of her hostess, carefully made sure all of her loose hairs went into her pocketbook to avoid possible sorcery. In the course of the very polite, friendly conversation it had become evident that her hostess might have been distantly related to a man with whom she had had an unsuccessful love affair seven years before, and she just might have continued to be resentful toward her.

Batek

The Batek are considered to be one of the Orang Asli peoples, and more specifically they are grouped with the Negritos. They number about 300 individuals and live in the watershed of the Lebir River in the state of Kelantan, in the mountains of the Malay Peninsula. Their economy has been based on gathering, hunting, and collecting forest products for trade, though the logging of their forests in the mid-1980s threatened to destroy their lifestyle. The Batek think of themselves as forest people, and have an egalitarian society based on sharing of food and a complete equality between the sexes. They avoid any possibility of interpersonal violence by immediate flight whenever hostility threatens. For recent information about the Batek, see the introduction to the section on the Orang Asli.

31   Endicott, Karen Lampell. "The Batek De' of Malaysia." *Cultural Survival Quarterly* 8(Summer 1984): 6-8.
       The Batek Negritos have a highly egalitarian society in which both men and women share the food which they procure. While the men normally hunt and the women gather vegetables, both foods are valued equally and are shared equally among men and women in their camps. Men sometimes gather vegetables, women sometimes (though rarely) hunt--they have no rigid rules separating their sex roles. Marriages are based on equality, compatibility, and affection; couples make joint decisions about movements and food getting. They live companionably, working together and enjoying their leisure time with one another. If the warmth of the relationship erodes, either can divorce the other and count on the support of the band to assist with child

support and food sharing. They recognize no formal leaders; individuals and families make their own decisions as to where to live, what camps to join, and so on, though people who are clearly wise or experienced may be looked up to for guidance.

32   Endicott, Karen Lampell. ''The Conditions of Egalitarian Male-Female Relationships in Foraging Societies.'' *Canberra Anthropology* 4(1987): 1-10.

Some anthropologists have maintained that all societies are, to a greater or lesser extent, dominated by men, with women fulfilling subordinate roles. One writer argued that sexual asymmetry predominates in hunter/gatherer societies because men are the hunters and the meat they provide is the most favored food. Endicott refutes these arguments based on her research work with the Batek and the literature about other peoples. Among the Batek, nuclear families are formed by men and women as equals, and a couple makes all decisions jointly-- though one or the other may be more vocal. The camp is an aggregation of autonomous families in which the leader, if there is one, will be a person who is respected for good sense, wisdom, persuasiveness and experience. This *de facto* leader may be a woman or a man. The Batek do not always favor meat as the preferred food--they will eat fruit, when it is in season, instead of everything else, including meat. Endicott concludes that the domination of men over women in many societies is actually based on their having established structures of male authority.

33   Endicott, Kirk. *Batek Negrito Religion: The World-View and Rituals of a Hunting and Gathering People of Peninsular Malaysia.* Oxford: Clarendon Press, 1979.

While Endicott focuses on religious beliefs of the Batek, he also provides insights into their peaceful social structure. For instance, each afternoon they carefully share the tubers and meat they have gathered and hunted that day; while meals are being cooked they send their children to other families with more plates of food, even though everyone has enough, which teaches the youngsters the importance of sharing. The Batek approach to one of their diseases, *ke'oy*, ensures that they treat each other peacefully and avoid interpersonal hostilities. The illness, which has symptoms consisting of fever, depression, shortness of breath, and weakness, is caused by the victim's frustration, mistreatment, fright, or perception that another person is angry without justification. The cure for the disease is for the person who is angry or has mistreated the victim to control his feelings and to perform a ritual in which he makes cuts in his leg, wipes the blood over the chest and back of the victim, blows on the victim's chest, tells his heart to be cool, and grasps and throws away the disease.

34   Endicott, Kirk. "Property, Power and Conflict among the Batek of Malaysia." In *Hunters and Gatherers 2: Property, Power and Ideology*, edited by Tim Ingold, David Riches, and James Woodburn, 110-127. Oxford: Berg, 1988.

The Batek are totally opposed to any interpersonal violence--they flee from enemies instead of fighting. As a consequence, Batek women as well as men are free from the threat of physical aggression. Their camps consist of autonomous families who share enough interests to prompt them to live together. Group issues are extensively discussed and they rely for advice on natural leaders--older people respected for their experience and judgment. These leaders can only be persuasive, since they have no authority. Their economy is based on gathering, hunting, and collecting forest products for trade, with occasional planting of crops. They have no concept of land ownership--the idea is absurd to them--and natural resources in the forest cannot be owned until someone harvests them. Once food is gathered, harvested or killed it becomes the possession of the individual who took it, but the Batek have a firm expectation that all food, including vegetables that are gathered, will be shared. The few lazy members of a band are simply tolerated, their spouses making extra efforts as if to compensate.

Birhor

The Birhor are a proto-Australoid aboriginal people of southern Bihar State in east central India. They are nomadic forest dwellers who live off their gathering and hunting, but who trade some of the forest products they gather for desired goods in villages. An important economic activity has been making ropes out of vines for sale to villagers. The literature on their peaceful ways emphasizes their love for the forest and their resistance to settling into permanent villages. Numbering 4,300 individuals in 1971, they speak a language that falls within the Munda group of languages.

35   Adhikary, Ashim Kumar. "Hunters and Gatherers in India: A Preliminary Appraisal of their Structure and Transformation." *Journal of the Indian Anthropological Society* 19(1984): 8-16.

Birhor relationships with neighboring Hindu agricultural villages are free of open conflicts because their forest-based economy--gathering a species of creeper that they make into ropes and hunting monkeys for food--does not interfere with the activities of the peasants. They are looked down upon by the low-caste villagers, and they accept the lower status as a necessary part of their social relations with their neighbors. They maintain a social distance from the peasants, yet they have adopted some Hindu ideas in order to keep relations stable. For instance, they avoid most foods that the Hindus would consider polluting, but they persist in eating monkeys, which their neighbors ridicule as unclean. Because the Birhor live successfully and simply at the edge of the forests, they have a reputation as experts in religious magic among their Hindu neighbors. These aspects of distinctiveness, mixed with carefully controlled social contacts, ensure their economic, social, and cultural survival.

36   Adhikary, Ashim Kumar. *Society and World View of the Birhor: A Nomadic Hunting and Gathering Community of Orissa.* Calcutta: Anthropological Survey of India, 1984.

Birhor society is characterized by economic cooperation, individual independence, altruism, and interpersonal relations which function within networks of kinship relations. The very elderly, who are highly respected for their knowledge of the forest, help the group with gathering and making ropes if they possibly can. Parents and children have relationships of affection and economic cooperation, while siblings have close ties that last throughout their lifetimes--perhaps the warmest relations in Birhor society. While they are young, elder brothers care for younger siblings in the absence of their fathers with a loving, affectionate attitude, while the younger ones look reverently to older brothers for their experience and wisdom. The Birhor also love the forest, where they are joyous, playful and easy-going. They react with respect toward the larger animals, and when poisonous snakes are encountered near their camps, the adults simply shoo them off like pets; children are sportive rather than fearful of them. Because of their feeling of communion with the forest, they will not cut branches from trees when they are blooming. Their name for themselves, Birhor, means men of the forest.

37   Bhattacharyya, Asutosh. "An Account of the Birhor of Palamau." *Bulletin of the Department of Anthropology (India)* 2(July 1953): 1-16.

The Birhor are honest, peaceful people who never become involved in crimes, seldom fight among themselves, and avoid conflicts with villagers. While they permit divorce and remarriage, both are rare. When a couple does have a dispute, they bring it to the headman in the group who makes a binding decision as to whether a divorce is warranted. One headman admitted that he had never had a case, such as adultery, that would be serious enough to cause a divorce. Couples appear to be loving and faithful to one another, affectionate toward their children, and supportive of their aged relatives. Elderly people try to be economically independent as much as they possibly can, but when an old man cannot accompany the younger men on a hunting party, or an old woman is unable to gather roots herself, their sons and grandsons will help by supplying them food. The Birhor never beg, since individual cases of hardship are handled by the group.

38   Chakraborty, Bhabesh. "Folksongs of a Folk Community: The Birhor of West Bengal and Bihar." *Bulletin of the Cultural Research Institute* 15(1982): 102-108.

The folk songs of the Birhor, some of which are summarized briefly, establish the importance of man's relationship to nature, the spirits, and other humans. Songs evoke the sylvan beauty of their forested environment, the relaxed Birhor attitude toward marriage and divorce, their love for their spouses, enjoyment of hunting, and appreciation of flowers, rivers, mountains and wild deer. One song recounts a legendary fight that resulted in a lot of bloodshed, the narration of which freshens Birhor dread for violence. Others display their customary hospitality and their concern for streams free of pollution.

39   Sarkar, R. M. "Eco-Cultural Perspective of Sedentarization of the Nomadic Birhors." *Man in India* 70(September 1990): 288-304.

The traditional Birhor economy was based on a nomadic lifestyle. They lived in temporary settlements at the edge of the forest, hunting and gathering food plus products for sale in the nearby agricultural markets. Their solution to problems--poor treatment by their neighbors or a lack of game and materials--was to move to another location. They cooperated with one another in all their activities. Their religious festivals particularly helped them to maintain harmony. Their life has been disrupted since the 1950s due to deforestation by outsiders and government attempts to settle them into permanent agricultural villages. These settlement efforts have been complete failures. The Birhor have been known to erect their traditional leaf huts next to the modern brick houses built by the government because the *bonga ore*, their god, will only protect them from evil spirits while they sleep in the huts. Despite decades of resettlement efforts, they still leave their homes early in the morning to wander in what's left of their beloved forests, only to return empty handed in the evenings.

40   Sinha, D. P. "The Birhors." In *Hunters and Gatherers Today: A Socioeconomic Study of Eleven Such Cultures in the Twentieth Century*, edited by M. G. Bicchieri, 371-403. New York: Holt, Rinehart and Winston, 1972.

The Birhor are much more conscious of the requirements of the group than they are of their own individual needs. For instance, they tell a legend of a Birhor man discovering a year's supply of creepers perfect for making ropes, but rather than hoarding the knowledge he quickly told everyone. In rare cases when a dispute threatens a settlement they simply split into two camps; disputes among residents of different camps are resolved by councils of elders from neighboring settlements. Members of a settlement normally gather and hunt together, but in order to hunt monkeys they will form cooperative hunting parties from several camps. They maintain a profitable trading economy at local markets with non-Birhor in order to obtain needed goods and food items in exchange for the ropes they make. The Birhor have adapted well to their subsistence forest environment-- although they experience periods when resources are scarce, they rarely starve. They are conscious of living in harmony with nature: when they have to take some bark off trees or collect vines, they are careful to not harm them.

Brethren

The Church of the Brethren developed in Germany in the early 18th century from Pietist and Anabaptist roots. Most emigrated to Pennsylvania starting in the 1820s and from there they spread out across the United States. Until the 20th century most were rural farmers and were called Dunkers, Tunkers or Dunkards after their belief in full immersion during baptism. They have been consistently opposed to fighting in the armed forces, and they have been grouped by most people, along with the Quakers and the Mennonites, as one of the three "Historic Peace Churches." In 1990 there were nearly 150,000 members of the Church of the Brethren in the United States, plus several thousand members of other Brethren churches.[2]

41   Bowman, Rufus D. *The Church of the Brethren and War, 1708-1941.* Elgin, IL: Brethren Publishing House, 1944.

   The Brethren have consistently taken the position that since war is contrary to the teachings, life, and spirit of Jesus, fighting is wrong. They do not litigate in courts, take oaths, or try to force their religion on others. Throughout their history they have been reluctant to articulate a creed, preferring to base their beliefs directly on the New Testament. A hallmark of their history has been their toleration for others, and particularly for their own members who do not strictly follow the recommendations of the church. However, they have suffered from government intolerance during periods of war. They were persecuted during the American Revolution and the Civil War because they refused to sign loyalty oaths and to fight. During World War I church officials were nearly sued for treason by the War Department due to their statement advising Brethren draftees against wearing uniforms and participating in military drills. The government only backed down after the church members explained their historic opposition to war, their love and loyalty for the government, and their intention to prevent any further distribution of the offending statement.

42   Clouse, Robert G. "The Church of the Brethren and World War I: The Goshen Statement." *Mennonite Life* 45(December 1990): 29-34.

   During the 19th century the Brethren began losing their distinctiveness, merging into the dominant American culture, and relaxing their traditional pacifist beliefs. When the U.S. entered World War I, some Brethren leaders advised draftees to uphold their nonresistant traditions by refusing military service, while others suggested they should be loyal American citizens and accept noncombatant service. A declaration issued at Goshen, Indiana, in January 1918 urged Brethren to work for nonresistance, Christian mission, and humanitarian efforts. It clearly told the Brethren "not to enlist in any service which would, in any way, compromise our time-honored position in relation to war ...'' In July church officials were notified by the War Department that the authors of the statement were being charged by the federal government with treasonable intent to obstruct the draft law. The members of the committee decided to buckle under to the government's demands and withdraw the statement with promises to stop circulating it. While church leaders were subsequently divided about the wisdom of the decision, they rebounded with an intense commitment to non-resistance, peace witness and social outreach.

43   Durnbaugh, Donald F. "Relationships of the Brethren with the Mennonites and Quakers, 1708-1865." *Church History* 35(March 1966): 35-59.

During the 18th century, Brethren doctrines were similar to those of the Mennonites, though unlike them they practiced full immersion during baptism. They seemed to exhibit more zeal for their faith so they were able to convert some Mennonites. Both groups strongly supported Quaker control of the Pennsylvania Assembly during the Colonial period. The Brethren suffered the same harassments and difficulties during the Revolutionary War as members of the other peace churches. Like the others, they felt the Bible required them to obey the authority of the state, but unlike the Quakers they were willing to pay war taxes. Because of the modest differences between Brethren and Mennonites, there have been periods of contention. During most of the 1850's, for instance, Joseph Funk, a Mennonite publisher, and John Kline, a Brethren elder, attacked and rebutted each other's published writings regarding baptism. But during the Civil War the differences among the peace churches were once again put aside as they all sought accommodations for their pacifist positions from the Union government and the governments of the Confederate states.

44   Durnbaugh, Donald F. "The Legacy of Suffering and Persecution in the Church of the Brethren." *Brethren Life and Thought* 37(Spring 1992): 73-86.

Most of the persecutions of Brethren over the past 300 years have been due to their refusal to fight and their commitment to peace. While Mennonites and Quakers were often summarily executed in the 16th and 17th centuries, religious dissenters since the beginning of the 18th century, when the Brethren emerged, only had to suffer expulsions, beatings, fines and confiscations of property. Brethren in America generally adopted neutral stances during the Revolution because they felt gratitude that the British government had accepted them as refugees from German persecution. During the Civil War the ones living in the South had more problems with the draft than those in the North because the Confederacy had a greater shortage of manpower. In World War I, Brethren were drafted, taken to military camps, and subjected to a range of pressures and tortures to get them to accept orders and serve the needs of the army. Brethren generally fared better during World War II and the Vietnam War. Their strength during their history of persecutions has been based on their belief that Christ commanded peacefulness and an attitude of nonresistance to persecutors.

Buid

About 6,000 Buid live in the highland forests of Mindoro, the seventh-largest island in the Philippines about 100 miles south of Manila. They practice shifting cultivation--swidden farming--on forested hills that look down on the denuded lowlands of their Christian Filipino neighbors. They attach highly negative values to aggressiveness, which they associate with the lowland peoples, and correspondingly positive values to their own peaceful behavior and individual autonomy. However, their interaction with the dominant Christian culture has upset their traditional egalitarian society and begun to modify their customary forms of conflict resolution; occasional violence has occurred.

45   Gibson, Thomas. "Meat Sharing as a Political Ritual: Forms of Transaction Versus Modes of Subsistence." In *Hunters and Gatherers 2: Property, Power and Ideology*, edited by Tim Ingold, David Riches, and James Woodburn, 165-179. Oxford: Berg, 1988.

The Buid avoid dyadic, one-on-one relationships as much as possible. When two individuals converse, they do not face one another or address comments or questions directly to the other person; instead, each makes comments that may not directly answer the previous comment. When they are preparing to engage in cooperative agricultural tasks, everyone will get together, face in the same direction toward a distant object, and each will address the group indicating his need for assistance. If conflicts are perceived, the two individuals do not confront each other: instead, each addresses the group as a whole. Since the speaker is always an individual and the listener a group, clashes of wills are avoided, confrontations and competition are minimized. When a family sacrifices a chicken or pig the meat is carefully and equally shared with every other family in the community. But even then, since the individual family is sharing with the whole community and not with another specific family, no direct obligations are made. Of course every family frequently receives ritual portions of meat from others.

46   Gibson, Thomas. "Raiding, Trading and Tribal Autonomy in Insular Southeast Asia." In *The Anthropology of War*, edited by Jonathan Haas, 125-145. Cambridge: Cambridge University Press, 1990.

The peaceful lifestyle of the Buid is compared, within a historical perspective of trading and slavery among the peoples of insular Southeast Asia, with the warfare, violence and aggression of the Ilongot of northern Luzon and the Iban of Sarawak. The Buid have learned that physical violence is produced by bragging, quarreling, competition, the expression of emotions, egotistical self-assertion, and aggression, all of which must be controlled. They castigate the *maisug* (aggressive) behavior of their Christian lowland neighbors, though the same word is used elsewhere in the Philippines positively to refer to such male "virtues" as courage and virility. The Buid do not have a positive word for courage when confronting danger, though they do have approving words for flight from danger. Whenever a Buid does act aggressively, the actions are condemned and the aggressor is assumed to lack proper control or have a weak mind. When courting women, Buid men completely ignore acts of courage and learn love poems instead. They have preserved an ancient script which they use to help them memorize their poetry, which is filled with gentle images.

47   Gibson, Thomas. *Sacrifice and Sharing in the Philippine Highlands: Religion and Society among the Buid of Mindoro*. London: Athlone Press, 1986.

While the Buid have a long history of external trade, they avoid economic transactions with one another. Such business dealings, they believe, foster feelings of debt and inequality; calculations of equivalent values are completely incompatible with their egalitarian ethos since they place people in situations of competition in which one or the other must lose. The central symbol of Buid social organization is a group of companions engaged in a cooperative task. Their relationships are based, not on kinship, common residence, or debt obligations, but on friendly relations and a desire to cooperate in a shared activity. Their religion is based on rituals such as seances, which are conducted by many mediums who have to cooperate with one another in an egalitarian fashion in order to understand the spirits, and pig sacrifices which reaffirm the companionship of humans and the earth spirits. These rituals provide the mystical vitality for their idealized image of tranquil, cooperative households free of domination, possessiveness, jealousy and quarreling. Gibson presents a general ethnography of the Buid covering many aspects of their peacefulness.

48   Gibson, Thomas. "Symbolic Representations of Tranquility and Aggression among the Buid." In *Societies at Peace: Anthropological Perspectives*, edited by Signe Howell and Roy Willis, 60-78. London: Routledge, 1989.

The Buid condemn violence and aggression in all human interactions, but they don't criticize aggressiveness in the worlds of animals and spirits. The spirit world serves as a model that explains the social world in which they live: hostilities between friendly spirit familiars and rapacious spirits represent mystically the hostility between them and their Christian lowland neighbors; the close, mystical linkages between humans and earth spirits symbolize the sharing, supportive relationships in their own communities. They believe they must live peacefully but within a context in which they are preyed upon by both the lowlanders and the spirits. In order to maintain the stable, predatory system that surrounds them, they have to commit aggression against animals and sacrifice them. They envision a continuum of animals, humans and spirits: the pigs eat the passive plants, people in turn eat pigs in rituals that try to control dangers from spirits, and the spirits eat the people. Violence is thus a normal part of the non-human world, and eating is symbolic of aggression, violence, and domination--a contrast with speech, which symbolizes two-way, mutual relationships.

49   Gibson, Thomas. "The Sharing of Substance Versus the Sharing of Activity among the Buid." *Man* n.s. 20(September 1985): 391-411.

The Buid have negative attitudes toward relations based on kinship and positive attitudes toward companionship relationships, which they feel foster personal autonomy, are easy to terminate, and are of a voluntary nature. Their social and moral order is based on the symbolism of companionship, particularly

their closely cooperative, companionable marriages. Both partners to the marriage own their separate swidden patches and
valuables, but they share ownership of their house and the
animals they raise cooperatively. Divorce is easy and common.
When a couple quarrels, the spirits of the earth may become
angered and terminate their protection of humans, which would
endanger life and fertility. Benevolence of the spirits is restored
through a ritual sacrifice of one of the couple's pigs, whose meat
is shared with the entire community, including the spirits. If they
have a serious conflict they appeal to a *tultulan*, a collective
discussion with the rest of the community, which either results
in a renewed commitment to their companionship or a divorce
agreement that includes appropriate compensation. These discussions and agreements serve to control quarreling and channel
potential violence into compromise and negotiation.

Chewong

The Chewong, a small Senoi tribe of about 260 people, part of the Orang
Asli grouping of peoples, live by gathering, hunting, and some shifting
agriculture in the mountainous interior of Peninsular Malaysia. They are
a completely peaceful people, with no history of warfare or fighting. For
recent information, see the introduction to the section on the Orang Asli.

50   Howell, Signe. "From Child to Human: Chewong Concepts of
      Self." In *Acquiring Culture: Cross Cultural Studies in Child
      Development*, edited by Gustav Jahoda and I. M. Lewis, 147-
      168. London: Croom Helm, 1988.
         The Chewong are completely peaceful, with no history of
      warfare; overt aggression is very rare. They withdraw from
      situations of conflict, moving to different settlements to avoid
      people with whom they have bad feelings. A key ingredient in
      the growth of children into humans (that is, adults), is the
      acquisition of practical and supernatural knowledge. For in-
      stance, a girl learning the techniques of weaving a carrying
      basket must learn to face the cane joints upward so that the breath
      of someone carrying it will not become trapped, which might
      have fatal results. Adolescence is a time of active learning,
      though society assumes that the adolescents will learn the skills
      of adults by the time they are grown without being specifically
      taught. As adults, men and women work together and have very
      flexible sex roles. Though the women bear children and nurse
      them and the men take on more of the hunting and heavy work,

no value judgments are assigned to either sex or their respective behaviors. Individual achievements are ignored by everyone, competition is absent, and personal proficiency is not noticed.

51   Howell, Signe. "Rules Not Words." In *Indigenous Psychologies: The Anthropology of the Self*, edited by Paul Heelas and Andrew Lock, 134-143. New York: Academic Press, 1981.

The Chewong always appear to be in control of their emotions. Their gatherings are reserved except for ritual occasions when the community may be involved in singing and drumming, but even then they enjoy themselves in a constrained, low-key fashion. They suppress their emotions by following rules very carefully. For instance, the rule *maro* implies that a visitor must immediately be offered tobacco and food, lest one be thought of as stingy. *Punen* requires the Chewong to avoid desires that might not be fulfilled. One can *punen* another by not sharing food with him, or by withholding something that the other person specifically desires, or by denying something from oneself. Due to *punen*, pleasurable events such as feasts are not discussed in advance, and one must make no outburst if an accident occurs. *Taladn* is a rule that prohibits anyone from laughing at animals or teasing them, whether they are living or dead. The Chewong feel there are no essential differences between human beings, supernatural beings, and the rest of nature. All have a comparable life-force, *ruway*, the essence of their beings.

52   Howell, Signe. *Society and Cosmos: Chewong of Peninsular Malaysia*. Singapore: Oxford University Press, 1984.

The Chewong never quarrel, show anger, or display emotion. Their language lacks words for aggression, war, crime, fighting, or punishment. When confronted with aggressiveness or threats, they immediately flee. One man, threatened by a Malay soldier, fled with his family to a remote mountain for ten years. The Chewong exhibit no rivalry or competitiveness, and they never make a point of one individual having greater ability than another. But while they do not compete, they also don't help one another, since they prefer to do their own work with their spouses. They have no political organization, no leaders, no system of authority, no formal sanctions, and no punishment. Group ideas of proper behavior are known by all, and someone who transgresses may have to move away to avoid the disapproval of the group. They ascribe no special status to male or female roles--hunting carries no more prestige or value then cooking, planting, gathering, or child care. The married couple cooperates closely in their economic activities. Chewong ideas of human relationships, relations with superhuman beings, consciousness, relativity, and the rules that govern behavior form the core of this book.

53   Howell, Signe. "'To Be Angry Is Not To Be Human, But To Be Fearful Is': Chewong Concepts of Human Nature." In *Societies at Peace: Anthropological Perspectives*, edited by Signe Howell and Roy Willis, 45-59. London: Routledge, 1989.

Quarrels and the expression of anger are rare among the Chewong, and crime is nonexistent. In one incident, a jealous woman got angry at her husband, who was apparently innocent of her accusations of adultery, so she broke his best blowpipe in half and trampled on it. This highly antisocial act upset everyone in the camp; they tried to avoid her and several families moved away because of the incident. They have no violence in their mythology, and could not conceive of murder. Even outsiders who are aggressive toward them and are not part of their social universe cannot be attacked. They believe health is based on maintaining the established order, and disease is a result of its disruption. Healing is assisted through the cooperation of non-human spirit guides which, during seances, provide help. The Chewong particularly appreciate the help of the "leaf people," spirit beings that live in the flowers and trees and look and dress like them. The Chewong have adopted Malay words for anger, quarreling, fighting and war, concepts they understand, but they have no words for coercion and competition.

Doukhobors

The Doukhobors number about 25,000 people living in the western prairie provinces of Canada and in British Columbia. They formed in Russia more than 200 years ago, accepting the central belief that the presence of God is immanent in every human being as the Christ spirit. Thus, they believe it is a sin to kill. Their leadership has been vested in hereditary dynasties of theocrats, most notably during the late 19th and 20th centuries in Peter Verigin and his son, also named Peter Verigin. During the early period of their settlement in Canada they were a communal people, but their communes collapsed; their economic activities are integrated with the mainstream of Canadian society, though they still speak Russian.[3]

54   Lyons, John E. "Toil and a Peaceful Life: Peter V. Verigin and
Doukhobor Education." *Communal Societies* 11(1991): 78-92.

The Russian Doukhobors believed in communal living, pacifism, and equality; God, they felt, directs their lives through their
inner voices. When they had a series of massive protest burnings
of weapons in the 1890s, persecution from the Czarist government intensified so they emigrated to Canada. There they soon
divided into those who wanted to meld into Canadian society,
others who continued to follow their leader, Peter Verigin, and
some who would only follow their own inner voices. Since they
believed that education should consist of learning peasant skills
taught to them by their parents, plus rote learning of the Psalms,
they began to come into conflict with provincial requirements
to attend public schools. In 1923 they responded to heavy
provincial pressure in British Columbia to attend schools by
keeping their children home; then some school buildings started
to be burned. These protest activities, clearly inimical to their
traditions of peacefulness, may have been aimed as much at
Verigin, who tried to foster a slow accommodation with Canadian society, as at the government for its attempts to force their
compliance with the laws.

55   Woodcock, George and Ivan Avakumovic. *The Doukhobors.*
Toronto: Oxford University Press, 1968.

Doukhobor pacifism and their rejection of the authority of the
state have frequently influenced their history. The sect arose in
southern Russia sometime before the 18th century, and went
through alternating periods of austerity, communal life, prosperity, toleration by the government, and persecution for their
beliefs. During the 1840s they were exiled to the Caucasus
where they prospered, gradually lost the fervor of their earlier
convictions, and in 1877, under government pressure, compromised their ideals by supplying transportation for imperial army
campaigns against the Turks. Beginning in the 1890s their exiled
leader Peter Verigin, influenced in part by the writings of
Tolstoy, began directing a moral and spiritual renewal. They
resumed communal living and held a massive burning of all their
weapons which symbolized their rejection of violence and all
their compromises of the previous half-century. Many emigrated to western Canada a few years later because of persecution. The colorful history of their difficulties with neighboring
peoples and hostilities from governments, their pacifism, their

nude demonstrations, terrorism, political intrigues and social developments are thoroughly described in this history.

Fipa

The 100,000 Fipa live on a treeless plateau region of southwestern Tanzania bordered on the west by Lake Tanganyika. The Bantu-speaking people cultivate finger millet as their primary crop, they raise goats, sheep, cattle and chickens, and they fish and trap to supplement what they raise themselves. Their system of compost farming allows them to have enduring, sedentary villages. Early European visitors in the 19th century commented on the evident prosperity of their land as well as the peacefulness of their communities.

56   Willis, R. G. "Kamcape: An Anti-Sorcery Movement in South-West Tanzania." *Africa* 38(January 1968): 1-15.
        Kamcape was the name adopted by an anti-sorcery movement that swept through the Fipa villages in 1963-64, a phenomenon that was very similar to outbreaks of sorcery in 1933-34, 1943-44, and 1954. When the proponents of anti-sorcery moved into a village, their accusations were founded on general social, political, economic, and religious differences rather than on interpersonal conflicts. The abrupt "cleansing" of a village by the anti-sorcerers was a partly magical revolution in which the lowest-status people temporarily assumed power and attacked the "sorcery" of the village elites. The process reaffirmed the moral values of the community--its traditional harmony and unity--at the same time as it resolved at the psychic level the internal conflicts. The elders and the prestige class of people were allowed to resume their normal roles when the leaders of Kamcape moved on to another village.

57   Willis, Roy. "Do the Fipa Have a Word for It?" In *The Anthropology of Evil*, edited by David Parkin, 209-223. Oxford: Basil Blackwell, 1985.
        Rather than focusing on division and dualism, the Fipa emphasize the processes that promote unity in their villages. During his 19 months of residence among them, the author did not witness any fighting. However, there is an undercurrent of competition in the villages between the major wealthy families and their supporters for additional alliances and power. Stresses related to this tense clandestine conflict are periodically resolved when cults arise that target the wealthy households. The

rich people are accused of using sorcery to kill livestock, crops, and other villagers, and in an effort to restore peace and the normal village unity they confess to these crimes. The villagers believe that the medicines of the cult leaders could be used to kill wealthy people--the "sorcerers"--if they repeated their offenses, while their own medicine would protect themselves. When the excitement dies down, the wealthy people remain in the villages and resume their normal social roles. These cultic public accusations of wealthy people, part of a continuing dialogue in the villages, arise every ten years or so.

58   Willis, Roy. "Executive Women and the Emergence of Female Class Consciousness: The Case of the Fipa." *Anthropology* 4(May 1980): 1-10.

The pre-colonial Fipa had two major states, which had dual political systems run by the men and the women. The non-coercive male system was based on peaceful local commerce between wealthy men, who provided food to poor people in return for their labor. These wealthy people used their surplus to acquire higher government positions and to gain access to the transcontinental trade. The women controlled the judicial system. The magistrates, normally older women, handled village sex crimes with the authority to place heavy fines on male or female offenders. They could retain one-third of the fine money. The people who worked hardest within the system, and derived least benefit from it, were the younger women of child-bearing age. Their resentment at being exploited erupted periodically whenever a woman died in labor or twins were born. They tore off their clothing, painted their faces, and, seizing their farm tools, rampaged through the villages plundering crops and killing animals. These brief attacks on the male economic system were sanctioned by Fipa cosmology, which associated force with sexuality and femaleness.

59   Willis, Roy. "Power Begins at Home: The Symbolism of Male-Female Commensality in Ufipa." In *Creativity of Power: Cosmology and Action in African Societies*, edited by W. Arens and Ivan Karp, 113-128. Washington: Smithsonian Institution Press, 1989.

Advancement among the Fipa has become contingent on peaceful, friendly social skills. The twice-daily meals and the frequent sessions of beer drinking symbolize this desirable sociability. Leisurely meals are eaten without haste and with a great deal of pleasant conversation among everyone present. People take food from the central bowls without intruding on their neighbor's space and without appearing to be too eager to eat. If a bowl is out of convenient reach of someone, subtle glances and casual conversation about other topics are sufficiently strong hints to prompt people to pass the desired food. Drinking rituals differ from the etiquette of eating meals, but the same basic principles apply: while everyone converses, bowls of beer are carefully and without haste passed around the assembled group, avoiding any appearance of greed or selfishness. Men and women participate as equals at meals and drinking occasions, an unusual custom among African societies. Even when people become quite inebriated during their drinking sessions, everyone maintains the correct forms of courtesy and no one ever becomes violent.

60   Willis, Roy. "The 'Peace Puzzle' in Ufipa." In *Societies at Peace: Anthropological Perspectives*, edited by Signe Howell and Roy Willis, 133-145. London: Routledge, 1989.

According to the oral traditions of the Fipa, they were constantly at war with one another until the mid-19th century, not long before contacts with Europeans. Their oral narratives recount numerous violent battles, and the archaeological evidence from abandoned villages confirms the impression of a warlike people. However, European explorers and colonists all commented on the orderly peacefulness of their society, where people respected the authority of their rulers but there appeared to be no oppression. These observers described the Fipa as friendly, talkative with strangers, outgoing, good-hearted, self-possessed, energetic, industrious and lacking violent crime. Out of the chaos of their warfare they evidently constructed new, indigenous states which embodied their dualistic cosmology in opposed, but complementary male and female administrative systems. The government of the Fipa state was run by a hierarchy of men who bid for their offices, and it existed parallel to a magistracy run by women who maintained the judicial and punitive systems in the villages. Despite their peaceful, orderly ways, however, the Fipa today are quite energetic and competitive.

Fore

At the time of first contact with Westerners in the 1950s, about 12,000 Fore lived in the mountains of Papua New Guinea. They became renowned in the West because of reports on their cannibalism, intervillage warfare, and the debilitating disease kuru, a degenerative, always-fatal illness of the central nervous system that was only known among these people. While several scholars described them as highly warlike, anthropologist E. Richard Sorenson found the Fore to be not nearly so aggressive as they had been portrayed. The North Fore had run out of unsettled forested areas to move to, and because of population pressures had been forced to accept settled agriculture. The North Fore had adopted some intervillage warfare because of the stress, though it was disorganized and disliked. The South Fore, however, still had virgin forest to move into when Sorenson first visited them, so they still practiced a protoagriculture consisting of hunting and swidden gardening. As tensions developed among the South Fore, people could easily leave their hamlets and move into new territories. While the other anthropologists focus on the aggressive attitudes of the Fore, Sorenson concentrates on their peaceful resolution of conflicts and their ability to raise their children without fighting.

61   Berndt, Ronald M. "Interdependence and Conflict in the Eastern Central Highlands of New Guinea." *Man* 55(July 1955): 105-107.

Warfare and other aggressive acts are major interests of the South Fore, though their social system fluctuates between conflict and cooperation. A primary aim of the socialization process is to produce warriors who enjoy fighting, aggression, self-assertion, and dominating others through force or threats. Conflict among the districts, an essential feature of their society, is always justified as revenge for injuries or slights. The districts constantly bribe others to be allies, or at least to be neutrals, and positions of alliance and hostility are regularly shifting. Since most relatives live in adjoining districts, the constantly shifting conflicts mark the interdependence of the districts with one another. The only peoples with which any given district are not potentially at war are the ones that live too far away to be related or to fight with. Control measures in each district operate to support conformity and regulation within the group, and to promote conflict with adjoining districts.

62   Glasse, Robert and Shirley Lindenbaum. "South Fore Politics."
In *Politics in New Guinea, Traditional and in the Context of
Change: Some Anthropological Perspectives*, edited by Ronald
M. Berndt and Peter Lawrence, 362-380. Seattle: University of
Washington Press, 1973.

Fore society highly admired physical aggression and aggressive leaders. A child who dominated other children--who would
bully, swagger, and throw tantrums to get his way--was highly
regarded by adults since he had the right characteristics to be a
Big Man, a leader. One Big Man proudly told how he resisted the
punishments of his initiation rite, fought back against the adults
trying to hold him down, and threw stones at them. The Fore tried
to prevent violence and internal aggression within their major
political units, the parishes; if people did fight they were
supposed to use only sticks and try to not kill one another.
Sometimes this ideal failed and opposite factions of a parish
clashed in open warfare. A major cause of Fore aggression was
their belief in sorcery, which they believed was the primary
cause of the mysterious, fatal disease kuru; when a new case was
detected the angry men would hunt for the sorcerer in other
hamlets, focusing particular suspicion on people who had
exhibited peculiar behavior, or who had had strained relations
with the victim.

63   Lindenbaum, Shirley. "Sorcery and Structure in Fore Society."
Oceania 41(June 1971): 277-287.

The Fore social system fosters constant flexibility and movement of peoples to different villages, with a corresponding
weakness of kinship relations. True kin are replaced by fictional
kin. Although the village may gain strength from newcomers,
the lack of a sense of solidarity leads to feelings of ambiguity and
the belief in sorcery. Kuru, the fatal disease unique to the Fore
in the 1970s and before, was among the major causes of sorcery
charges. The author concludes that the exceedingly flexible
South Fore social system, exacerbated by this mysterious disease, "contributes to mutual mistrust among men at close
range" and has led to sorcery and violence.

64   Sorenson, E. Richard. "Cooperation and Freedom among the
Fore of New Guinea." In *Learning Non-Aggression: The Experience of Non-Literate Societies*, edited by Ashley Montagu, 12-
30. New York: Oxford University Press, 1978.

The Fore were a protoagricultural hunting-gardening people

of highland New Guinea who had a peaceful, cooperative lifestyle in which individuals associated with others with whom they could get along, and moved further into the forests when they came into conflict with hostile peoples. An important aspect of Fore peacefulness was the way their children were raised. Infants were held all the time, and all of their babies needs were satisfied immediately. This constant level of physical communication, even before they could talk, minimized infant frustration and protest. Fore mothers, as well as other adults and older children, responded to displays of aggression by children by diverting them playfully and affectionately--through "distraction by affection," as Sorenson characterizes it. Thus, Fore children learned from their society to place no value on aggressive behavior. As the Fore began to be crowded, however, and ran out of new forests that they could move into, they were forced to settle into more stable agricultural communities, which prompted them to begin fighting with neighboring groups.

65   Sorenson, E. Richard. "Socio-Ecological Change among the Fore of New Guinea." *Current Anthropology* 13(June-Oct. 1972): 349-383.

Years ago the small, isolated groups of Fore accepted rules of give and take; they would move to new territories if conflicts arose. Introduction of the sweet potato about 100 years ago significantly raised the yield of food from their gardens, which allowed population densities to grow. This population increase inhibited the free movement of peoples, forcing them to live in close proximity with others they did not get along with. In areas that became densely settled, conflicts became severe and warfare common. The sweet potato cultivation also fostered an increase in their stocks of domestic pigs, so the villagers tried to defuse tensions by inviting neighboring peoples to large pig feasts, though the feasts were usually tense affairs. Since they had not adopted coping mechanisms for their increasing warfare, when the first Australian patrols arrived in the mid-1950s the Fore welcomed them: they quickly gave up their fighting, appealing their conflicts to the white people for resolution, they dropped their habits of aggressive posturing and talk of manliness, and they adopted an anti-fighting ethic.

66   Sorenson, E. Richard. *The Edge of the Forest: Land, Childhood and Change in a New Guinea Protoagricultural Society*. Washington: Smithsonian Institution Press, 1976.

This large, well-illustrated book about the Fore provides a full description of the geographical, social, economic, agricultural and cultural conditions of Fore existence, both in their earlier, shifting-agricultural lifestyle, and in their more recent, settled situation. Most of the book concentrates on the South Fore groups who retained their shifting ways into recent decades. The author describes two different forces which appeared to help shape the Fore feelings of trust and affection for the other residents of their villages: growing up in a milieu of personal regard and understanding; and the territorial freedom to move about easily. Many photos illustrate his thorough analysis of the way their children developed: he shows how children were held all the time, not only by their mothers but also by the older children who carried them around on their backs; how older children deferred to the desires of the younger; how their play lacked competition; behavioral strategies employed by older children to quickly deal with feelings of anger, and so on.

G/wi

The 2,000 G/wi, one of the San peoples of southern Africa, live as hired laborers on Botswana ranches owned by whites and to some extent they still subsist in the Central Kalahari Game Reserve on their traditional hunting and gathering economy.

67   Hold, Barbara C. L. "Attention-Structure and Behavior in G/wi San Children." *Ethology and Sociobiology* 1(1980): 275-290.
        Observations of G/wi children during their play activities focused on the circumstances of group dominance--which children were most often the center of attention, which were the most highly regarded, which had the highest rank. The results are compared with groups of German and Japanese children. The ranking G/wi children, as in Germany and Japan, most frequently initiated and organized activities, but unlike the other two societies they did not attempt to dominate their playmates. And in contrast to the German children, where the highly ranking children displayed significantly more aggression than the rest, there was no such correlation among the G/wi. Older G/wi children protected and mediated conflicts among the younger ones, regardless of rank, though most often disputes among the children resolved themselves or adults intervened. Children in Germany and Japan shared with the dominant children, while among the G/wi they shared with intimate

playmates; German and Japanese children helped their ranking peers most often, while among the G/wi there was a negative correlation between being helped and dominance.

68 Silberbauer, George. "Political Process in G/wi Bands." In *Politics and History in Band Societies*, edited by Eleanor Leacock and Richard Lee, 23-35. New York: Cambridge University Press, 1982.

G/wi band decisions are normally reached through informal discussions: conversations among friends, or in larger groups if the issue is involved or contentious. In those larger group discussions, people with strongly held views may speak forcefully and everyone will signal their assent or dissent through body language, murmurs, and grunts, but not through open disagreement. Sometimes a person will present his views loudly, ostensibly just to his group but obviously intended to be heard by everyone in the band, and an opponent may respond, with equal volume to another group, both ignoring the other's comments and answering arguments without seeming to directly confront another person. If passions during a discussion become too strong, the G/wi will back off from the topic for a while to allow emotions to cool down--an effectively presented piece of rhetoric may be received by a man who is suddenly very busy picking an invisible thorn from his foot. Decisions are reached through consensus--which is neither democratic nor unanimous, but which is arrived at when there is no significant opposition to a proposal.

69 Silberbauer, George B. "The G/wi Bushmen." In *Hunters and Gatherers Today: A Socioeconomic Study of Eleven Such Cultures in the Twentieth Century*, edited by M. G. Bicchieri, 271-326. New York: Holt, Rinehart and Winston, 1972.

G/wi social relationships are cooperative, peaceful, and friendly. Before they have children, a young couple will live with the wife's parents, who take on the role of affectionate teachers and advisors. Infants are given constant security and affection, and as they grow their training is managed in a supportive fashion: when children misbehave they are allowed to sense the upset that their behavior causes and the brief, slight lessening of warmth from the band. As they become older, children will be admonished to be cooperative and gentle, or someone will distract them into acceptable behavior. Tensions and conflicts in the band are usually dispelled through gossip and joking, or sometimes through talking out the issues. When an individual antagonizes the group and refuses to heed its judgments and standards, the band may have to gently ease him out. This is done through subtle frustration--by purposely misunderstanding his wishes or not hearing him--in effect rejecting him without causing him to feel rejected or offended. As he grows disgusted with the band, he'll leave without feelings of anger to live with another group.

Hutterites

A communal, pacifist, Anabaptist group originating in southern Germany and Austria in the early 16th century, the Hutterites have been forced to make numerous moves due to persecutions: to Moravia in 1528, to Transylvania in 1621, to Wallachia in 1667, to Russia in 1770, to the United States in the 1870s, and to Canada in 1918. By 1974 there were 229 Hutterite colonies in North America: Alberta had 84 colonies, Manitoba 53, Saskatchewan 28, South Dakota 34, Montana 23, and a few existed in other states. They contained, in all, over 21,000 people. By 1990 they had grown to 38,000 people in 375 colonies. The colonies engage in large-scale farming and ranching operations. Because of their strongly pacifist beliefs, they fled from Russia in the 1870s when the government instituted universal military service, and many fled to Canada from the United States in 1918 because of the tortures inflicted on their young men when they refused to fight in the army.[4]

70   Bennett, John W. *Hutterian Brethren: The Agricultural Economy and Social Organization of a Communal People*. Stanford, CA: Stanford University Press, 1967.

Adaptability to change among the Hutterite colonies in Saskatchewan is an important asset for their farming economy. The author examines the economic and social systems of six colonies, particularly their resource utilization, decision making, management styles, control of pressures, and administrative techniques. These colonies manage to avoid interpersonal conflicts and preserve a cooperative spirit despite divisive forces. While tensions exist between colonies, the Hutterites don't allow them to become too important, and they utilize a variety of techniques to build friendly relations with their non-Hutterite neighbors. They avoid the growth of factions by relying on their institutional structures and good leadership. They train their children to be non-competitive--if an outside teacher makes a special point of praising one of the pupils, the entire class reacts with embarrassment, since they have already learned not to emphasize differences in intelligence and skill. The competition that does exist in the Hutterite colony is never overtly between individuals. Rather, managers of the different colony enterprises may try to compete for resources; colony executives have to make decisions for the good of the whole.

71   Bennett, John W. "Social Theory and the Social Order of the Hutterian Community." *Mennonite Quarterly Review* 51(October 1977): 292-307.

The most important aspect of Hutterite social control is that it is not inflexible and unchanging. Instead, Hutterites regularly review and adapt their social structures in response to external and internal pressures. Children learn that their actions will be monitored all their lives, but they also learn the need for inner controls--the individual must suppress hatreds, jealousies, and wants in order to be an effective part of their society. The Hutterite system of guaranteed equality forbids individuals from seeking honor and status, but it has marginal privileges and covert recognitions that do not violate the order. Restless young men are encouraged to leave the colony to try life on the outside, though 95 percent of the time they return to the colony. Despite pressures of discipline and seemingly a complete lack of individualism, Hutterites actually allow a great deal of individuality, an essential psychic need for the health of the colony. They never witness oral or physical aggression and do not have the opportunity to learn patterns of aggressive responses, but occasionally they do have problems caused by repressing their aggressions.

72   Deets, Lee Emerson. "The Origins of Conflict in the Hutterische Communities." *Publications of the American Sociological Society* 25(May 1931): 125-135.

The spirit of the Hutterite colony is organization and cooperation. Jobs are rotated on a weekly basis so that a woman, for instance, will spend one week out of three milking cows, one week out of twelve in the bakery, and so forth. The leaders of the colony have complete authority, and gossip does not play any role in social control. There is no adult quarreling, conflict, or individualism. Each colony is able to maintain Hutterite social values because of its isolation, and they have solved the problem of overpopulation by their practice of dividing the colonies. A history of persecutions over the centuries has held them together and carried them through times when leadership was weak. One potential source of conflict in the Hutterite colony might be between the interests of the family and the needs of the colony, while other sources of conflict might include access by individuals to money, adoptions of customs or conveniences from the outside, the fairness and nature of work assignments, privileges, and punishments meted out to rule breakers.

73   Hostetler, John A. *Hutterite Society*. Baltimore: Johns Hopkins University Press, 1974.

In the first third of the book, Hostetler chronicles the migrations of the Hutterites from the early 16th century until their move to America in the 1870s. Periods of growth followed times of persecution, eras of renewal succeeded intervals when they became lax about discipline and abandoned their communal living. The rest of the book covers their culture, social organization, and strategies for survival. While little of the material is directly about their pacifism, most relates indirectly to their peaceful lifestyle. For instance, the author shows how they view individualism as evil--they teach their children an unquestioning obedience to authority and acceptance of punishment. By the age of three, children attend a kindergarten where they learn to pray, obey, respect authority, and get along with others. From age six to fifteen they attend separate German and English schools daily; in the one they learn German, the Bible, and Hutterite beliefs, and in the other they learn all the subjects of the public school curriculum. The German language and culture--the life of the commune--dominates the outside language and customs.

74   Sawka, Patricia. "The Hutterian Way of Life." *Canadian Geographical Journal* 77(October 1968): 126-131.

Hutterites started moving into Canada from the United States in 1918, settling in Manitoba and Alberta. During World War II they refused to serve in the military of their country, and they suffered from the hostility of their neighbors. Alberta passed a law in 1942 that forbade the sale of land to them, which was revised in 1947 to limit the closeness and size of their colonies. While their neighbors respected them as good farmers and religious people, opposition was based on their pacifism, the impression that they did not support local businesses, and the fact that they showed no concern for community welfare outside their colonies and would not participate in civic duties. Within the colonies relationships between Hutterite spouses are normally good, with no quarreling and divorce very rare. Couples usually have nine or ten children, with whom they have good relations. The author observed, on visiting a colony as a health practitioner, that the children were very cooperative, intelligent, and obedient, though they lacked an urge to excel.

75   Thielman, George G. "The Hutterites in Contemporary Society." *Mennonite Life* 25(January 1970): 42-46.

The Hutterites have suffered a lot of persecution because of their strict belief in nonresistance and their communal style of living. They fled Russia in the 1870s and came to the United States to escape the Czar's pressures for militarization, but they were subject to so much hatred in the U.S. during the First World War that they emigrated to Canada, primarily Alberta, which appeared to be more amenable to their ways. But during World War II they received similar discrimination in Alberta as they had experienced earlier in the U.S. Canadians resented the negative attitude of the Hutterites toward their war effort, and even more importantly they resented their desire to keep expanding and buying more large tracts of land for new colonies to take care of their growing population. They were disliked for a host of other reasons: their communal lifestyle, their old-fashioned dress, their refusal to allow their children to be educated. A more positive attitude prevailed in Saskatchewan, so a big colony was established there.

76   Unruh, John D. "The Hutterites During World War I." *Mennonite Life* 24(July 1969): 130-137.

Hutterite draftees in 1917-18 would not cooperate with the military in any way: they refused to wear uniforms or to do any work assignments except to keep their quarters clean and neat. Army personnel were determined to break them of their obstinacy, and would not listen to their repeated statements that, as members of the Hutterian Brethren Church, they could not participate in any form of military service. They were frequently ridiculed and abused, and many were harassed through such means as being made to stand in the sun all day. Some were tortured: lowered head-first repeatedly into water until nearly drowned, beaten, dragged about by the hair, held in a cold shower at length then thrown outside, and so on. Two men who were sent to Fort Leavenworth military prison for refusing to obey orders died from the inhuman abuse they received. The

Hutterites never bent to the demands for cooperation since they felt that even obeying orders given by a military officer to do routine work would have compromised their peaceful beliefs.

77   Van den Berghe, Pierre L. and Karl Peter. "Hutterites and Kibbutzniks: A Tale of Nepotistic Communism." *Man* n.s. 23(September 1988): 522-539.

The Hutterite colonies, along with the Israeli kibbutzim, are perhaps the only communes in Western history to have achieved indefinitely self-sustaining communal societies. The primary reason the Hutterites have been able to maintain their egalitarian communal societies in the face of pressures from outside temptations and the disruptions of nepotism is that individuals perceive their society as superior to the alternatives that surround them. Factors that foster this perception of superiority include the life-long security of their society, and, for the men particularly, the more varied, self-fulfilling, self-paced, and autonomous quality of their work compared to outside factories. The small size of the colonies ensures that everyone's contributions are essential to the welfare of the group; small size also allows the group to monitor and control informally (or sometimes formally) the behavior of individual members. While an emphasis on collective prosperity and informal monitoring of individual behavior is a clear source of tension. the Hutterites control open conflict through strong constraints that prevent the expression of hostility.

Ifaluk

Over 400 people live on an atoll of less than one-half a square mile in area, located about 400 miles south of Guam in the Pacific Island nation of the Federated States of Micronesia. The Micronesian people on the island subsist on fish, coconuts, breadfruits, and the taro produced in their gardens. Several anthropologists, most recently Catherine Lutz, have noted the social values of the Ifaluk which emphasize sharing and cooperation; these ethnographers have observed a complete lack of aggressiveness on the island, though an article by Betzig and Wichimai [78] notes one incident of violence many years ago.

78   Betzig, Laura and Santus Wichimai. "A Not So Perfect Peace: A History of Conflict on Ifaluk." *Oceania* 61(March 1991): 240-256.

The record of violence on Ifaluk in the past is not clear--some European writers mentioned peaceful conditions while others wrote about violence. Legends of former wars are still told involving Ifaluk warriors wiping out the people of other islands and resettling them with Ifaluk. However, the distance between the islands would have militated against interisland wars. The second author, an Ifaluk native, provides insight into, and stories about, the roles of chiefs and sorcerers. While the chiefs gained advantages from the tributes of their subjects, they resolved conflicts, pressured their subordinates to treat one another as equals, urged them to share in communal fishing, persuaded them to do public works projects, and convinced them not to take resources from others. Traditionally, the chiefs could impose penalties, and they might pay a sorcerer to kill an offender or even an entire household. The Ifaluk author is able to narrate one verifiable story of violence in island history: the grandson of a man who got hurt is still alive. Many years ago a man (the grandfather) tried to sneak into a village at night after a woman, was set upon by the village guards, chased across the island, caught finally and severely beaten up.

79   Burrows, Edwin G. "From Value to Ethos on Ifaluk Atoll." *Southwestern Journal of Anthropology* 8(Spring 1952): 13-35.

Ifaluk clans are ranked according to certain traditional privileges, and within the clans people have ranks as well. The lines of division are extremely subtle, however: instead of being a stratified society, the ranking system produces a graduated continuum in which each individual has a known place. In practice, this helps maintain law and order--the atoll is without crime. The most prominent Ifaluk characteristic is kindliness (according to the author, a better term than nonaggression), which produces courteous speech, a particularly important attribute of the clan chiefs. If the chiefs speak kindly, setting the tone for everyone, the Ifaluk will enjoy long lives. The author never heard any expression of anger, even when people had had too much to drink, and although legends tell of violent periods in the distant past there is no memory of violence. Visitors between Ifaluk and the neighboring atolls give and receive only kindness and hospitality to and from one another. Ifaluk social ranking structures and beliefs in kindliness together produce a successful governing structure and a peaceful society characterized by cooperation, generosity, and courtesy.

80   Lessa, William A. "Sorcery on Ifaluk." *American Anthropologist* 63(August 1961): 817-820.

Although he admits he has never been to Ifaluk, the author questions the accuracy of Burrows and Spiro's report that there is no sorcery on the island (Burrows, Edwin G. and Melford E. Spiro. *An Atoll Culture: Ethnography of Ifaluk in the Central Carolines*. Reprint. Westport, CT: Greenwood, 1970). He bases his reasoning on his field work on Ulithi, another atoll in the area, where the people of Ifaluk have a reputation as being skilled, aggressive sorcerers. One Ulithi informant who had been to Ifaluk three times reported a number of instances of rumored attacks of sorcery, in most of which the sorcerer also seems to have become as ill as his victim or to have died also. Lessa points out that these reports undermine Spiro's argument [91] that the Ifaluk have turned away from sorcery to relying on the spirits as scapegoats for their aggressiveness, and Spiro might want to revise his theory accordingly.

81   Lutz, Catherine. "Cultural Patterns and Individual Differences in the Child's Emotional Meaning System." In *The Socialization of Emotions*, edited by Michael Lewis and Carolyn Saarni, 37-53. New York: Plenum, 1985.

The gentleness that characterizes human relations among the Ifaluk can be witnessed right in the birth hut. At one birth, the infant's first cry was immediately labeled by onlookers as peevishness. "It's pissed off," they said. The child would subsequently be taught to avoid that behavior pattern. The author discusses the patterns in which Ifaluk children learn emotions by focusing on the concept of *nguch*, which combines the English feelings of being bored and fed up. She gives tentative reasons, for instance, why adopted children--which are quite common on Ifaluk--feel *nguch* more frequently when they do not have enough chores to perform, while children who are not adopted have the opposite reaction. It is clear that emotion concepts are learned by Ifaluk children not just as words but as a consciousness of social relationships within the value system of the people.

82   Lutz, Catherine. "Depression and the Translation of Emotional Worlds." In *Culture and Depression: Studies in the Anthropology and Cross-Cultural Psychiatry of Affect and Disorder*, edited by Arthur Kleinman and Byron Good, 63-100. Berkeley: University of California Press, 1985.

The Ifaluk views of emotion are very different from Western psychoanalytic concepts. The Ifaluk predicate their emotional well-being on their connectedness with others. Since they have an egalitarian society, they conceive of stress and loss using concepts that distinguish whether or not relationships are moral and valid. They live densely together on a small atoll in large families that have many connections with other families through the widespread practice of adopting and raising one another's children. They do not separate thoughts from emotions, and their word *nunuwan* (thoughts/feelings) also carries implications of their cultural values. A person with lots of *nunuwan* is compassionate, responsive, and considerate of the effects of his or her actions on others. They frequently talk about their emotions/thoughts, constantly verbalizing their moral views of events. Seven words that deal with helplessness and loss are examined in terms of their basic Ifaluk meanings, which relate in various ways to people as the objects of the loss. The words that deal with the frustration of loss distinguish between the legitimate justification for anger about it and losses that are unavoidable.

83   Lutz, Catherine. "Ethnopsychology Compared to What? Explaining Behavior and Consciousness among the Ifaluk." In *Person, Self, and Experience: Exploring Pacific Ethnopsychologies*, edited by Geoffrey M. White and John Kirkpatrick, 35-79. Berkeley: University of California Press, 1985.

All of the traits which the Ifaluk highly value--reciprocal sharing, nonaggression, cooperation, and minimizing jealousies--as well as negative characteristics are expressed by words which reveal their psychological concepts. They describe a person who is quiet, calm and gentle as *maluwelu*, a word which is also used to describe the lagoon when the wind is still. The calm person is respectful, kindly, and obedient, and he or she has enough *metagu*, defined as both fear and anxiety, to produce calmness in response to provocation. The Ifaluk esteem generosity and friendliness (*mweol*); they value the ability to effectively express opinions and feelings, to purge the emotions; they discourage impoliteness or loudness; and they prohibit any expression of violence. The person who has angry inner thoughts and emotions must *goli* (hide) them, without even looking irritated or angry. The Ifaluk do not make a sharp distinction between emotions and thoughts, which they link together in the work *niferash*, "our insides," and they do not have a fixed boundary between self and other, frequently using the first person plural rather than the singular.

84   Lutz, Catherine. "Goals, Events, and Understanding in Ifaluk Emotion Theory." In *Cultural Models in Language and Thought*, edited by Dorothy Holland and Naomi Quinn, 290-312. New York: Cambridge University Press, 1987.

The Ifaluk theory of emotion is based on certain words which signify concepts that include their cultural propositions. These concepts are embedded within a system of goals and expected human roles. Ifaluk concept words imply events which have meaning for them, and they take actions based on their perceptions of the concepts. They negotiate their interpersonal relationships on both semantic and pragmatic levels--what is the emotional concept for the issue at hand; do circumstances warrant use of a particular concept? For instance, a family was undecided how to handle a conflict of ideals when a daughter was expecting a baby, but a relative was quite ill on another island. Whom should they be with? After much negotiation over whether rules would be broken and which scenarios would provoke justifiable anger if they stayed or left, two sisters and the father went. When the father returned his daughter had delivered her baby, so he visited her to break the emotional impasse and to acknowledge that she would have a reasonable ground for justifiable anger, a necessary part of their reconciliation.

85   Lutz, Catherine. "Morality, Domination and Understandings of 'Justifiable Anger' among the Ifaluk." In *Everyday Understanding: Social and Scientific Implications*, edited by Gun R. Semin and Kenneth J. Gergen, 204-226. London: Sage, 1990.

Song, justifiable anger, is a powerful emotional concept on Ifaluk used to describe the reaction to morally condemned actions. The concept is essential in maintaining peaceful values on the island--where there is no record of violence. *Song* differs from the English word "anger," however, since it is prosocial rather than antisocial, and it does not carry other meanings of annoyance about unpleasant, frustrating events. Feelings of *song* get back to others through gossip, and they respond by feeling *metagu*, a fear of what the angry person will do. Anticipation of justifiable anger thus prompts adherence to the island's social codes, such as sharing or quiet speech. When someone violates a major value, he may incur the *song* of the chiefs, who are the final arbiters of morality and whose emotional leadership is linked to their authority over Ifaluk politics. While justifiable anger flows downward in the hierarchical structure, people lower on the social scale can invoke *song* in return for affronts or in attempts to change power structures. Proper understanding of the emotion of *song* is essential in raising children.

86   Lutz, Catherine. "Parental Goals, Ethnopsychology, and the Development of Emotional Meaning." *Ethos* 11(Winter 1983): 246-262.

The Ifaluk maintain their sharing, cooperation and nonaggression values with their emotional concept *metagu*, which is defined by the situations that produce it--such as entering an unfamiliar environment, finding oneself in a large crowd, or facing the justifiable anger (*song*) of someone who feels that a cultural value has been violated. While they believe that children will learn about *metagu* naturally, they reinforce that learning by actively teaching them about the antisocial, aggressive actions associated with it. For instance, children are taught to beware of the *metagu* that comes from strangers outside the house. Adults display justifiable anger whenever the child misbehaves. They teach them that a special kind of ghost will "get them" if they wander away from the house or misbehave, and when a child acts aggressively, one of the women will dress up in a costume to impersonate a ghost, appear menacingly at the edge of the compound, and threaten to kidnap and eat the wayward child. When the child reacts in terror, a protective adult assures the ghost that the child will not misbehave any more.

87   Lutz, Catherine. "The Domain of Emotion Words on Ifaluk." *American Ethnologist* 9(February 1982): 113-128.

The most important values on Ifaluk are sharing, cooperation, and nonaggression. In one year the most serious act of aggression consisted of one man touching another on the shoulder, which resulted in a stiff fine. Murder is unknown. In order to investigate the ways the Ifaluk conceive of their emotions, the author wrote 31 of their important emotion words on cards, asked literate informants to sort them according to the ways the words related to each other, and interviewed each individual to find out the reasons for their arrangements. Analyzing the results to ascertain the cognitive meanings of their emotional concepts, she found that the Ifaluk group their emotion words into five clusters: words for good fortune, emotions involving danger, words for connection and loss, a group related to human error, and emotion words concerned with inability. Her analysis shows that the Ifaluk are most concerned about the characteristics of particular situations and social activities in the definitions of their emotions, in contrast to Americans, who define emotions as internal feelings.

88   Lutz, Catherine A. *Unnatural Emotions: Everyday Sentiments on a Micronesian Atoll & Their Challenge to Western Theory.* Chicago: University of Chicago Press, 1988.

The ethnopsychological emotional values of the Ifaluk contribute to their peacefulness. While interpersonal violence is almost nonexistent among them, whenever people become justifiably angry (*song*), they recognize the possibility of aggression at the same time that they expect mechanisms of self-control to prevent it. For instance, they expect the adult to have the *nunuwan*--thought and emotion--of the mature, moral person. When they refer to a person as *maluwelu*--quiet, calm, and gentle--they are paying the highest compliment, since gentleness promotes their respectful, egalitarian ethos. They think of *fago* (compassion/love/sadness) as a link between the needs of one person and the nurturing feelings of others. *Fago* promotes nonviolence since it implies a feeling of love for the potential victim. Children are raised with the constant feeling of *fago* for other children: a toddler, making a threatening gesture toward another is immediately told by the adults nearby to *fago* the other. The Ifaluk frequently feel *song* (justifiable anger) toward others whose moral behavior doesn't meet community standards--for instance, when people fail to share as they are supposed to do.

89   Lutz, Catherine and Robert A. LeVine. "Culture and Intelligence in Infancy: An Ethnopsychological View." In *Origins of Intelligence: Infancy and Early Childhood*, 2d edition, edited by Michael Lewis, 327-345. New York: Plenum, 1983.

The Ifaluk word *repiy* means intelligence, in the Western sense, but the meanings also include other major values such as nonaggression, hard work, food sharing, cooperation, compassion, emotional maturity, and a ranked social and political system. *Repiy* implies not only the knowledge of values but their performance. *Repiy* people are constantly aware of the consequences of their actions, particularly the importance of avoiding conflict. While they have words for more specific values such as hard work, having an even temperament, and generosity, all may be subsumed within the concept of *repiy*. Thus, in their way of thinking, an intelligent person is a good person who abides by social values. The Ifaluk believe that children's intelligence, beginning at about two years of age and growing considerably at about five, should be fostered through adult lecturing about correct behavior. Since not all adults teach their children evenly, the youngsters do not all achieve equal measures of intelligence/proper values. Also, the boisterous behavior that children learn in school is at odds with their values of calmness and nonaggression.

90   Spiro, Melford E. "A Psychotic Personality in the South Seas." *Psychiatry* 13(May 1950): 189-204.

The Ifaluk, who had lived without aggression all their lives and were only accustomed to kindly speech, were controlled harshly by the Japanese while they owned the Caroline Islands. Speaking from raised platforms, the Japanese addressed the chiefs bluntly, demanding men to serve on work gangs on Yap Island. The Ifaluk men impressed into these gangs were subjected to harsh speech and physical abuse, a disturbing experience to them which resulted in two men becoming afflicted with severe mental disorders. One of the men, whom the author counseled over a period of four and one-half months, was quite aggressive, had severe hallucinations, felt everyone was against him, and was a constant strain on the other members of the village. The author surmises that because Ifaluk upbringing socializes people in ways that preclude aggressiveness and foster cooperation, mutual assistance, and peace, this man was unable to cope or respond to the sort of hostility he had experienced in the Japanese labor gang. The Ifaluk knew of only these two men who had ever had this kind of aggressive psychosis.

91   Spiro, Melford E. "Ghosts, Ifaluk, and Teleological Functionalism." *American Anthropologist* 54(Oct.-Dec. 1952): 497-503.

The Ifaluk ethic especially values nonaggression, helpfulness, cooperation, and sharing, all of which provide them with a high degree of physical and psychological security. They attribute abnormalities, which include aggressiveness and diseases, to possession by malevolent ghosts. This belief survives because it allows the Ifaluk to displace and suppress their aggressive drives into fear and hatred for the ghosts. On a tiny, crowded island where people cannot possibly escape from social pressures by withdrawing from one another, or escape into intoxicating beverages (since there were none when the author visited the island), this belief in evil ghosts provides an outlet for hostilities, an essential component in preventing mass neuroses. The belief also helps them to cope with their anxieties--which are identified with the ghosts--through rituals and other pre-scribed manipulations.

92   Spiro, Melford E. "Ghosts: An Anthropological Inquiry into Learning and Perception." *Journal of Abnormal and Social Psychology* 48(July 1953): 376-382.

Ifaluk infants are loved and protected, given the breast at the slightest whimper, held virtually all the time, and never re-strained. However, they are taken every morning at dawn from the warm blankets between their parents and washed in the freezing-cold waters of the lagoon, which even adults avoid until after sunrise. From these experiences children learn that the world is both satisfying and threatening, pleasant and painful. When the next baby is born, the period of indulgence suddenly ceases for the child: crying is ignored, needs are frustrated, adults no longer seem to be concerned. The children react with temper tantrums and other aggressive behaviors. These experi-ences prompt children to accept the cultural beliefs in benevo-lent and malevolent ghosts, who both protect and harm, cure and make ill, cause pleasure and pain, provide security and anxiety. Adult experiences continue to reconfirm their beliefs in ghosts: since men are intrinsically good and their society is peaceful, human anxieties, with their hostile and aggressive thoughts, are obviously caused by the alien ghosts and can thus be easily rejected.

93   Spiro, Melford E. "Some Ifaluk Myths and Folk Tales." *Journal of American Folklore* 64(1951): 289-302.

The Ifaluk chiefs, who are responsible for ethical instruction, take great delight in relating folk tales about their gods. The Ifaluk god Wolphat carries on in a manner that is completely at odds with their ethos of peacefulness. The stories display him as hostile, petulant, vengeful, lusty, aggressive, and self-centered. In some of the stories, when one member of a group is kind to a stranger (Wolphat) but everyone else is hostile, the god responds by punishing or killing everyone except for the kind person. And while the gods instituted the Ifaluk ethic of peace, Wolphat was born of a human mother, which excuses his behavior. Other folk tales relate the adventures of different characters, frequently focusing on the theme of stupidity. In one story, for instance, a group of women were fishing all night long but in the morning one found her basket filled only with seaweeds. Her husband and brother were angry with her, but the other women gave her ten fish so she would not be ashamed when the chiefs divided the catch for the village.

94   Spiro, Melford E. "Sorcery, Evil Spirits, and Functional Analysis: A Rejoinder." *American Anthropologist* 63(August 1961): 820-824.

Responding to Lessa's criticism [80] of his earlier works, Spiro indicates that he and Burrows may well have missed evidence of sorcery on Ifaluk during their work there, though it is possible Lessa's informants imputed sorcery to Ifaluk based on their own experience with black magic. But he does dispute Lessa's conclusion that the presence of sorcery would vitiate his theory about the belief in ghosts as an outlet for aggression on Ifaluk. Spiro maintains that a belief in spirits could well exist along with the practice of sorcery as outlets for aggressiveness-- he did not suggest in his earlier paper [91] that the belief in ghosts was the only way to relieve aggression. However, the Ifaluk belief in spirits that he describes is a superior approach since it does not foster the interpersonal hostility and insecurity the way sorcery does: it is the more effective peace-keeper on the island. Furthermore, since interpersonal hostility is not allowed on the island, if sorcery did exist there it would provoke animosities at the same time it released aggressiveness, which could only strengthen their belief in spirits.

Inuit

Inuit (Eskimo) peoples live in Greenland, Arctic and Subarctic Canada, northern and western Alaska, and the eastern tip of Siberia. Most of them traditionally hunted, trapped, traded, and fished, though virtually all are now part of the cash economy and rely on other sources of income as well. The literature about them is extensive, including numerous accounts by explorers, missionaries, traders, anthropologists, other social scientists, and popular writers. For several years a Canadian anthropologist, Jean Briggs, studied the Utkuhikhalingmiut (Utku), a small band of Inuit who lived, at the time of her research in the 1960s, on Chantrey Inlet in the Central Canadian Arctic. She also spent over a year in the 1970s among the Qipisamiut, an Inuit band living in Cumberland Sound, Baffin Island. Her book *Never in Anger* [101] describes the absolute prohibition on violence, aggression, or even on the expression of anger among the Utku. The other papers, chapters, and articles by Briggs amplify her psychological research among both Inuit groups. The selection of works by other writers in this section provides additional insights into the control of conflict among the Inuit.

95　　Briggs, Jean L. *Aspects of Inuit Value Socialization.* Ottawa: National Museums of Canada, 1979.

For Inuit adults, play is an essential method of creating, maintaining, and internalizing nonviolent, nurturing values among children. While it promotes a sense of right and wrong, it also fosters complex, ambiguous sets of contradictory emotional meanings and uncertainty for each value. In Western society, play is an activity for coping with the real world; in Inuit society, the real world is composed of play. Play is a form of expressing and controlling negative values: it shows that the individual has feelings under control. The Inuit in the Central Arctic do not even scold their children--they feel bad behavior by children may be caused by scolding. They prefer to maintain playful relations with children, thus demonstrating their carefully controlled, reasonable, nurturant values. Even the play aggression by adults is a form of loving behavior. Adults do not attempt to correct misbehaviors nor to impose their will: they will joke instead of confronting a child, and turn confrontations into games. By the time they are two, children learn to respond to potential anger from adults in the same fashion, by playful behavior.

96　　Briggs, Jean L. "Eskimo Family Life." In *Configurations: Biological and Cultural Factors in Sexuality and Family Life*, edited by Raymond Prince and Dorothy Barrier, 71-77. Lexington, MA: D.C. Heath, 1974.

Family behavior has to be evaluated in its cultural context, since conduct in two different cultures may have very different motivations and be interpreted quite differently by participants and observers. To Western observers, Eskimos appear to be inconsistent in the way they demonstrate open attention and affection for their infants, yet ignore children after they reach about three years old, when their demands, formerly met, are now ignored. Westerners also feel that Eskimo parents do not exert enough authority over their children, who do as they wish even when parents do say "no." Eskimos, however, value the fact that their children become controlled, quiet, undemanding, and independent by the age of six or so, in large part because of the example set by adults. Children learn that parents are usually right in the actions they recommend or the warnings they give. To the Westerner, Eskimo parents appear to be both authoritarian and permissive, a superficial inconsistency that is not apparent to the Eskimos, who think of obedience as a simple recognition of the greater wisdom of older people.

97   Briggs, Jean L. "Eskimo Women: Makers of Men." In *Many Sisters: Women in Cross-Cultural Perspective*, edited by Carolyn J. Matthiasson, 261-304. New York: Free Press, 1974.

In traditional Inuit culture there is no institutionalized gender conflict and very little tension between the sexes, though men and women feel some ambivalence about loving and being loved. Inuit couples have clear sex roles: men are the hunters who provide for their families, they do all the heavy work, and they repair things; the women do the lighter physical tasks such as cooking, child care, and sewing. Both spouses value the contributions of the other--the woman believes that she could not live without the hunting skills of her husband, and the man realizes he could not survive without the warm clothing sewn by his wife. While there are some exceptions, most feel they are incapable of doing the other's work. The husbands make the major decisions after consulting their wives. In public, men and women socialize in separate groups, but in private during the evenings Inuit couples frequently have close, companionable relationships in which they talk, play cards, or share special foods that they don't bring out for the neighbors--delicacies that symbolize the closeness of the husband, wife, and children.

98   Briggs, Jean L. "Expecting the Unexpected: Canadian Inuit Training for an Experimental Lifestyle." *Ethos* 19(September 1991): 259-287.

In the pragmatic worldview of the Inuit, people and objects are highly adaptable and without fixed characteristics. In order to develop this worldview, they train their children, both directly and indirectly, in *isuma*--human thought, reason, judgment, and emotional control. A particularly important aspect of *isuma* is the ability to contain anger, an emotion that is never admitted or acted upon. People with proper *isuma* do not need to have directions imposed by others--they automatically anticipate needs and respond without being asked. Adults expect children to learn at their own speed, and they use indirect means of instruction to promote the child's independent behavior. They play teasing games with their children in order to help instill in them Inuit values. They feel that seriousness and strong emotions--joy, excitement, worry, grief and anger--are all dangerous, so they emphasize happiness, joking, laughing, and playing. Laughing is often a way of releasing tensions about distressing events, such as the man who broke down in laughter when his tent started to burn--he said he couldn't do anything else but laugh.

99   Briggs, Jean L. "In Search of Emotional Meaning." *Ethos* 15(March 1987): 8-15.
        Two major values guide Inuit behavior. *Nallik-* is translated by the English concepts for love, pity, and nurturance, with a strong implication of attachment, protectiveness, and total suppression of hostility. *Isuma* translates as complete rationality, the ability to control impulsive behavior, to think calmly through problems, to predict the consequences of events and actions. To reinforce among children these desirable behaviors, the Inuit use a form of "benevolent aggression." Examples might include making hostile, suggestive comments such as telling a child that her new shirt is lovely and if she'd die the adult could have it, or suggesting that she might consider killing a new baby brother. The suggestion in these games of hostile, aggressive actions helps to create in the child the opposite effect--the games promote the positive, loving emotions. The games maintain an awareness that there is a danger in having possessions that others don't have, and that one must love and protect baby brother. They create a sense of the peril in wanting what is clearly wrong; correct, loving behavior is thus reinforced with strong internal controls.

100   Briggs, Jean L. "Living Dangerously: The Contradictory Foundations of Value in Canadian Inuit Society." In *Politics and History in Band Societies*, edited by Eleanor Leacock and Richard Lee, 109-131. New York: Cambridge University Press, 1982.
        Contradictions are an important aspect of Inuit society: the violent killing by the hunters and the nonviolence of the group,

the self-sufficiency of the hunter but the nurturance he shows toward others. The Inuit generate and maintain contradictory values such as these through their management of conflicting psychological needs and socializing techniques. They clearly enjoy killing--their eyes shine with excitement when they tell hunting stories--yet they react with horror to any form of interpersonal aggression such as shouting. They learn to associate danger with aggression and aggressive behavior with nurturance. Inuit children are socialized with teasing games in which they are challenged to be selfish or aggressive toward others. They are encouraged, through their behavior with animals, to engage in contradictory activities--to love, cuddle, and protect a baby duckling, and then to injure or even kill it. These games and activities create feelings of conflict and danger about the nurturant, nonviolent values, thereby creating doubt that society is predictable, that one is secure in the love of others--which strengthens their commitment to their values.

101   Briggs, Jean L. *Never in Anger: Portrait of an Eskimo Family.* Cambridge: Harvard University Press, 1971.

The author describes her life for one and one-half years as a family member in a small Inuit village in northern Canada. The book is filled with many rich details of daily living, related with a particular focus on the warmth, peacefulness, and displays of affection among the Inuit family members for their small children. She observes the lack of discipline of their children, especially during the first three years, when the parents attempt to meet all the demands that their small children make. However, when the next baby is born, usually when the youngest child is about three years old, the special closeness to mother ends and the father becomes much closer to the three-year old. The author includes in her narrative extensive descriptions of how the Inuit tried to handle her (and she them), how they tried to integrate her and the equipment and supplies she needed into their nomadic lifestyle. The complete absence of anger in their culture, in fact their fear of anger, showed up forcefully when she became angry at a visiting fishing party of whites that was exploiting her host family. She briefly displayed anger at the whites. This action cast her into the position of social pariah, which was the one way the Inuit could deal with her display of anger.

102   Briggs, Jean L. "The Creation of Value in Canadian Inuit
Society." *International Social Science Journal* 31(1979): 393-
403.

Inuit adults play teasing games with their children which help
socialize them to accept and maintain the core values of their
culture--nonaggression, nurturance, and generosity. As an example, a mother hands a candy to her three-year-old daughter
and tells her that since it is the last piece, she must eat it all
quickly without telling her older sister, who is playing outside.
The girl responds by breaking the candy in half, eating one piece
and taking the other outside to her sister. While the child makes
the right decision, which is approved by the adults present, the
game produces an internal conflict in her over her selfish desires
versus the ideal of giving. Other games similarly focus on love
versus hostility, or on nurturing versus hurting. Games such as
these succeed in attaching a positive emotion to social values so
they are intrinsically rewarding. They also promote correct
behavior by emphasizing the ambiguities of values, intensifying
the child's fear of her own negative feelings, and instilling in her
a fear of rejection unless she adheres to the approved standards.

103   Briggs, Jean L. "The Issues of Autonomy and Aggression in the
Three-Year-Old: The Utku Eskimo Case." *Seminars in Psychiatry* 4(November 1972): 317-329.

The crisis period of the two- to three-year-old Utku Eskimo
child contrasts with the Western psychosocial life crises analyzed by Erikson. Problems for the child during this period do
not relate to toilet training, which is a relaxed, supportive
development, but rather to a sudden separation from mother. For
more than two years the child has been held constantly, the
center of family attention. Weaning begins while the mother is
pregnant again and it is accomplished after the next is born
through persuasive, affectionate means. During this period the
child learns the socially approved qualities of *naklik-*: self-
subordination, self-restraint, helpfulness, patience, generosity,
and particularly, nonaggression and lack of hostility toward
others. The new baby is an excellent object on which to practice
these virtues. Adults show and instruct the child how to hold the
infant gently, how to give up things, restrain anger when the
baby interferes, and delay needs for attention in favor of the
younger child. Adults reinforce, with their approval, affectionate, generous, patient play with the baby, and disapprove of
anger or demands.

104   Briggs, Jean L. "The Origins of Nonviolence: Inuit Manage-
       ment of Aggression." In *Learning Non-Aggression: The Expe-
       rience of Non-Literate Societies*, edited by Ashley Montagu,
       54-93. New York: Oxford University Press, 1978.

The Inuit conception of fear (*ilira*) is an important aspect of
their nonviolent society. Briggs argues that the Inuit view fear
as both undesirable and desirable: undesirable because it is
uncomfortable for both parties and it promotes aggressive
behavior, but desirable because it promotes reassuring, protective, comforting behavior by both parties. The Inuit teach their
children ambivalence toward affection and fear by acting aggressively at the same time they are loving them--by overfeed-
ing them to the point where they vomit, by roughly cleaning
them while they nurse, by mistreating a favorite child rather
harshly, and so on. Older children may act competitively to see
who loves a baby the most and gets to carry it, to the point where
the baby cries in confusion and fear. This confusion of affection
and fear that the Inuit build up in their young people appears to
be their way of insuring a continuing peaceful society. The
author argues that they teach their children these ambivalent
feelings in order to develop in them a fear of disruptive human
social relationships--i.e., violence. This chapter represents a
condensation and rewriting of Briggs' chapter "The Origins of
Nonviolence: Aggression in Two Canadian Eskimo Groups,"
which appeared in *The Psychoanalytic Study of Society*, vol. 6,
edited by Warner Muensterberger and Aaron H. Esman (New
York: International Universities Press, 1975), p. 134-203.

105   Condon, Richard G. "The Rise of Adolescence: Social Change
       and Life Stage Dilemmas in the Central Canadian Arctic."
       Human Organization 49(Fall 1990): 266-279.

The last Inuit family on western Victoria Island moved into
the community of Holman Island in 1969 to settle around the
Hudson's Bay Company store; the small, isolated community of
the 1970s was transformed by the introduction of television in
1980, which has been a major factor in tying the hamlet to
Canadian national culture. While the number of jobs has increased, many adolescents and young adults get by on part-time
work of short duration and welfare support. The economic
security of wage employment or government assistance has
eliminated the uncertainty of traditional Inuit existence, but the
price of the security has been greater individualization of the
families and less dependence on sharing and cooperation--

values that are no longer imparted to the younger generation. Even without the opportunity for jobs in Holman, most young people prefer to remain there. Since 1978 the hamlet has experienced a steady growth of alcohol abuse and the attendant social disintegration, violence, and attempted suicides among the youth. The formerly quiet, peaceful community finally gained the protection of a police detachment in 1988.

106   Damas, David. "Central Eskimo Systems of Food Sharing." *Ethnology: An International Journal of Cultural and Social Anthropology* 11(July 1972): 220-240.

Food sharing practices among the Copper River, Netsilik, and Iglulik Eskimos were complex and varied from group to group. The Copper River and Netsilik peoples (though not the Iglulik) depended heavily on the capture of ringed seals, which they shared through a system of sharing partners. Each hunter had partners named after different parts of the seal: for instance a Copper River hunter might have a "lower back companion," a "flipper companion," and so on, who received the appropriate portions of the carcass. *Payuktuq* involved taking portions of seal meat to households in the village not included in the primary network of hunting companions. Another type of food sharing practiced in the central Arctic was communal eating, in which people that had food available hosted others at their meals; there did not appear to be a set pattern to this practice. *Payuktuq*, which was completely voluntary, did not operate as extensively during periods of plentiful food supplies, but there is little doubt that, throughout the whole year, a substantial portion of the food supply was shared.

107   Eckert, Penelope and Russell Newmark. "Central Eskimo Song Duels: A Contextual Analysis of Ritual Ambiguity." *Ethnology: An International Journal of Cultural and Social Anthropology* 19(January 1980): 191-211.

Song dueling at feasts was an Inuit technique for bringing conflicts between men out into the open before they became serious enough to provoke violence. The beginner would step forward with his drum and, directing himself to the audience as well as to his opponent, appeal to the emotions of the listeners by combining his substantive accusations with the artistry of his performance--story, tune, repetitive refrains, rhythms, drum beating, and dance steps. While the song described the singer's own virtues and the accusations against the opponent, frequently with biting irony and innuendo, it had to be humorous enough in its insults to be funny: the aggressiveness of the verbal attack had to be couched in humor. When he was finished, his opponent had his turn, and the dueling continued until the general laughter of the audience either signaled a victory by one of the contestants, or a victory by both. The expected result of the song duel was to laugh off animosities and return to friendship, an effective therapy that allowed the men to return to the normal ambiguities of social life.

108   Irwin, C. "The Inuit and the Evolution of Limited Group Conflict." In *Sociobiology and Conflict: Evolutionary Perspectives on Competition, Cooperation, Violence and Warfare*, edited by J. Van Der Dennen and V. Falger, 189-226. London: Chapman and Hall, 1990.

Inuit in Central Arctic Canada have difficulty conceptualizing or discussing war since they have no word for it. While the literature refers to murders among them, they have had few conflicts with other Inuit or Indian groups. Speculating on the reasons, the author suggests that they specialized in hunting game animals in their own limited territories, and since they would have had difficulty surviving in the territories of their neighbors, they had no incentive for attacking them. Furthermore, because only a small number of men were highly skilled hunters on whom survival of their groups depended, the Inuit were reluctant to risk losing them in conflicts. Within groups, potential conflicts were avoided through having flexible sexual relationships, sharing material goods among group members, and believing that attacks were carried out through magic rather than direct physical violence. When two Inuit did have a grievance, they might engage in a song duel--mutual, musical ridicule. Failing to resolve a dispute that way, they could start exchanging blows, but in a carefully controlled fashion, first one and then the other.

109   Jayewardene, C. H. S. "Violence among the Eskimos." *Canadian Journal of Criminology* 17(1975): 307-314.

Many studies of the Inuit have emphasized the role of alcohol in causing violent behavior. Reviewing the literature, the author finds communities where alcohol and violence was unknown, others where deviant behavior and mental aberrations caused disorder, and some where violence was unrelated to alcohol or mental problems. Some of the early explorers, portraying themselves as totally peace loving, told of treacherous sneak attacks by the Inuit, though these attacks were probably provoked and they were obviously the actions of people who felt highly threatened. The literature shows that Inuit children were raised without physical discipline; the adults were rarely violent, preferring to withdraw from situations of conflict and to deal with trouble-makers through ridicule or ostracism. The author admits the possibility that drunken, boisterous Inuit men might become violent if police ignored them, but that is speculation. Reports of alcohol-induced violence among the Inuit contain a lot of exaggerations, since many of the studies appear to be based on conjecture and a lack of factual data on actual violence.

110   Kleivan, Inge. "Song Duels in West Greenland--Joking Relationship and Avoidance." *Folk: Dansk Etnografisk Tidsskrift* 13(1971): 9-36.

Song duels among the Inuit of western Greenland were always held between individuals living in different settlements. They brought hostilities out into the open before they could develop into violent conflicts, and they fostered open communications and peaceful social relationships between the communities. The challenger's satirical ditties poked fun at the defender, mocked his abilities or habits, taunted or jeered at him; the defender listened patiently with a pleasant demeanor until his turn came, when he could retaliate with his satirical songs, revealing whatever choice gossip or unpleasant facts he could muster. They would continue taking turns, making their points, and while no loser was declared, the winner was clearly the most skilled satirist. The song duels sensitized people to reproach, prompted them to exercise caution and self-control, and thus helped inhibit physical violence. They were abandoned soon after contact with Europeans due to disapproval by the missionaries, who presumed that the Inuit might engage in immoral activities when so many of them had assembled together unsupervised. The missionaries also disliked the idea of the Inuit controlling their public morality through satirical singing.

111   Langgaard, Per. "Modernization and Traditional Interpersonal Relations in a Small Greenlandic Community: A Case Study from Southern Greenland." *Arctic Anthropology* 23(1986): 299-314.

The overall impression of the traditional Greenland village, in contrast to the towns, is one of silence, peacefulness, beauty, and equanimity among the people. Villagers interact constantly, sharing common feelings of solidarity, the importance of kin, respect for older people, appreciation for nature, and the value of traditionally established social patterns. Children are very well behaved, helpful to one another, and peaceful in their manners; while they sometimes quarrel, they never have serious fights and are never punished. Adults avoid conflicts through a variety of strategies: the many different social alliances they maintain; joking relationships; the tradition of inviting everyone, including people with whom they have bad relations, to parties on special occasions, which forces people to face even their foes periodically; the social obligation to exchange pleasantries when passing any group of people; and the prohibition of self-promotion and leadership. In order to avoid conflicts in informal groups, Greenlanders may lie, refrain from discussing controversial issues, or give oral approval to ideas they disapprove of. However, heavy drinking in the villages is undermining the traditional structures of reciprocal assistance.

Jains

About 3.5 million Jains live in India, mostly in the western part of the country where many of them are prosperous merchants. An ancient Indian religion that dates from the sixth century B.C., there are two major sects of Jainism--the Svetambara, whose ascetics dress in white garments, and the Digambara, whose ascetics are naked. They all believe in *ahimsa*, nonviolence, as the highest virtue. Since their belief in nonviolence includes all living things, the Jains are widely known for their extreme care in preventing harm to any insect or animal and for promoting animal welfare. Little sociological research has been done on the actual peacefulness of the Jains other than the book by Sangave [122], which discusses the issue briefly. Only a selection of the numerous works on the place of *ahimsa* in Jain philosophy is included. The influence of Jainism on the philosophy of Gandhi forms an important additional aspect to the study of Jain peacefulness.[5]

112   Bhanawat, Narendra, Prem Suman Jain and V. P. Bhatt, editors. *Bhagwan Mahavira and His Relevance in Modern Times*. Bikaner, India: Akhil Bharatavarshiya Sadhumargi Jain Sangha, 1976.

A collection of 29 essays about Jain ethics and related topics, gathered for this volume in celebration of the 2,500th anniversary of the nirvana (death) of Lord Mahavira, founder of Jainism. While many of the essays contribute to an understanding of the Jain philosophy of nonviolence and related ethical issues, the four that are particularly useful are no. 1, "Mahavira and His Philosophy of Life," by A. N. Upadhye [123], no. 8, "Bhagwan Mahavira's Ahimsa and World Peace," by S. C. Diwakar [114], no. 16, "World Problems and Jain Ethics," by Beni Prasad [121], and no. 25, "Jainism in Economic Perspective," by S. L. Mandawat [118].

113   Carrithers, Michael. "Passions of Nation and Community in the Bahubali Affair." *Modern Asian Studies* 22(October 1988): 815-844.

In 1983 a temple complex on a hill in southern Maharashtra, India, became the scene of a highly acrimonious dispute between the two major Jain sects, the Digambars and the Svetambars. The two groups had competed over the previous century in constructing ever larger temples, and as their rivalry intensified relations grew worse. In 1981 a gang of Digambar youths vandalized the Svetambar facilities, and each side began to escalate the dispute. The outspoken religious leader of the Digambars, a naked ascetic, went on hunger fasts to dramatize his side; the Svetambars succeeded in arousing a larger group in the area, the Marathas, who decided they wanted to build their own temple on the hill. The police intervened several times in 1983, and only the intervention of Prime Minister Indira Gandhi cooled the situation. The whole affair was tied in with the symbols of nationalism. The techniques of the Digambar religious leader--holding silent marches, closing shops, fasting--harkened back to the nonviolent methods of Mahatma Gandhi, who was the symbol of Indian nationalism and who derived his doctrine of *ahimsa*, nonviolence, from Jainism.

114   Diwakar, S. C. "Bhagwan Mahavira's Ahimsa and World Peace." In *Bhagwan Mahavira and His Relevance in Modern Times*, edited by Narendra Bhanawat, Prem Suman Jain and V. P. Bhatt, 53-59. Bikaner: Akhil Bharatavarshiya Sadhumargi Jain Sangha, 1976.

The Jain belief in *ahimsa* (nonviolence) is the critical aspect of their ethics. The author explains that householders and monks will reach different levels of perfection, but the avoidance of violence to all living things is the ideal. Thus, Jains are complete vegetarians. The essay explains that Gandhi's belief in *ahimsa* came from Jainism, and that this belief in nonviolence is perhaps the most important contribution of the faith to the rest of the world.

115 Dundas, Paul. "The Digambara Jain Warrior." In *The Assembly of Listeners: Jains in Society*, edited by Michael Carrithers and Caroline Humphrey, 169-186. New York: Cambridge University Press, 1991.

The *Adipurana*, an 8th-century Jain text, provides through its stories and legends insights into the relationship of medieval Jainism to the warrior caste and militarily aggressive kings who embraced the faith but carried out many violent military conquests. It is apparent from the text that conquest was the primary image of Jainism, which points to the ambivalence in the Jain community between peace and war, violence and nonviolence. The belief in *ahimsa* (nonviolence) was important for ritual reasons, as long as it did not interfere with the military conquests of rulers. The *Adipurana* provides descriptions of the idealized Jain king, who should rule a model kingdom which adheres to Jain principles, and in which the Jain religious community provides moral direction. It indicates that the ideal Jain warrior is a fighter for spiritual victories. Dundas concludes that the non-violence of Jainism did not distinguish that faith from Buddhism or Hinduism, which also partly accept the principle of nonviolence.

116 Gandhi, Raj S. "The Rise of Jainism and its Adoption by the Vaishyas of India: A Case Study in Sanskritisation and Status Mobility." *Social Compass* 24(1977): 247-260.

Jainism developed as an anti-Brahmin (priest) reaction to sacrificial killing. It focuses on asceticism and *ahimsa* (non-violence), which is an essential part of the commitment of Jains to a practical ethical code prohibiting adultery (*bramacarya*), and greed (*aparigrah*). Jainism arose in the Kshatriya (warrior) caste but the Jain ethics were difficult for the Kshatriyas to follow since killing was an integral part of their profession. Jainism came to have more appeal to members of the Vaishya (merchant) caste, whose prosperous members found they could enhance their status vis-a-vis the Brahmins and Kshatriyas by adopting the faith and taking actions that it advocated, such as patronizing monks and making charitable contributions. For them, adopting *ahimsa* was a way to challenge both the Brahmins, with their animal sacrifices, and the Kshatriyas. Jainism did not condemn the Vaishyas' accumulation of wealth--only dishonesty or the unwise use of money. The adoption of Jainism by the merchant class was thus an aspect of wider changes in the social and economic patterns of Indian society.

117   Laidlaw, James. "Profit, Salvation and Profitable Saints." *Cambridge Anthropology* 9(1985): 50-70.

Ritual practices at a temple in Jaipur to the Dadagurudevas, saints in a cult of the Karataragaccha sect of Svetambara Jainism, help explain how the basic Jain philosophy of renunciation of worldly things is reconciled with the daily activities (and achievements) of the Jain business community. The businessmen who enter the temples do not feel any contradictions since the practices of their daily lives are totally separate from the minutiae of their religion. For instance, they honor the rule of *ahimsa*, nonviolence, in terms of exclusively religious, minute details that prevent harm to the slightest insects, such as restrictions on diet, not stepping on ants, or wearing cotton rather than silk, but they see no dichotomy in supporting the state with its capital punishment or warfare. The temple rituals integrate, for the businessmen who stop briefly each morning, their basic beliefs in karma, magic, the personal help of the saints, and their practical daily lives. The temple affords an opportunity for renewal and integration of belief and daily practice.

118   Mandawat, S. L. "Jainism in Economic Perspective." In *Bhagwan Mahavira and His Relevance in Modern Times*, edited by Narendra Bhanawat, Prem Suman Jain and V. P. Bhatt, 167-176. Bikaner, India: Akhil Bharatavarshiya Sadhumargi Jain Sangha, 1976.

The focus of this essay is the economic implications of Jain ethics. The author argues that *aparigraha* (self-control), which forbids the acquisition of possessions other than those which are absolutely necessary, is really oriented toward controlling the motive of greed. Jains can acquire wealth as long as they don't take any joy in its acquisition. *Asteya* (honesty or, more literally, non-stealing), leads to a belief in honest business dealings. *Ahimsa* (nonviolence) prevents the pursuit of any business that might endanger life, such as many industries and, for some Jains, agriculture. These Jain ethics, in the view of the author, lead to an economics of peace, the "practical value of the doctrine of non-violence." Furthermore, Jainism includes a dualistic community, of monks at its spiritual core who practice all of its principles, and householders, comprising the rest of the faithful, who abide by only modified virtues. This system leads both to austerity and to economic prosperity for the whole community.

119 Misra, Rajalakshmi. "The Jains in an Urban Setting: The Ascetics and the Laity among the Jains of Mysore City." *Bulletin of the Anthropological Survey of India* 21(Jan.-June 1972): 1-68.

The Jaina community in Mysore exemplifies some of the conflicts among Jains between traditional and modern practices. For instance, although they traditionally resist military service, a Jain engineering student took a competitive examination offered by the army and was selected to receive a salary while he finished his education. His parents strenuously opposed the arrangement (and prevailed in their wishes) because military service might have required him to kill human beings, a contradiction to their ethics. Traditional Jains do not normally accept modern medicine since, they feel, it does violence to the human body as well as to microbes within the body; but modern Jain doctors justify their practice of medicine with the argument that taking the small lives of germs is necessary to save the large life of a human. While Jain householders try to avoid violence to any living creature, they recognize that occasional acts of self-defense may be unavoidable. And if discipline is needed for a servant or child, they feel that physical punishment may be justifiable.

120 Mittal, S. K. "Jain Influences on Mahatma Gandhi." *Quarterly Review of Historical Studies* 21(July-September/October-December 1981): 26-35.

Many of Gandhi's ideas can be traced to Jain influences, such as his concept of Satyagraha, his vegetarianism, his belief in *brahmacharya* (sexual purity), and his limitations on personal possessions. As a child he was exposed to many Jain monks who visited his father's house in Gujarat, and when he returned to his community as a young lawyer in 1891, a Jain relative from Bombay, Raichandra Ravjibhai, inspired him profoundly. A poet, saint, and man of encyclopedic learning, Raichand guided Gandhi's reading and, after the young man left for South Africa, gave him spiritual advice via letter. Troubled by conflicting claims from Christians and Hindus, Gandhi asked Raichand

such questions as "What is the soul?" and "What is God?"
While most of the correspondence has not been preserved,
Gandhi's belief that religion is the realization of soul shows
distinct evidence of Jain and Hindu thought (Gandhi himself did
not distinguish between the two). Though Gandhi's ideas were
influenced by many different religious and philosophical traditions, his beliefs in *ahimsa* (nonviolence) and truth throughout
his political career were particularly inspired by Jainism.

121   Prasad, Beni. "World Problems and Jain Ethics." In *Bhagwan
       Mahavira and His Relevance in Modern Times*, edited by
       Narendra Bhanawat, Prem Suman Jain and V. P. Bhatt, 97-106.
       Bikaner: Akhil Bharatavarshiya Sadhumargi Jain Sangha, 1976.
          The five major ethical principles, the *anuvratas* (little vows)
       of Jainism, are explained in detail. The author argues that *ahimsa*
       (nonviolence), the most important of all five, offers a positive
       alternate to the violence of both internal and international
       affairs, which have been based on the rule of force. *Satya*
       (truthfulness) and *asteya* (honesty) are essential companion
       virtues to *ahimsa* on both the individual level and the level of
       society if nonviolence is to prevail. Likewise, the other two
       essential Jain ethical principles, *brahmacharya* (celibacy) and
       aparigraha (self-control), are important parts of an inner moral-
       ity that would eliminate self-aggrandizement and materialism,
       which foster grave social problems. All five virtues are quite
       positive in nature; together they lead to an ethical wholeness that
       can prevent the problems of societies.

122   Sangave, Vilas Adinath. *Jaina Community: A Social Survey*, 2d
       edition. Bombay: Popular Prakashan, 1980.
          An overview of Jain society based on survey data and thor-
       ough personal knowledge of Jainism. The book describes the
       demography of Jains, their predominantly urban lifestyle, their
       religious divisions, their caste system--which is not as rigid as
       that of the Hindus--and the social effects of their belief in
       nonviolence. According to the author, women have a more
       favorable position among the Jains than among their Hindu
       neighbors for several reasons: having male heirs is not an
       imperative; female infanticide is unknown because of the
       prohibition of violence (*himsa*); and Jain women can inherit
       their husband's estates. The author points out that petty crime is
       less in the Jain community than among surrounding Indian
       peoples, that major or violent crime is extremely rare, and

habitual criminals are unknown. Because of their faith, Jains are also noted for founding and generously supporting numerous charitable organizations such as rest houses, schools, colleges, libraries, and other humanitarian causes. The author concludes that the major contribution of Jainism to world civilization is the culture of *ahimsa*.

123　Upadhye, A. N. "Mahavira and His Philosophy of Life." In *Bhagwan Mahavira and His Relevance in Modern Times*, edited by Narendra Bhanawat, Prem Suman Jain and V. P. Bhatt, 1-12. Bikaner, India: Akhil Bharatavarshiya Sadhumargi Jain Sangha, 1976.

An introduction to the volume on Jainism, Upadhye provides a brief overview of the life of Mahavira, founder of the faith. He describes the four categories of Jains (monks and householders, both men and women), and the basic beliefs of the faith. Most of the essay is devoted to an introductory explanation of the five major ethical virtues of Jainism: *ahimsa* (nonviolence), *satya* (truthfulness), *asteya* (honesty, or non-stealing), *brahmacharya* (avoiding sexual promiscuity), and *aparigraha* (self-control that avoids unnecessary pleasures or materialism). The author emphasizes that *ahimsa*, nonviolence, is the most fundamental of all beliefs of the Jains. It leads to toleration and is the basis of their humanitarian outlook.

Kadar

The Kadar live in India at an elevation of about 2,000 feet near the southern end of the forested mountains known as the Western Ghats, on the border between the states of Kerala and Tamil Nadu. Their territory is quite near that of the Paliyan and about 60 miles north of the Malapandaram (see those sections). Their lives and economy, as described in 1952, included impermanent villages with people moving in and out as they wished. They had no village leaders, except for the ones required by government agencies, and they lived on the food they gathered from the forest plus the foods they exchanged for so-called "minor" forest products such as honey and cardamom. They also kept some animals, including dogs, fowl, and a few cattle and goats. As of the 1941 *Census of India* they numbered 565 people.

124　Ehrenfels, Umar Rolf. *Kadar of Cochin*. Madras: University of Madras, 1952.

The Kadar have never experienced murder or crime, and they

normally settle their disagreements peacefully to avoid physical violence. For instance, during a very loud fight one evening, a woman berated her husband because he had bought nice presents for his two children by a previous marriage but a worthless one (she felt) for their own daughter. She accused him of having affairs with a younger cousin and a widow in another village, all of which he quietly denied to the listening villagers. In the morning she was gone but a week later she returned and settled in with him again. Traditional Kadar society accorded equality to the sexes, but this ideal is fast being lost due to the influence of the larger Indian society that devalues women. Kadar families have very close relationships, particularly between parents and their children. Parents are normally quite permissive toward their children, though they will interfere and distract them affectionately if they get into too bad a mood. Children's non-competitive games are based on simple enjoyment of physical activities.

!Kung

The publication of Elizabeth Marshall Thomas's popular book *The Harmless People* in 1959 [357] cast an image of the San peoples, and particularly the !Kung, as being completely peaceful, despite the fact that the book recounts incidents of mounting tensions and flaring anger along with impressions of peacefulness. Thomas's mother, Lorna Marshall, wrote a series of pioneering, scholarly anthropology works which include critical analyses of !Kung peacefulness. Many of the social scientists associated with the Harvard Kalahari Research Group have done research which provides additional understanding about the !Kung means of conflict resolution, gift exchange, and child socialization. However, Richard B. Lee's major book [147] makes it clear that in the past there were a significant number of murders among the !Kung, and that fighting is a persistent phenomenon. The !Kung, about 15,000 of whom live in Namibia, Botswana and Angola, are included in this bibliography, despite the convincing data in Lee's book, because other scholars have described them as peaceful, and because those scholars, including Lee himself, have depicted the significant strategies the !Kung use to promote their peacefulness.

125   Biesele, Megan. "The Old People Give You Life." *Parabola* 5(1980): 39-46.
       One of the !Kung folktales describes the way a few droplets of blood came on the wind to grandmother after the death of

elephant girl, her granddaughter. The old lady cared for them as elephant girl had previously instructed and they steadily grew, first in a bottle, then in a skin bag. One day, while the rest of the band, including elephant girl's little daughter, was away gathering, grandmother removed her granddaughter from the bag and fixed her up properly with new clothing and ornaments; when everyone returned, there they sat laughing and telling stories together, to everyone's joy. This story dramatizes the warm, caring relationships that the !Kung have with their elders. Old people who are physically able help as much as possible with food gathering, they are respected for their knowledge of local resources, and they entertain children with games, joking, teasing, and storytelling when their mothers are away. They teach important skills, social attitudes, and traditions to the children; when they are ill or infirm, the members of the band care for them since they have given generously to others throughout their lifetimes.

126   Biesele, Megan and Nancy Howell. "'The Old People Give You Life': Aging among !Kung Hunter-Gatherers." In *Other Ways of Growing Old: Anthropological Perspectives*, edited by Pamela T. Amoss and Stevan Harrell, 77-98. Stanford, CA: Stanford University Press, 1981.

A scholarly version of [125], with more details provided than in the popular article. Despite the physical limitations of old people in !Kung society, they are frequently healthful, active, and valuable to their camps because of their detailed knowledge of animal and plant resources; they also have the best understanding of how to maintain patterns of community sharing and how to prevent conflicts from arising over resources. They are particularly helpful and loving toward their grandchildren, whom they teach invaluable practical knowledge, culture, lore, and social values. The elderly !Kung do not accumulate any more goods than anyone else, since they remain dependent on relationships based on mutual assistance, giving gifts (*hxaro*), and reciprocal visiting. Grandparents are primarily responsible for instructing their grandchildren in the *hxaro* system by demonstrating the proper !Kung way of giving away parts of their possessions, such as a portion of a string of beads. As the children become young adults, they maintain *hxaro* ties with the old people in order to gain secure access to resources and land for gathering and hunting.

127   Christiansen, Kerrin and Eike-Meinrad Winkler. "Hormonal,
        Anthropometrical, and Behavioral Correlates of Physical Ag-
        gression in !Kung San Men of Namibia." *Aggressive Behavior*
        18(1992): 271-280.
            Aggressiveness among the San peoples was studied in 1987
        through an examination of the violence among the !Kung at the
        settled community of Tsumkwe. Out of 114 men interviewed
        and measured, 37 had visible scars on their heads, most of whom
        admitted that their wounds had been a result of interpersonal
        violence. The quarrels, either men against men or men against
        women, were mostly due to adultery, though some were caused
        by thefts or money problems. Comparing the physically violent
        and the nonviolent men (many of whom may have exhibited
        aggressiveness in other ways), the results showed: there were no
        statistically significant differences between the two groups in
        the mean values of their sex hormones; the more violent men
        tended to be more physically robust; abstainers from alcohol
        were less violent than the moderate consumers; and the levels of
        acculturation to outside society did not appear to influence the
        amount of physical violence.

128   Draper, Patricia. "!Kung Women: Contrasts in Sexual Egali-
        tarianism in Foraging and Sedentary Contexts." In *Toward an
        Anthropology of Women*, edited by Rayna R. Reiter, 77-109.
        New York: Monthly Review Press, 1975.
            Significant differences have developed among the !Kung in
        their attitudes toward women. Those who are still nomadic
        hunters and gatherers maintain their egalitarian views, while
        those who have settled into permanent villages have begun
        devaluing females. Among the nomadic people, women derive
        a lot of self-esteem from the fact that they gather most of the
        food, which requires a fair amount of skill. The vivacious, self-
        confident women forage many miles from the men without
        weapons, despite the possibility of encountering lions and
        leopards. They retain control over the food they gather, they
        have no need for permission or assistance from men, and they are
        absent from camp about as much as men are. A division of labor
        between the sexes is not followed rigidly, as men may help the
        women with their work, and fathers are not viewed as patriarchal
        figures. !Kung values that disapprove of anger, fighting, wealth,
        and competition are easy to maintain in the face-to-face camps.
        All of these factors, which promote equality for women, have
        eroded in the villages.

129   Draper, Patricia. "Crowding among Hunter-Gatherers: The !Kung Bushmen." *Science* 182(October 19, 1973): 301-303.

The !Kung inhabit the Kalahari sparsely, about one person per 10 square miles, yet within each camp they live very closely together. They establish circular spaces for their settlements and build grass huts so closely together around the perimeter that people sitting in front of them can hand items to their neighbors without getting up. The camps have an average population density of 188 square feet per person; people can carry on conversations across the settlement at normal speaking volume. They are careful to remove all plants and obstructions in the central area of the settlement to remove any sense of privacy. When they sit together and talk their bodies are often touching. A band of 30 people thus spends a lot of time living closely together, as if in a single room. People who have difficulty accommodating to a particular group can resolve conflicts by moving to another band. A potential source of stress in modern cities, close contact with strangers, is also not an issue since the !Kung settlements are so far apart that they are unlikely to encounter strangers.

130   Draper, Patricia. "Social and Economic Constraints on Child Life among the !Kung." In *Kalahari Hunter-Gatherers: Studies of the !Kung San and Their Neighbors*, edited by Richard B. Lee and Irven DeVore, 199-217. Cambridge, MA: Harvard University Press, 1976.

Draper characterizes the !Kung camp as isolated, intimate, and close. The 30 or 40 people in a band erect small huts backed up to the bush and clear a central area for the eating, sleeping, and living space of the village. While each family has its own hearth in front of the hut, there is no privacy between families. The children engage in non-competitive games, in part because there are so few of them that the age differences would not allow even-aged competitions to take place. Adults are very tolerant and patient toward their children; though they don't supervise children closely, they do intervene to discourage their displays of aggressiveness, particularly among children of different ages. Draper explains how the ecology and food-gathering practices militate against having children helping out with adult work, with the exception of carrying water.

131   Draper, Patricia. "The Learning Environment for Aggression and Anti-Social Behavior among the !Kung." In *Learning Non-*

Aggression: The Experience of Non-Literate Societies, edited by Ashley Montagu, 31-53. New York: Oxford University Press, 1978.

The !Kung people of the Kalahari Desert rarely display aggression for their children to emulate. Whenever children show signs of aggression adults quickly intervene to diffuse their hostilities, take them away from a fight, and try to distract them. The close physical proximity of the huts means that children seldom get to play away from the ear of an adult and aggression never has a chance to develop. Since the !Kung live in a hostile desert environment, they do not have any periods of plenty, and they have no way of storing food supplies. One of Draper's key points is that the security of the !Kung rests in the solidarity of their groups--the group's peaceful cohesiveness is its stored surplus. They cannot tolerate the braggart, the nonconformist, the unstable, violent or unpredictable person. They do bicker constantly, apparently as a safety valve for their aggressive feelings, and they constantly badger each other for gifts. The hunter who has to share the meat after a successful hunt has to withstand verbal abuse from everyone about the smallness of their portions.

132   Draper, Patricia and Elizabeth Cashdan. "Technological Change and Child Behavior among the !Kung." *Ethnology: An International Journal of Cultural and Social Anthropology* 27(October 1988): 339-365.

Measured observations of behavior and socializing by !Kung children in both the traditional nomadic camps and in recently settled villages showed a number of significant differences in the two environments: 1) children in the settled villages are put to work more than the ones in the bush, and there is less adult time available for children; 2) in the bush, children of different ages and sexes tend to play together and roughhousing is engaged in equally by girls and boys; in the villages, children play more with their peers and the amount of roughhousing increases among the boys, who can easily get out of adult earshot, but decreases among girls who appear to be more restrained; 3) adults have more social interactions with children and more opportunity to supervise in the bush camps than in the settled villages; and 4) attention by mothers to their children is significantly less in the sedentary villages than in the bush camps.

133   Katz, Richard. "Accepting 'Boiling Energy': The Experience
        of !Kia-Healing among the !Kung." *Ethos* 10(Winter 1982):
        344-368.

   !Kung healing takes on spiritual, social, physical, and psychological levels and is essential for individuals, the whole group,
and relationships with the surrounding environment. It is an
integrating force, an inclusive rather than an exclusive process,
that is an essential aspect of their sharing, egalitarian, commu-
nity-focused tradition. The healing takes place at a dances which
last all night, usually with women sitting around the fire singing
and men, sometimes joined by women, dancing around the
circle of singers. The growing warmth of the dancing generates
n/um, a powerful energy that wells up within the dancers and
expands to fill the whole community. For those who are healers,
this *n/um* leads to *!kia*, an altered state of consciousness, which
permits the healing. The healers focus on individuals who are ill,
but the healing process also helps resolve divisive issues and
reunites the group into a greater spiritual union. The onset of *!kia*
intensifies the emotions of the dancers so that they may see
illnesses within others, see great distances, handle live coals,
walk into the fire without harm, or interact with their gods.

134   Katz, Richard. "Healing and Transformation: Perspectives
        from !Kung Hunter-Gatherers." In *Altered States of Conscious-
        ness and Mental Health: A Cross-Cultural Perspective*, edited
        by Colleen A. Ward, 207-227. Newbury Park, CA: Sage, 1989.

   Egalitarian life in the !Kung band is based on sharing of all
resources, minimal personal possessions, and no disparity in
wealth. The healing trance dances, their primary ritual, epito-
mize and foster these social characteristics. Healing--defined as
the process of making a transition toward wholeness, balance,
meaning, and a sense of being connected--is based, among the
!Kung, on an enhancement of consciousness developing in the
healer which is shared throughout the community. Healing
promotes, enhances, and integrates the health of individuals and
groups at all levels--physical, spiritual, psychological, social.
The healing dance may cure an individual's body or mind, mend
the fabric of society by promoting social cohesion, protect the
community from environmental troubles, and foster well-being,
fulfillment and growth. Healing integrates these functions into
the fabric of daily gathering and hunting; it is part of everyone's
life and serves to establish the sense of community. The author

uses data on the !Kung healing to establish a transformational model, in which enhanced consciousness may be accessed and applied within a community in order to interrelate and merge development and education.

135   Katz, Richard. "Toward a Paradigm of Healing: Data from the Hunting-Gathering !Kung." *Personnel and Guidance Journal* 61(April 1983): 494-497.

Healing among the !Kung is a routine part of their daily existence, a mark of their feelings toward one another as a community, and an important aspect of their egalitarian culture. At the all-night trance dances when the healing takes place, the men dance around the circle of chanting, clapping women, who sometimes also join the dancing. As the dancing increases, the *n/um* (energy) rises in the healers until they reach a state of *!kia* (altered consciousness) in which they can begin to heal people. The healer must learn to manage his psychological, emotional, and physical states during the dance so that he can control the *n/um*. Powerful healers admit their fear, since the success of the *!kia* is a result of facing death and feeling a rebirth--a departure from familiar reality and rebirth into a state where they can lay their hands on the sick person and pull out sickness. The powers of *n/um* are shared widely, as the dance assists in the promotion of social cohesiveness, mends the fabric of society, and releases hostilities.

136   Lee, Richard. "Politics, Sexual and Non-Sexual, in an Egalitarian Society." In *Politics and History in Band Societies*, edited by Eleanor Leacock and Richard Lee, 37-59. New York: Cambridge University Press, 1982.

This is the same article that appeared in *Social Science Information* in 1978 [140] with only minor editing changes and the addition of a photograph of a !Kung woman orator.

137   Lee, Richard. "The Gods Must Be Crazy, But the State Has a Plan: Government Policies Towards the San in Namibia." *Canadian Journal of African Studies* 20(1986): 91-98.

The major forces that are changing !Kung society in Namibia include the efforts of missionaries and government officials to convert them and make them part of the cash economy, and the recruiting by the South African military forces into patrol and regular army units. The most serious threat is the armed conflict between the South African government and SWAPO, the Namibian liberation forces. South African propaganda promotes the benefits the San receive from their enforced enculturation by the army, and the importance to them of preserving freedom and democracy by their fighting in the territorial forces. Many !Kung, however, would agree with the sentiment expressed by one man who approved of SWAPO and expressed his fear of the government soldiers, who bring to them the values of anger, fighting, and killing. The only viable future for the !Kung is in a free Namibia, so the best way to help is to support the SWAPO-led independence movement. The portrait of the !Kung in the movie *The Gods Must Be Crazy* as noble, timeless savages untouched by the modern world is a cruel joke.

138   Lee, Richard and Susan Hurlich. "From Foragers to Fighters: South Africa's Militarization of the Namibian San." In *Politics and History in Band Societies*, edited by Eleanor Leacock and Richard Lee, 327-345. New York: Cambridge University Press, 1982.

In order to improve their control over the border zone of Namibia with Botswana in the early 1960s, the government of South Africa gathered the !Kung from the border area into a new settlement, Chum!kwe. Since the South Africans could not distinguish between !Kung individuals when they distributed rations, they issued numbered metal dog tags to identify people from Namibia so they could exclude other !Kung from across the border in Botswana. But the !Kung traded their dog tags, as they did everything else, so everyone could share in the largesse. During this decade, the South Africans introduced wage labor, Christianity, and alcohol to the Chum!kwe !Kung in order to convert them to Western ways. In 1970 the South African military forces started using !Kung bands as trackers to monitor guerrilla activity along the border, and in 1974 they started incorporating them directly into army units. This brutalization of the !Kung--such as instruction in hand-to-hand combat--led to seven cases of murder between 1978 and 1980, about five times the figure for the 35-year period from 1920 to 1955.

139   Lee, Richard B. "!Kung Spatial Organization: An Ecological and Historical Perspective." *Human Ecology* 1(1972): 125-147.

The organization of hunter-gatherer bands needs to be examined in terms of both spatial and social boundaries. Arguments by anthropologists that many hunting and gathering peoples have exclusive territories and closed social boundaries are challenged by data from the !Kung. Among the !Kung, camp compositions are quite flexible, people visit other camps frequently and share their food resources, and territorial boundaries are vaguely defined and undefended. The environmental reason for their flexibility is the wide variation in annual rainfall, which varies by as much as 300 percent from one year to the next in any given location. The ability of people to move during drought conditions to other inhabited areas which have had greater rainfall ensures their survival. This flexibility implies a reciprocity in the use of resources; it also allows individuals to avoid violence by separating from one another into different camps. Contact with Bantu and white peoples, particularly their economic and military systems, has prompted the !Kung to modify these social and spatial patterns, however. A modified version of this article appears as chapter 12 of [147].

140   Lee, Richard B. "Politics, Sexual and Non-Sexual in an Egalitarian Society." *Social Science Information* 17(1978): 871-895.

The egalitarian !Kung society is based on complete willingness to share everything, to give without the presumption of an equal return until one has nothing left. !Kung groups regard stinginess with hostility, and they are even more strongly opposed to arrogance. Hunters who announce their successes to the camp and women who make a point of displaying their gifts are equally arrogant, but their society has elaborate leveling devices to maintain egalitarian norms such as self-deprecating conversation, put-downs, and back-handed compliments. While leadership qualities vary, traditional leaders are never aloof, boastful, overbearing, or arrogant--characteristics that they can't accept--and they live no differently than anyone else, exerting their guidance through indirect and subtle means. However, new-style leaders who have to deal with outsiders need to be aggressive and articulate, traits which contradict the traditional leadership qualities of generosity, modesty, and egalitarian behavior. Husband-wife relationships are based on relatively equal amounts of hard work, though the women predominate in child care and housework and the men in hunting and tool making. See also entry [136].

141   Lee, Richard B. *The Dobe !Kung.* Fort Worth: Holt, Rinehart and Winston, 1984.

A 170-page distillation, rewritten for college students and a general audience, of the material found in the author's more technical and slightly older monograph, *The !Kung San* [147]. The wealth of research details contained in the larger monograph are generally omitted, though this volume does contain numerous tables, figures, maps and photographs that amplify the presentation about !Kung life. The concluding chapters have more recent information about the situation of the !Kung in the early 1980s than the earlier work. The book includes a chapter on conflict among the !Kung which is based on the extensive investigation presented in the 1979 volume. Contains an appendix which reprints the article "Eating Christmas in the Kalahari" [145].

142   Lee, Richard B. "The Sociology of !Kung Bushman Trance Performances." In *Trance and Possession States*, edited by Raymond Prince, 35-54. Montreal: R. M. Bucke Memorial Society, 1968.

Soon after they are married, young !Kung men become seriously interested in learning how to go into trances and heal. For several years they will be apprentices to an older healer--father, uncle, etc.--who helps them, dance after dance, gradually learn how to go into a trance. Finally, when a young man is successful, he will go very deeply into a trance seizure. At that time his mentor and other healers, also in trances, will place their hands on him and allow their medicine to pass into him. He may react violently during this first real seizure, punching and kicking the older men who are trying to help him. The others explain his aggressive behavior in terms of the overwhelming nature of his experience, and they feel a lot of pleasure that another healer is joining the band. The !Kung trance healing, within a context of Altered States of Consciousness (ASC) theory, can be seen as a ritualized expenditure of energy and an outlet for behaviors that their social ethics would not otherwise approve. Much of this article, except for the sections on apprenticeship and ASC theory, appeared in a somewhat reorganized version in [143].

143   Lee, Richard B. "Trance Cure of the !Kung Bushmen." *Natural History* 76(November 1967): 30-37.

!Kung healing takes place as part of marathon, all-night dances. For the first several hours they sing and dance in a casual fashion, but as the intensity picks up, some individuals will start going into trances. They place their hands in turn on everyone present, the sick and the well, and rub their sweat into the bodies of others, thus transferring the healing to them. These ceremonies are cooperative efforts characterized by mutual aid and the absence of secrecy. Their beliefs and practices differ from those of many other societies, where people believe that illness is due to the malevolence and witchcraft of others, and where the shamans, who receive their healing ability from outside spiritual contacts, may form separate priest classes. The !Kung, in contrast, believe that misfortunes are caused by spirits who generate problems with humans for their own reasons. They feel the benevolent healing powers of their healers are due to the social group itself rather than to spiritual forces. Their healers--half of the adult men and some women--are fully part of the community. A somewhat reorganized version, with the addition of numerous photos, of [142].

144   Lee, Richard B. and Irven DeVore, editors. *Kalahari Hunter-Gatherers: Studies of the !Kung San and Their Neighbors.* Cambridge, MA: Harvard University Press, 1976.

This is a substantial, scholarly collection of 15 essays by anthropologists participating in the Kalahari Research Group of Harvard University. Most of the essays provide excellent information about the !Kung people from the perspectives of the differing research interests of the authors. The first five essays give a thorough background to the !Kung environment and society. The next three papers focus on population and health, and the third section deals with childhood among the !Kung. In that section, Marjorie Shostak's paper, which narrates a !Kung woman's recollections of her childhood, throws light on the issue of how the people view themselves. In the fourth section on behavior and belief, an essay on the extensive knowledge of animal habits by the !Kung reveals how closely they are attuned to their environment. Patricia Draper's essay on the social and economic constraints in the village in section three [130] and Lorna Marshall's paper on the !Kung style of talking, sharing and giving in section four [152] are particularly relevant to the study of !Kung peacefulness.

145   Lee, Richard Borshay. "Eating Christmas in the Kalahari." *Natural History* 78(December 1969): 14-22, 60-63.

In order to repay the !Kung for their goodwill, the author purchased a huge ox to be slaughtered for a Christmas feast. Soon, however, individuals started coming to him and commenting on how badly he'd been gypped, how thin the beast was, how they'd all go hungry on Christmas, how the ox was really only good for its soup bones. Then they started indicating that the thinness of the feast would probably provoke fights. Thoroughly spooked by their unanimous opinion of his colossal error, the author tried unsuccessfully to buy another, and he even considered spending Christmas day in the bush. He was astonished when the ox was butchered: it was as fat and meaty as he had first judged. He learned later that the joking put-down was standard !Kung technique. Every kill is too small, old, or thin. No one brags, everyone puts down the success of others in order to control arrogance, which might lead to boasting, pride, and violence. By denigrating the kill, or in this case the Christmas ox, they cool the proud heart and prompt gentleness--and they forced a lesson in humility on the author. Reprinted in [141].

146   Lee, Richard Borshay. "Male-Female Residence Arrangements and Political Power in Human Hunter-Gatherers." *Archives of Sexual Behavior* 3(March 1974): 167-173.

Research among the !Kung discredits a theory that the dominance of males in Western society is derived from the hunter-gatherer past. These theorists argue that hunter-gatherer society is characterized by male-sibling groups defending exclusive territories; in contrast, the !Kung have flexible band structures which adjust for differing availability of resources, and which split when necessary to avoid conflicts. The !Kung structure of flexibility is possible because women have significant economic importance derived from the fact that they gather extensive amounts of vegetable foods. Another factor strengthening the power of marriageable women is their scarcity--they can afford to be selective. The husband has to live with his bride's family for many years, perhaps for a lifetime, while he proves his prowess as a provider. During this period he is extremely well treated by the bride's family, in hopes that he'll remain with them. Thus, the flexibility of the band structure operates to recruit and enlarge personnel rather than to exclude, as the male-dominance theorists argue.

147   Lee, Richard Borshay. *The !Kung San: Men, Women, and Work in a Foraging Society*. Cambridge: Cambridge University Press, 1979.

While several writers have described !Kung peacefulness, Lee argues in this book that they have a fairly violent society. Their bantering and arguments about interpersonal issues are normally kept at a humorous level, but occasionally two people become angry and start to "talk," in which both pour out extravagant comments at a rapid rate. Sometimes the level of argument escalates still farther into trading insults and physical fighting or splitting of the group. During his three years of living among the !Kung, Lee recorded 58 arguments, of which 34 led to physical fights. Discussing past violence with many informants, he learned that 22 murders occurred between 1920 and 1955, a homicide rate of 29.3 per 100,000 person years. While this compares with the murder rate in American cities, he presents other arguments showing the greater violence of United States society. !Kung fights were characterized by spontaneous anger, general hysteria, a temporary group insanity, and more fatalities among innocent bystanders than active combatants. The !Kung now have such a fear of violence that they split their groups in order to avoid it. Chapters in the book describe in detail the !Kung environment, people, technology, usage of plants and animals, production, and relations between men and women. Chapter 12, on !Kung spatial organization, is a modified version of an earlier article [139].

148   Lewin, Roger. "New Views Emerge on Hunters and Gatherers." *Science* 240(May 27, 1988): 1146-1148.

The basic presumptions of Richard Lee, Irven DeVore and the other anthropologists who studied the !Kung during the Harvard University project of the 1960s and 1970s have been widely challenged and generally supplanted. Their basic premise was that the !Kung represented a living example of technologically primitive hunting and gathering people as they existed before the advent of settled agriculture. DeVore admits today that they were a bit romantic at the time, infused with the spirit of the 1960s, as they generalized about the peaceful harmony and sharing that prevailed among the !Kung to other foraging peoples. Critics charge they ignored data available at the time that indicated considerable variations in the evolutionary patterns of hunter-gatherers and their interactions to settled agriculturalists. The views of other anthropologists, who advocate an evolutionary approach or who are historical particularists--those who deny that what is learned about one people can be generalized--are presented.

149   Marshall, Lorna. "!Kung Bushman Bands." *Africa* 30(October 1960): 325-355.

The !Kung have no tales of battles, no warrior heroes, and no mythology of territorial fighting. The bands are quite rigid about only gathering food on their own territories. Encroaching on the territory of another would be equivalent to stealing, a very dangerous action which could provoke fighting. One tale is told of a man who was killed by another for stealing honey that he had already marked as his own. He was easily identified by his footprints. The fact that everyone can identify footprints of everyone else helps prevent stealing since the culprit would be immediately known to all. The headman of the band is the owner of the food and water, but all members of the band have equal rights to those resources. There is no advantage to being a headman--he eats and works equally with others, and he has no special honors. Decisions about band movements and gathering are made by group consensus rather than by the headman. The headman does not necessarily organize hunting expeditions, and doesn't act as judge when problems arise; people initiate, arrange, and solve issues themselves. Also appears as a chapter in [154].

150   Marshall, Lorna. "!Kung Bushman Religious Beliefs." *Africa* 32(July 1962): 221-252.

The !Kung associate Gao!na, their great god, and old Gao!na, the hero of their folktales, as one individual, but they whisper the name of the great god, and will talk loudly about the exploits, pranks, and good and evil deeds of the old hero. //Gauwa, the lesser god, inflicts both good and evil on humans, sometimes in response to the directives of Gao!na and sometimes on his own volition. The //Gauwasi, the spirits of the dead, live with Gao!na in the sky and do his and //Gauwa's bidding, such as coming to earth, interfering with human lives, and causing sickness and accidents. To the !Kung there are no distinctions between good and bad people when they die--all become //Gauwasi and join the great god. People fear them, though they are not terrified: the gods may respond to their prayers; the //Gauwasi may be bad, good or indifferent to people. Further, they can be challenged: during the trance dances, the healers often take burning brands and charge out into the darkness loudly driving away the lurking //Gauwa and //Gauwasi.

151   Marshall, Lorna. "Marriage among !Kung Bushmen." *Africa* 29(October 1959): 335-365.

!Kung co-wives share the same hut and cooking fire, and they normally cooperate in gathering food, hauling water, nursing one another's babies, and living as harmoniously together as possible by repressing jealousies and discords. Controlling anger is a highly approved ideal, though sometimes tempers flare, particularly in the case of adultery. They fear the possibility of a fight with their poisoned arrows, for which they are not aware of an antidote, so they consider uncontrolled anger to be extremely dangerous. When adultery does occur and come to light, everyone tries to resolve the resulting conflicts before serious fighting erupts. In one incident, a young widower had tried to take a wife away from another man, but others intervened, the tragedy of an open fight was averted, and both parties camped out next to the anthropologists for several days with the obvious knowledge that neither would probably resort to open conflict next to the visitors. After a few days the widower left the area peaceably. Everyone highly desired peace and harmony and was willing to try to calm the situation. Also appears as a chapter in [154].

152   Marshall, Lorna. "Sharing, Talking, and Giving: Relief of Social Tensions among the !Kung." In *Kalahari Hunter-Gatherers: Studies of the !Kung San and Their Neighbors*, edited by Richard B. Lee and Irven DeVore, 349-371. Cambridge, MA: Harvard University Press, 1976.

Marshall describes several key elements that she feels help the !Kung maintain their peacefulness. They talk constantly to keep communication open and maintain group norms; when contentious issues threaten stability, a spontaneous "talk," in which the parties to the problem participate, helps resolve the difficulty. Proper manners are extremely important to them, such as the importance of people correctly welcoming visitors to the fire, and for visitors the necessity of their correctly receiving offerings of food. The author describes in detail the processes !Kung use to share meat after a successful hunt, an important aspect of group cohesion, and she also explains the role that gift-giving has for fostering friendship and generosity, as well as for relieving the tensions of envy and jealousy. Also appears as a chapter in [154].

153   Marshall, Lorna. "Sharing, Talking, and Giving: Relief of Social Tensions among the !Kung Bushmen." *Africa* 31(July 1961): 231-249.

This same paper, with only slight modifications of writing style, appears in *Kalahari Hunter-Gatherers: Studies of the !Kung San and Their Neighbors*, edited by Lee and DeVore [152]. An appendix listing !Kung Bushmen artifacts was included only in this version.

154 Marshall, Lorna. *The !Kung of Nyae Nyae*. Cambridge, MA: Harvard University Press, 1976.

A thorough description of the lives of the !Kung of western Namibia near the Botswana border, based on eight expeditions from 1950 through 1961 by the Marshall family, which included the author's husband Laurence Marshall, son John Marshall and daughter Elizabeth Marshall. Elizabeth Marshall Thomas wrote her own book about the San peoples [357], and four of the chapters in this volume appeared previously in the journal *Africa*, three of which, on the family and band [149], on !Kung marriages [151], and on sharing, talking and giving [153] are noted separately. Other chapters describe the environment in which the !Kung live, their style of gathering plants, their hunting techniques, their kinship structure, behavior patterns, play, games and music. The descriptive text is enriched by numerous black-and-white photos, and the analytical discussions are amplified by detailed lists, charts, and other scholarly apparatus.

155 Marshall, Lorna. "The Medicine Dance of the !Kung Bushmen." *Africa* 39(October 1969): 347-381.

The only activity in the lives of the !Kung that draws everyone together, regardless of kinship ties, is the medicine dance; everyone in the band participates and, if other bands are camped nearby, many of them will walk over a mile in the dark to be part of it. Healing dances occur as spontaneous decisions of the band, and there are no leaders of the dancing--anyone will start singing the first line of a healing song and others will join in. The dancing starts, pauses, and stops on the signals of any member of the group. During the dance, the healer will often scream his hostilities at the spirits out in the darkness, showing off his aggressiveness toward them by throwing firebrands at the circling spirits. The healing dance provides a lot of strength for the band: whatever the state of friendliness or hostility among them, as they sing, clap, and dance together to drive away the spirits that bring illnesses, tensions are put aside and they unite in actions that will benefit them all.

156   Rosenberg, Harriet G. "Complaint Discourse, Aging, and Caregiving among the !Kung San of Botswana." In *The Cultural Context of Aging: Worldwide Perspectives*, edited by Jay Sokolovsky, 19-41. New York: Bergin & Garvey, 1990.

Although old people are cared for very effectively in !Kung society, they complain ceaselessly about perceived slights or lack of caregiving by others. Their relatives expect them to complain: it shows they are still healthy and it helps to keep the elderly complainer visible. Complaining serves to keep services and goods circulating, to reinforce their traditional group sharing and egalitarian society. Sometimes the complaining takes the form of elaborate stories. For instance, an old man spun a lengthy yarn about how he was once caught in a trap and no one cared; when confronted with the facts in the case, however, everyone enjoyed a hearty laugh. Truth was not the issue: he had told a fine story that exemplified the caregiving obligations of !Kung society. When asked why she cared for old people to whom she was not directly related, one !Kung lady replied that she didn't think about the issue--if an old person was there and needed help, she provided it.

157   Wiessner, Polly. "Risk, Reciprocity and Social Influences on !Kung San Economics." In *Politics and History in Band Societies*, edited by Eleanor Leacock and Richard Lee, 61-84. New York: Cambridge University Press, 1982.

While the !Kung generally eat well, there is a lot of uncertainty due to the fluctuations of wild vegetables and game. They reduce these dangers through a reciprocal method of exchanging gifts called *hxaro* which cements social obligations and pools the risks. *Hxaro* gifts are valuable, useful and attractive objects that express the warmth of a friendship--generous but not overly so since they must not arouse resentment or jealousy. Infants are socialized into *hxaro* exchanges by their grandmothers, who remove the child's beads so they can be given to a relative; she then gives the child new ones. Children soon start to place a value on the gifts they give and receive, and as they begin to establish their own relationships with their playmates they learn lifetime lessons of toleration for imbalances. Adults spend an enormous amount of time sitting around fabricating gifts, working slowly in groups, laughing, talking, and telling stories-- which adds value to the gifts. In order to inhibit freeloaders and foster return giving, at times hard workers have to sit back, limit their work, and become needy.

Ladakhis

The traditional, peaceful lifestyle of the Tibetan Buddhist people of Ladakh is based on their belief in living in harmony with the land and with one another. Ladakh is located in the northern Indian state of Jammu and Kashmir, on the north side of the Himalayas, and is composed of the district of Leh, which is primarily Buddhist, and Kargil, which is mostly Muslim. There are about 50,000 Ladakhi people. The focus of the literature in this section is on the Buddhist people who inhabit the high mountain valleys, all over 10,000 feet in elevation, in the Leh district. Despite the high, arid conditions of their valleys, the Ladakhis are able to live on small family farms of about five acres growing primarily barley, wheat, and some other crops, depending on elevation. The settlements in the highest valleys cannot grow food, and depend entirely on their livestock. Completion of a road into Ladakh and opening the area to tourism in the mid-1970s has significantly altered the economy, society, and peaceful harmony of the people, a trend which is analyzed in Helena Norberg-Hodge's book [161].[6]

158   Harvey, Andrew. *A Journey in Ladakh*. Boston: Houghton Mifflin, 1983.

The author makes many observations on the Ladakhis--their dislike for competition, their opposition to cruelty, their toleration for others--but he emphasizes his personal search for the wisdom of Ladakhi Buddhism. According to one of the chief lamas he visits repeatedly, the true motivation of the seeker after learning should be to love all of creation and to seek perfection oneself in order to help others to similarly become perfect. According to this Ladakhi Buddhist, the ideal of personal escape from suffering is not acceptable: instead, one must seek to free all of creation from the pain and prison of the self; one must renounce personal salvation for the pleasure of working to liberate others. A pure spirit of inner strength and peace is necessary in order for one's love to have effect and bring peace and strength to others. The man who is in the world but not part of it, not stained by it, can be the most helpful. The lotus flower rises from the mud, but it is not composed of mud and has no mud on its petals.

159   Mann, R. S. "Intra and Inter Family Relations among the Ladakhis of Ladakh." *Bulletin of the Anthropological Survey of India* 21(Jan.-June 1972): 88-106.

Social relations among Ladakhis are easy, frank, and free of tensions. Spouses are normally cooperative and affectionate with one another, as are parents with their children, though fathers do administer corporal punishment on occasion. Siblings have such close relationships that brothers frequently share a wife in a polyandrous union. All of the potential fathers in such a union are very affectionate toward their children, who refer to the eldest as "elder father" and to each of the others as "younger father." Cooperation, mutual assistance, and sharing make Ladakhi life easier in the face of the difficult natural environment they live in, and are integral aspects of their kinship groupings and social brotherhoods. People share bullocks for plowing, assist others when asked, and raise orphans if both their parents die. Individuals who do not follow the social norms, who thus pose threats to the community, will be boycotted: cut off from participation in religious observations, rites, ceremonies, cooperative endeavors, shared food, and social relationships until they correct their behavior.

160   Mann, R. S. *The Ladakhi: A Study in Ethnography and Change.* Calcutta: Anthropological Survey of India, 1986.

Peacefulness among the Ladakhis is a result of their Buddhist beliefs and their adaptation to the harsh natural environment: cooperation is essential for survival. Major crimes are unknown, and when individuals violate important social norms without repenting, villages may, as a last resort, ostracize them. The lamas may stop serving the religious needs of the offender, and no one may visit, support, or assist him or his family. Largely due to their practice of polyandry, in most respects Ladakhi women and men are treated equally. Women have considerable authority in the home, manage the domestic economy, and speak freely in social situations, though they lack the ability to travel outside Ladakh and they do not have village leadership roles. They do have equal rights with men to divorce, and in divorce situations they are compensated fairly. Ladakhis enjoy village archery competitions which frequently form the basis for their festivals. Everyone who hits the target wins a prize out of the pooled entrance fees of all the participating archers, and with the music, dancing, singing, and socializing, everyone enjoys the festivities.

161   Norberg-Hodge, Helena. *Ancient Futures: Learning from Ladakh.* San Francisco: Sierra Club Books, 1991.

Aggressive behavior--even arguing--is exceedingly rare in the traditional Ladakhi villages, where relations are based on getting along with one another. They make vigorous efforts to avoid offending others, and when someone does suffer because of the thoughtless actions of another, the offense will be excused placidly. Ladakhis normally ensure the peaceful resolution of human interactions by relying on third parties to act as arbiters. If two people are trying to reach a deal, a neutral person, perhaps unknown to both, will intervene and help them reach their agreement. Conflicts are resolved by the elected head of the village who listens to both sides of a case and makes a decision. In addition to family ties, they have formally established groupings of families which help one another on many occasions; the small-scale village environment helps people to unite, share the work in a cooperative fashion, and remain flexible to each other's needs. However, the introduction of a money economy and modernization over the past few decades has fostered competition, social disruption, strife, and a loss of traditional values.

Lepchas

The 23,000 Lepchas are the original inhabitants of the mountainous valleys of Sikkim, a district in the Himalayas of northeastern India. Their land was invaded by Tibetan and Nepali peoples and a Sikkimese king was established in the early 17th century. Since that time, as a subject, minority people they accepted the Tibetan Buddhist faith but retained many elements of their previous shamanistic practices. Their villages spread out for thousands of vertical feet along the sides of their valleys, which provides the altitudinal variety that allows them to practice settled agriculture and raise widely varying crops; they also do some shifting cultivation. Hunting, formerly common, is not practiced much any longer.[7]

162   Gorer, Geoffrey. *Himalayan Village: An Account of the Lepchas of Sikkim*, 2d edition. New York: Basic Books, 1967.

The Lepchas almost completely suppress aggression and competition, foster daily cooperation in their farm work, and exhibit little jealousy toward each other. Their love is based on the satisfaction of mutual needs for food. A boy will express love for his mother in the same way as a man once expressed his affection for his wife: "I am pleased in my belly." The Lepchas strongly disapprove of quarreling, and when quarrels do occur, mutual friends try to resolve the problems. If that fails, village leaders will discuss the issues and threaten heavy fines to force the people to patch up their differences. They believe that quarreling is the work of an evil spirit which must be destroyed each year by the lamas in a vividly dramatic exorcism ceremony. A large image of the quarrel spirit is first shot through the heart with an arrow, another is hacked to pieces and burned, then a third is cast away by the lama. These actions to purge the community of quarreling are accompanied by a variety of prayers and rituals. This book describes many such aspects of Lepcha life.

Malapandaram

The Malapandaram live on about 1,000 forested square miles of the Pandalam Hills, which are located near the southern end of India's Western Ghats in the state of Kerala. Some authorities have claimed that, although they speak dialects of Malayalam and Tamil, they are remnants of a pre-Dravidian people. The evidence is not conclusive. The 1,569 Malapandaram (in 1971) are closely related to the Paliyan people who live in the Western Ghats to the north; but though they may intermarry with the Paliyans, they dislike being confused with them. They are a nomadic people who live off the foods they find in the forest and the products they gather for trade in the markets. Their religion and culture have traits in common with the surrounding Hindu peoples of the plains; this trait is particularly noticeable among the Malapandaram who live at the edges of their territory.[8]

163   Fürer-Haimendorf, C. "Notes on the Malapantaram of Travancore." *Bulletin of the International Committee on Urgent Anthropological and Ethnological Research* 3(1960): 45-51.

Traditionally the Malapandaram lacked weapons of any kind, hunting only small game that could be caught by dogs and killed with sticks. They used vegetable poisons in streams in order to gather fish, plus they ate roots, tortoises, iguanas, and hares. Before embarking on a honey-collecting expedition they offered a coconut to the gods of the local forest; they worshipped a variety of male and female deities associated with local hills and other natural features.

164   Morris, Brian. *Forest Traders: A Socio-Economic Study of the Hill Pandaram.* London: Athlone, 1982.

In Malapandaram society men and women treat each other equally and cooperate in each other's economic endeavors-- men help women with their gathering, hauling, and cooking, while women help men hunt small animals. While spouses are very warm and affectionate toward one another, their relation- ships are also transient and ephemeral. Couples frequently move apart for lengthy periods and casually take up relations with others. They will similarly treat their children with considerable affection, yet show indifference for their welfare, such as a mother--who was normally quite affectionate with children-- allowing her son to walk through a column of soldier ants without bothering to warn him. By the time they are five or six years old, children have lost their close emotional ties with their parents and have been socialized into a pattern of individual autonomy, balanced with warmth and affection for close family members. Adults will only limit children's autonomy by con- trolling expressions of aggression such as physical violence against other children or adults. Family composition is primarily determined by how well people get along rather than by kinship relations.

165   Morris, Brian. "Hill Pandaram." In *Encyclopedia of World Cultures, Volume III, South Asia*, edited by Paul Hockings, 98- 101. Boston: G. K. Hall, 1992.

The Malapandaram are mostly a nomadic people who live by gathering, hunting, and trading forest products for outside goods. While certain gathering activities and tasks are primarily men's or women's, the division is not rigid, the sexes are equal, and both men and women work together in many of the domestic and gathering activities. They associate certain areas with particular individuals, but do not assert territorial rights--the forest is the property of everyone. The basic social unit is the nuclear family; settlements normally consist of several such families, though a single family may live by itself for a length of time. Marriages are primarily monogamous, though they tend to be fragile. Individuals are self-sufficient, autonomous, and egalitarian in their relations with others. They highly emphasize their lack of aggressiveness by separating and fleeing from conflicts. They do not have a formal means of resolving disputes, though individuals do act as mediators informally.

166   Morris, Brian. "Settlement and Social Change among the Hill Pandaram." *Man in India* 56(June 1976): 134-151.

Government agencies have been trying for decades to induce the Malapandaram to quit their nomadic existence and settle down to an agriculturally based economy. Many decades ago their isolation ended when forest workers and agricultural peoples came into the hills and when the forestry department established a market for so-called minor forest products--especially wax, honey and cardamom. In the 1960s the government of Kerala tried to settle some of them into a village with brick homes, a school, and a local agricultural agent to teach them to grow tapioca as a cash crop. This attempt failed since the Malapandaram did not see any benefit to themselves from raising cash crops. They were able to gather enough products in the forest to trade for goods they wanted--shirts, blouses, oil lamps, cloth, tobacco--so they didn't need to devote time to settled agriculture. Besides, they always had plenty to eat from the forest, including a varied diet and regular sources of proteins. They resisted giving up this relative affluence for the poverty of settled, cash-crop, small farming.

167   Morris, Brian. "Tappers, Trappers and the Hill Pandaram (South India)." *Anthropos* 72(1977): 225-241.

Although some writers have maintained that the hill tribes of South India lived until recently in a completely isolated, purely gathering-hunting lifestyle, historical evidence shows that they have had extensive contacts with outside traders for hundreds if not thousands of years. Government regulations today give complete monopolies to particular contractors for trading with the Malapandaram; as a result, the hill people receive only nominal prices for the "minor" forest products that they gather. They tend to trade primarily for luxuries such as tobacco, chewing items, and beverages and not much for staples, so the trade represents only a supplement for them. The forest contractors employ agents who aggressively patrol their territories and attempt to cajole, sometimes coerce, and, at times in the past, to physically assault the Malapandaram to induce them to gather more forest products. Their shyness and timidity is a response, and they still hide from the agents when they are about in the forest. Thus, the individualistic nature of their culture is largely a result of their being bound to the trading system of the larger society.

168   Morris, Brian. "The Family, Group Structuring and Trade among South Indian Hunter-Gatherers." In *Politics and History*

in Band Societies, edited by Eleanor Leacock and Richard Lee, 171-187. New York: Cambridge University Press, 1982.

The Malapandaram live together in small bands consisting of one to six families. Individuals from different families may cooperate in the daily foraging for food and trade goods, or they may forage alone. Meat, tobacco, and honey gathered from collective expeditions are shared generally among families, but otherwise people eat or trade what they gather themselves, sharing only within their families. They are a nomadic people with a strong emphasis on equality of the sexes, individual autonomy, frequent separation and forming of new groups, no group formation above the family level, and no assertion of territoriality. Their nonviolence and timidity result primarily from the bullying and harassment they get from the farming people in the lowlands. However, their trade links with the plains people are important factors in forming the fragmentary pattern of their social structure, which is geared to their dual-purpose economic activity: gathering for both subsistence and for trade. Theoretical analyses of the nature of hunter-gatherer social structures need to factor in the existence of external trade linkages.

Mbuti

Approximately 35,000 Mbuti Pygmies live in the Ituri rainforest of northeastern Zaire. Most of them are still engaged in gathering and net-hunting when they live in the forest, but they periodically move to settlements of Bantu villagers in forest clearings where they temporarily provide labor and meat in exchange for vegetable foods and outside products. Turnbull's very popular book *The Forest People* [174], supplemented by his other writings, forms the basis for understanding the generally peaceful ways of the Mbuti. He relates numerous fights among them, but he evaluates the resolution of their conflicts within a broader context of peaceful social relations and their harmony with their forest home. Their forest environment, along with that of the neighboring Efe Pygmies, who hunt with bows and arrows, is threatened by logging, though a reserve is being established for the Efe.[9]

169   Mosko, Mark S. "The Symbols of 'Forest': A Structural Analysis of Mbuti Culture and Social Organization." *American Anthropologist* 89(December 1987): 896-913.

An abstract discussion of theoretical and ethnographic issues related to the symbolic Mbuti conceptions linking the forest with kinship relationships. The pregnant Mbuti woman avoids noise and disharmony and sings lullabies to her unborn child to acquaint it with the forest spheres in which it will live. The center of their world is the quiet forest (*ndura*) and the family hut (*endu*), both of which are linguistic metaphors for the womb (*ndu*). At the center of each family hut is the family hearth (*kuma*), also their word for vagina. The layout of the hut follows the same spatial pattern as the design of the camp, and both symbolize the relationships of different bands to each other and to the forest. In an idealized sense, the family hut, with parents and children, is comparable to the whole natural environment, with the forest as parents and Mbuti as children. The Mbuti view of the forest as both father and mother, lover and sibling, expresses the contradictions of their social system, which incorporates both endogamy and exogamy.

170 Singer, Merrill. "Pygmies and Their Dogs: A Note on Culturally Constituted Defense Mechanisms." *Ethos* 6(Winter 1978): 270-277.

The Pygmies treat their dogs quite harshly, despite the fact that they are very important to them for assistance in hunting. The author speculates that the reason for such harsh treatment is their tightly knit, cooperative, sharing society: the Pygmies need a release for their aggressive tendencies--a "culturally constituted defense mechanism"--and the vicious beating of their canines forms part of that outlet. The Pygmies dislike aggression or disharmony, and when disputes do occur they are settled with a primary focus on restoring peace among the people, without much regard to right versus wrong. Their aggression is displaced onto the dogs since open aggression might split the band. The Pygmies do not displace their aggressive drives onto the supernatural, as Spiro suggests the Ifaluk do (see entry [91]), since to them the forest is associated with supernatural benevolence and they would feel mentally uneasy believing in malevolent ghosts living around them. A modest amount of aggressiveness is appropriate for the Pygmies since it helps to keep their band sizes from growing too large.

171 Turnbull, Colin. "Liminality: A Synthesis of Subjective and Objective Experience." In *By Means of Performance: Intercultural Studies of Theatre and Ritual*, edited by Richard Schechner and Willa Appel, 50-81. Cambridge: Cambridge University Press, 1990.

To the Mbuti, the liminal state, which is coexistent with the normal one, can be activated through the group *molimo* ritual. The author participated repeatedly in the *molimo*, sitting with them and listening to their deeply moving music; after he was moved to get up and walk around outside the circle, to listen to the forest as it echoed the voices of the singers (who were echoing the forest), they told him they were glad he had danced as they did, in a spontaneous, solo fashion. He found that all of the senses are involved in the ritual, and that the opposition of opposite concepts (passive versus active, etc.) and the discreetness of the senses began to change. They sing their *molimo* songs to make contact with the spirits, to symbolize their exclusion of the rest of the world except for the surrounding forest of sounds, movements and smells--the essence of their lives. The mood of the *molimo* festival varies, depending on the mood of the people: it may express sadness, joy, mourning, and other emotions.

172   Turnbull, Colin M. "Human Nature and Primal Man." *Social Research* 40(Autumn 1973): 511-530.

The Mbuti's social relationships, and their view of the forest, require them to maintain an attitude of cooperativeness. They live so closely to their forest world that they associate abnormalities such as witchcraft, violence, aggression, and hostility with the outside world of their neighboring farmers. This is contrasted with the Ik, mountain-dwelling peoples of Uganda, who live in a much harsher environment and have a social system that denies any value in sharing, loving relationships and teaches that the only value is self-survival. Turnbull examines the conflict between self and society in modern, Western, technological society in light of the values held by these two African cultures.

173   Turnbull, Colin M. "Mbuti Womanhood." In *Woman the Gatherer*, edited by Frances Dahlberg, 205-219. New Haven: Yale University Press, 1981.

The major value of Mbuti society is interdependence. While sex and age differentiations are important aspects of their social organization, neither carries any sense of superior or inferior status. When conflict does occur among the Mbuti it is often between men and women. Nursing mothers normally restrict sexual intercourse with their husbands, who often have affairs with other women during that period. While not forbidden in their culture, if affairs are discovered they provoke noisy disputes. Gender conflicts are averted through dances and rituals. In one ritual the men dress as women and vice versa, each side ridiculing the other's sex organs. Another strategy that diffuses sex conflicts is to have a tug of war between the sexes: if the men start to win a man will join the women and ridicule the female sex while helping their side; if the women start to win, a woman will join the opposite side while ridiculing the sex of her new team. The contest continues until it breaks down from the laughter of the contestants. The effect is to ridicule conflict itself.

174   Turnbull, Colin M. *The Forest People.* New York: Simon and Schuster, 1961.

The Mbuti invade each other's territories every year during the annual honey flow, and while the group whose territory has been invaded may threaten warfare, no harm is done. If the different groups meet, the invaders flee back to their own territory without fighting. The Mbuti have no leaders, formal councils, chiefs, or methods of resolving disputes or crimes. But the people react cooperatively to difficult situations, publicly disapprove of fractious behavior, and ridicule or punish offenders in order to prevent disruptions in social relations. An offender who was permanently driven out of the camp for a serious infraction was surreptitiously cared for by relatives for several days until he could quietly come back and resume his life. Sometimes serious fights break out, and they will continue until an older person wades in and breaks up the fighting. But their most important relationship is with the forest, which they consider to be their god. They sing songs to it, appreciate that it cares for them, have faith in its goodness. They feel their songs of rejoicing, devotion, and praise serve to make the forest happy.

175   Turnbull, Colin M. *The Human Cycle.* New York: Simon and Schuster, 1983.

Turnbull defines a society as a group of people whose members are tied together by a set of mutual responsibilities and obligations. He examines the customs of several societies--American, English, Hindu, and the Mbuti of Zaire--in terms of the five stages of life: childhood, adolescence, youth, adulthood, and old age. Turnbull describes the peacefulness of the Mbuti with obvious affection, including their worshipful attitude toward the forest they live in, their views of their place in the universe, and their harmony and cooperativeness with each other and their children. He describes the completely non-competitive games the children play, the nature of their interdependence, and the role of their puberty rites in tying them together as a people.

176   Turnbull, Colin M. "The Importance of Flux in Two Hunting Societies." In *Man the Hunter: Symposium on Man the Hunter, University of Chicago, April 6-9, 1966,* edited by Richard B. Lee and Irven DeVore, 132-137. Chicago: Aldine, 1968.

The supportive environment of the Ituri forest is an important factor in determining the social structure of the Mbuti, particularly the process of people moving from group to group. Two different hunting styles are followed: Net hunters live in larger bands, of six to thirty nuclear families, while archers live in much smaller bands which may include only two or three families. Both types of Mbuti bands regroup during the brief, annual honey-flow season--the net hunters break up into smaller groups since they feel that game is so plentiful that they can easily hunt without large parties, and the archers form larger bands since they believe that game is scarce and they have to cooperate in communal hunts. The reforming of groups that occurs during the honey-flow season allows the Mbuti to move in with other bands if they wish. Peaceable relations are maintained and tensions dissipated because people have this annual opportunity to move away from others with whom they may have problems and live with different groups.

177   Turnbull, Colin M. "The Politics of Non-Aggression." In *Learning Non-Aggression: The Experience of Non-Literate Societies,* edited by Ashley Montagu, 161-221. New York: Oxford University Press, 1978.

The Mbuti children learn that the security they feel in the forest, their dependence on one another and the interdependence within the group, their ways of coordination and cooperation are all values which foster peacefulness and militate against aggression. They view their forest as sacred--they talk and sing to it reverently, they address it both as father and mother, they express affection for it and need from it. Pregnant Mbuti women sing special lullabies to the infants in their wombs, reassuring them about the goodness of the forest and the supportiveness of the human world into which they will soon be born. This feeling of support, dependence, and interdependence is reinforced throughout childhood, particularly during the children's non-competitive play activities. One of the major strategies of the Mbuti which dissipates conflict is the use of laughter, jokes, and ridicule. When they do discuss issues they prefer to interact in the spirit of *ekimi*, quiet or calm, rather than *akami*, noisy disturbance. *Akami* is associated with bad temper, noise, hunger, arguments, and damaging winds, while *ekimi* is associated with happiness and gentle winds. About half of this chapter was reprinted under the title "The Ritualization of Potential Conflict Between the Sexes Among the Mbuti," which appeared in *Politics and History in Band Societies*, edited by Eleanor Leacock and Richard Lee (New York: Cambridge University Press, 1982), p. 133-155.

178   Turnbull, Colin M. *Wayward Servants: The Two Worlds of the African Pygmies*. Garden City, NY: Natural History Press, 1965.
        Turnbull recorded 124 disputes during the year he lived in a Mbuti camp, not counting daily, petty squabbles, and he recounts 35 of them in considerable detail. Despite the number of disputes, the author concludes that most of them served to air problems before they became too serious. The Mbuti think it is not good to keep their discomforts or irritations to themselves, since it makes their hearts feel better to voice their antagonisms. However, they have a strong dislike for noise, which they define as the sound of people fighting loudly. Noise not only disturbs the camp, it also kills the hunt and the forest. Most Mbuti camps have a person who acts like a clown and takes on the unique responsibility of actively trying to end conflicts. He uses mime, ridicule, and other antics to revive other, more minor disputes which get everyone laughing, thus focusing the conflict on himself and diverting attention from the conflict in progress. *Wayward Servants* is a much more detailed volume on the Mbuti than the popularly written *Forest People* [174], though the author is careful not to repeat his stories or information from the earlier work.

Mennonites

The term "Mennonite" derives from the name of Menno Simons, an early Anabaptist leader. Traditionally, Mennonites have held a dualistic view that they should live in the world but not of it--they should obey the dictates of the state unless it contradicts one of the mandates of Christ. To them, one of Christ's most important commands was for people to live in peace. If anyone tried to force them to serve in an army, they should simply refuse, and not resist the judicial or punitive actions carried out against them--the doctrine of nonresistance as exemplified by Christ's going to the cross. The more conservative Mennonites continue to work on their farms, living and dressing in a plain fashion and selectively rejecting the values and technologies of modern society, while others have moved into urban areas, attained non-farming skills and professions, and joined the mainstream of contemporary American life. Various streams of Mennonites have entered the United States and Canada--from Switzerland and Germany starting in the 18th century, and from Russia starting in the 1870s. There were about 370,000 members of the various Mennonite churches in 1988 in over 3,600 congregations in the United States and Canada.[10]

179   Albrecht, Paul. "Civilian Public Service Evaluated by Civilian Public Service Men." *Mennonite Quarterly Review* 22(January 1948): 5-18.

Just after World War II, the author sent questionnaires to Mennonites who had chosen alternative service in Civilian Public Service camps during the war. The 712 returns revealed a generally positive attitude among the men toward their camp experiences. Appreciation for their Mennonite heritage had increased among 66 percent of the men, while 81 percent felt that their understanding of nonresistance had become clearer. They felt that exposure to other Mennonite groups in their camps would be beneficial (67 percent), though only 46 percent decided that such exposure would allow them to understand their own beliefs more strongly. While the results were split in terms of whether the men believed their home congregations understood their camp experiences, the men felt overwhelmingly (77 percent) that they had gained an understanding of the "Christian life" that would be needed by their home church. The experience increased the importance of personal devotions for 55 percent of the men. In camps that had councils which worked with the staff to solve problems, 70 percent of the men felt that the councils helped resolve conflicts.

180   Appavoo, David. "Ideology, Family and Group Identity in a Mennonite Community in Southern Ontario." *Mennonite Quarterly Review* 59(January 1985): 67-93.

Despite the fact that it is no longer a rural community, Mennonites living in a suburban town on the edge of a major metropolitan area in Ontario still define themselves by their traditional values of nonresistance and service. While all responded to the author's study by expressing a preference for taking a voluntary service assignment instead of serving in the military, if that option were available to them, 90 percent of their older non-Mennonite neighbors indicated they would choose the military option. In contrast to the individualism of their neighbors, the Mennonites turned out to be more strongly oriented to their group, and while they avoid direct participation in politics, they are involved in the issues of their larger society. In order to develop service and nonresistance values in their children, Mennonite organizations train young people in volunteer service, disaster relief, peace work, and child care. While Mennonites effectively maintain close ties within their families and their kin groups, they also cultivate close ties with everyone else in their religious community without any lessening of family closeness.

181   Augsburger, David Wilbur. "The Control and Management of Hostility in a Nonviolent-Nonresistant Community." Claremont, CA: PhD Dissertation, School of Theology at Claremont, 1974.

While a large majority of the 414 Ohio Mennonites tested for their levels of hostility, anger, and aggression were strongly committed to nonviolence and nonresistance, a minority had served in the military or had low nonresistance values. These minorities exhibited statistically significant higher levels of verbal hostility and assaultive behavior than did the majority. Mennonites over 60 years of age reported the lowest instance of assaultive behavior but the highest responses of suspicion and guilt; people over 50 appeared to admit their hostilities and express them more freely than younger ones. Nonresistance values did not, however, result in increased passivity or higher levels of indirect hostility, as had been suspected, though the Mennonites did have a higher level of guilt than normal, with a greater degree of overcontrolled hostility in some people. The author concludes that his results disprove theories that hostility must be released; instead, they show that nonviolence, nonresistance, and controlling aggression reduces assaultive behavior, active hostility, and the verbal expression of anger, without a corresponding rise in indirect or passive hostile behavior.

182   Becker, Mark. "Mennonite Resistance to Draft Registration." *Mennonite Life* 40(December 1985): 19-21.

In contrast to the earlier Mennonite practice of registering for the draft but refusing to serve in the army, in 1980 when

President Carter reinstituted the registration process, a number of young Mennonites refused even to register. Of the three Mennonite men whom the government decided to prosecute, one pleaded not guilty but he was convicted by a jury; on appeal, his conviction was overturned. The second, because of his belief in nonresistance, refused to enter a plea and stood mute during his arraignment. The third argued in court that he had already, in effect, registered with the government through all of his correspondence with officials explaining his reasons for refusing to register. The judge pressured the government to drop the case and just register him anyway. At least 60 to 80 other students at the Mennonite colleges were also involved in the registration resistance movement.

183   Bush, Perry. "'We Have Learned to Question Government'." *Mennonite Life* 45(June 1990): 13-17.

Drafted Mennonites at the start of World War II had the option of choosing alternative service in the Civilian Public Service (CPS) camps, which were run by Mennonites and the government. At first, most draftees reflected the passivity of their elders, that the best way to deal with violence in society was to pray, that it was important to oppose evil but inappropriate to put pressure on government. But increasing numbers began questioning Mennonite cooperation with the government; they wondered if total non-cooperation would be a better way of presenting a peace witness. During a series of meetings in 1945, many CPS men openly indicated disagreement with church leaders, saying that CPS was simply an aspect of conscription and thus a part of the act of war. Some indicated that alternative service was a way for Mennonites to endorse war "for everybody but themselves." This turmoil led, in the decades after the war, to a much stronger Mennonite activism for peace and social justice, as well as an increasing discontent with the concept of alternative service.

184   Driedger, Leo. "Community Conflict: The Eldorado Invasion of Warman." *Canadian Review of Sociology and Anthropology* 23(May 1986): 247-269.

A Canadian company, Eldorado Nuclear, proposed the construction of a uranium processing plant near the Mennonite community of Warman, Saskatchewan. The company secretly accumulated land for the project and developed support from key business, political, and labor leaders before revealing their plans to the community. Company representatives indicated that the refinery would provide jobs, increase tax revenues, and be totally safe. The community, composed of many different Mennonite branches, quickly became alarmed because the production of uranium appeared to be completely at odds with their traditional peace values. Mennonite leaders who combined traditional values of their faith with extensive networks of contacts formed a group to spearhead the opposition. At a federal government hearing the company was overwhelmed by the range and quality of opposition testimony, which included experts who focused on Mennonite theology, ethics, and the social implications of such a plant. The final success of the opposition was based on effective leaders who were able to shift the conflict from economic and technical issues, the company's prepared stance, to the traditional peaceful values of the community.

185   Driedger, Leo. "Native Rebellion and Mennonite Invasion: An Examination of Two Canadian River Valleys." *Mennonite Quarterly Review* 46(July 1972): 290-300.

Indian and Metis (mixed Indian and white) residents of the prairie regions of Canada had major conflicts with the federal government in Manitoba in 1870 and in Saskatchewan in 1884-85. The latter was settled only after considerable bloodshed by Federal troops. Following both of these conflicts the government promoted settlement, and numerous Mennonites accepted the invitations. The government encouraged them to establish their own communities, schools, and societies; it offered them private ownership of surveyed land; it promised transportation for the marketing of their farm production; and it protected them by a stable government which would allow them to maintain their own traditions and peace position. While the displaced Indians and Metis felt bitter toward the settlers who had taken lands they considered to be theirs, the Mennonites became condescending and prejudiced toward these outgroups, seemingly unaware that they had settled on their lands after government violence. The Mennonites were unconcerned that they had benefitted from the intervention and protection of the Canadian government. These historical developments, which need further study, show how Mennonites have compromised their peace-loving, nonresistant principles.

186   Driedger, Leo. "The Peace Panorama: Struggle for the Menno-
        nite Soul." *Conrad Grebel Review* 10(Fall 1992): 289-317.
            In 1989 the author and J. Howard Kauffman conducted a
        survey of the attitudes of Mennonites toward issues such as
        peace, politics, urbanization, and secularization, and published
        the results in their book *The Mennonite Mosaic: Identity and
        Modernization* (Scottdale, PA: Herald Press, 1991). This article
        summarizes the responses of over 3,000 Mennonites and Breth-
        ren in Christ members related to peace and political issues, and
        provides some comparisons to a survey conducted 17 years
        earlier. Driedger discusses historical reasons for the different
        attitudes among Mennonites living in the East and the Midwest,
        Canada and the United States, urban areas and rural areas. He
        concludes that a large majority of Mennonites are firmly com-
        mitted to their traditional peace attitudes and a minority believe
        social activism should be an aspect of their peace commitment;
        but only a very small number will consider any radical activism.
        Another minority, the Mennonite fundamentalists, reacted nega-
        tively to concepts and issues related to peacemaking, social
        justice, welfare, and the Mennonite Central Committee. Driedger
        argues that fundamentalism opposes and depresses peacemak-
        ing among Mennonites, who need to reconcile these divergent
        attitudes toward the meaning of the kingdom of God.

187   Driedger, Leo and Dan Zehr. "The Mennonite State-Church
        Trauma: Its Effect on Attitudes of Canadian Students and
        Leaders." *Mennonite Quarterly Review* 48(October 1974):
        515-526.
            Surveys of Canadian Mennonite conference leaders and uni-
        versity students showed that the leaders were primarily con-
        cerned with the historic peace witness of their churches and their
        nonresistance to violence, while the students were more inter-
        ested in peace and social concerns. The leaders were much less
        willing than the students to support peace or social issues that
        would involve interaction with the state, probably because of the
        history of conflicts between the Canadian government and the
        Mennonites earlier in the century, as well as conflicts with the
        Russian government from which many had emigrated. The
        university students supported more strongly than the leaders
        actions to ameliorate problems of violence and social justice,
        such as the prevention of war, opposition to capital punishment,
        and support for the United Nations, even though these actions

would involve interactions with the state. The survey results did reveal some differences between the various Mennonite conferences, however.

188   Durnbaugh, Donald F. "Religion and Revolution: Options in 1776." *Pennsylvania Mennonite Heritage* 1(July 1978): 2-9.

American church denominations are often grouped into those which supported the American Revolution, such as the Calvinist denominations, those opposed to it such as the Anglican and Methodist clergy, and neutral groups such as the members of the peace churches. The reality was much more complex and many faiths were split, with individual loyalties often determined by other factors such as regional tensions, minority issues, and political problems. The Mennonites of Pennsylvania and Maryland were neutrals with a decidedly pro-loyalist leaning during the Revolution. Evidence suggests that an underground loyalist movement claiming up to 6,000 supporters flourished in these two states, and that the Mennonites, much as later historians might not be proud of the fact, supported it. Hessian mercenary prisoners captured by the colonialists were well received by the Anabaptists, who were instrumental in drawing up a petition to the king during the war affirming their loyalty.

189   Entz, Margaret. "War Bond Drives and the Kansas Mennonite Response." *Mennonite Life* 30(September 1975): 4-9.

U.S. government campaigns to sell liberty bonds during World War I were designed to raise money and to foster patriotism and popular support for the war. Initially, most Mennonites were opposed to buying bonds voluntarily since that would signify support for the war effort, though some felt they had to comply because the government seemed to be demanding the money. Public opinion in Kansas was quite hostile to the "Germans" who refused to buy the bonds. An Amish bishop who wrote to his newspaper to denounce purchase of the bonds was indicted and fined for violating the Espionage Act. Mobs threatened, beat, tarred and feathered Mennonite leaders who refused to buy them. Mennonites attempted to work out compromises with government officials to avoid violating their consciences, but compromise was not allowed. Many of the Mennonites who gave in under pressure and did buy the bonds immediately donated them to worthy causes such as relief programs, so they would not profit from them. But as the war progressed the degree of Mennonite participation in the successive Liberty Loan campaigns increased.

190   Friesen, Duane K. "Peace Studies: Mennonite Colleges in the North American Context." *Mennonite Life* 35(March 1980): 13-18.

Peace studies programs at American colleges and universities are part of a worldwide phenomenon of peace research and teaching. The major Mennonite colleges have active peace studies programs, though the emphases differ. At Goshen College the peace studies co-major includes, in its core curriculum, a course on "War, Peace and Nonresistance" and a psychology course on "Violence and Nonviolence." The Institute of Peace and Conflict Studies, located jointly at Conrad Grebel College and the University of Waterloo, offers a comprehensive program which emphasizes the sources and resolution of interpersonal and intergroup conflict. Bethel College has a major in peace studies which allows students to focus on a variety of themes such as international war and peace issues, Third World development, theological perspectives on peace, and rural development. The other Mennonite colleges also offer a variety of courses and programs which support peace studies. The programs at the Mennonite Colleges are focused on the humanities, particularly theology, history and ethics, while peace studies at the public and non-Mennonite private institutions tend to focus on the social sciences.

191   Friesen, Steven K. "Mennonite Social Consciousness, 1899-1905." *Mennonite Life* 30(June 1975): 19-25.

Articles in three Mennonite periodicals from 1899 to 1905 reveal the growing social consciousness of many Mennonites during this period. Though their stands on issues varied, they became increasingly concerned about international peace, condemning the Boer War in South Africa and the Russo-Japanese War in East Asia. Articles covered domestic issues such as poverty, the lack of social justice, and the human environments and institutions that seemed to be responsible for these problems. While *The Review* and *The Mennonite* were more action oriented, publishing news about the substance of the issues, the *Herald of Truth* took a Biblical stance, and was more concerned about the religious solutions to social problems. They all covered the temperance and prohibition movements. Because nonresistance implies a lack of participation in the political process, their opinions differed on how much Mennonites should vote in order to produce social changes. By 1905 *The Mennonite* began to advocate their voting: "The man who prays for his country will vote as he prays and the vote of the praying man is the Salvation of the nation," it wrote in November that year.

192   Hershberger, Guy F. "Historical Background to the Formation of the Mennonite Central Committee." *Mennonite Quarterly Review* 44(July 1970): 213-244.

The 19th-century revivalist movement fostered a Mennonite awakening which led to a new spirit of evangelism and outreach. In 1873-74 Mennonite churches cooperated, briefly, to help the Russian Mennonites immigrate, and in the 1890s they again cooperated for several years to provide famine relief to India. During World War I, Mennonites supported the work of the American Friends Service Committee in Europe with money and volunteers, which provoked the ones working for the AFSC to agitate for a program within their own church. A group of young Mennonites formed a worldwide Mennonite Young Peoples Movement and went to France for an organizing conference, which articulated ideals--closer cooperation of Mennonites worldwide, support for social reforms, and an active peace program--that significantly influenced church leadership. The different branches of the church continued to support their separate relief programs until the situation in Russia became desperate, in 1920, and they were not really able to assist the Russians separately. They formed the Mennonite Central Committee (MCC) that year to coordinate relief service there. This article is part of an "MCC Anniversary Issue."

193   Hershberger, Guy F. "Mennonites in the Civil War." *Mennonite Quarterly Review* 18(July 1944): 131-144.

Mennonites had very strong convictions about nonresistance during the 18th century and the American Revolution, but some of that strength was lost during the 19th century. During the Civil War, both the Union and Confederate governments allowed conscientious objectors to provide substitutes when they were drafted, which Mennonites generally were willing to do, though fairly late in the war some church leaders began to oppose the practice. The Mennonites had almost no special publications on pacifism until 1863 when a couple of pamphlets were issued, soon followed by a new journal, the *Herald of Truth*, which carried a renewed vision of nonresistance. In the South, Mennonites living in the Shenandoah Valley of Virginia experienced active warfare when Sheridan's raid brought intense fighting to their farms. Many Virginia Mennonites had to flee into the mountains or hide in their homes when search parties came looking for them. Others who were drafted were willing to obey orders and drill, but they agreed among themselves to not aim correctly. They were soon taken out of the front ranks and assigned to support roles.

194   Hershberger, Guy Franklin. "Nonresistance and Industrial Conflict." *Mennonite Quarterly Review* 13(April 1939): 135-154.

Industrial confrontation in 20th-century America is primarily a class struggle, a battle for power in which labor unions seek economic and social justice for their members. This conflict is diametrically opposed to the Biblical ideal of nonresistance. In order to obtain the justice they seek, American unions feel they must coerce their employers. Undoubtedly compromises are often reached peacefully, as when trade agreements are reached, or, when disputes threaten, arbitration is used to settle the issues of contention. Even strikes and boycotts can be peaceful. For their part, employers may infiltrate their spies into union membership or even into leadership positions, or lock employees out of the shop--peaceful strategies on their part. But these methods are coercive, and when they fail both sides may resort to violence. The author sees no real difference between nonviolent coercion and actual violence--both violate the principle of nonresistance and should be avoided by Mennonites who should try to remain on farms or working for small businesses.

195   Hershberger, Guy Franklin. *The Mennonite Church in the Second World War.* Scottdale, PA: Mennonite Publishing House, 1951.

The Mennonite Church is the correct name for one of a number of Mennonite denominations. The history of this denomination during World War II covers a wide range of issues, including Mennonite services, missions, peace outreach, group relationships, the work of the Peace Problems Committee, relations with the Selective Service system, and the establishment and operation of the Civilian Public Service (CPS) camps. Many of the CPS camps were involved with soil conservation work under the direction of the Soil Conservation Service, while others worked with the Forest Service, the National Park Service, and the Bureau of Reclamation. During the early period of the war the church groups experienced a lot of freedom in developing the programs and regulations of the men at the camps, but in time the Selective Service began to assume a stronger hand, prompted in part by some discipline problems. The government felt the churches had not handled difficulties properly; however, the camps had to accept men who were conscientious objectors but were not in their churches, and they were responsible for some of the problems.

196   Hildebrand, Mary Anne. "Domestic Violence: A Challenge to Mennonite Faith and Peace Theology." *Conrad Grebel Review* 10(Winter 1992): 73-80.

An unpublished study of Canadian Mennonite families showed that they experience as much domestic violence as the population in general. Over 25 percent of the Mennonite women surveyed reported that they had been abused sexually. The author argues that the underlying beliefs of the Mennonite faith, particularly the peace theology, perpetuate this domestic violence. This theology has argued for a patriarchal family structure, a male God, a passive acceptance of persecution, particularly for women, self-sacrifice, and a view that to accept suffering without complaint is Christ-like. Hildebrand maintains that the love-your-enemy model acculturates women to accepting abuse. Mennonite women have traditionally been valued for their endless, uncomplaining service to their families and their weakness in the face of dominating men. They have been socialized to be nice, feminine, shy, and obedient in all situations. This pattern has fostered abusive family relations.

197   Homan, Gerlof D. "Mennonites and Military Justice in World War I." *Mennonite Quarterly Review* 66(July 1992): 365-375.

During World War I, Mennonite conscientious objectors had to report to army camps, but many decided that their beliefs would not permit them to do routine work which might draw them into supporting the military. As a result, they were ridiculed and physically mistreated; after April 1918, 136 were court-martialled as required by an order from the Department of War. At their court-martial hearings, most of the Mennonites could explain their ethical beliefs, but they had difficulties with the "what if" questions, such as, "what would you do if the 'Huns' invaded the U.S. and threatened your mother?" Since the

military court-martial serves not to secure justice but to investigate accusations and report findings to the camp commander,
all but one of the C.O.s were convicted; one was dismissed on
a technicality. The enthusiasm for instilling discipline and
satisfying hostile public opinion toward the Mennonites varied
from camp to camp. Sentences ranged from three months to 40
years in prison, though all of the convicted men were released
in 1919.

198   Hostetler, Beulah Stauffer. "Nonresistance and Social Respon-
       sibility: Mennonites and Mainline Peace Emphasis, ca. 1950 to
       1985." *Mennonite Quarterly Review* 64(January 1990): 49-73.

       From 1950 on American Mennonites have had to deal with
       major peace-related issues. As more and more Mennonites have
       served in international relief work, they have increasingly
       questioned the social effectiveness of the traditional, nonresis-
       tant pacifism of their faith. By the 1960s many were asking for
       direct action, comparable to the activism of Jeremiah, Jonah and
       Jesus, to right social wrongs, to support civil rights, and to
       oppose the Vietnam War. These concerns spread not only
       among church intellectual leaders but also at the local level,
       where resolutions condemned militaristic Civil War history
       anniversaries, racism, and hate groups. As the level of church
       involvement with the government increased, however, anxiety
       and opposition among conservative Mennonites grew as well.
       They were committed to living separately from the rest of
       society, and were opposed to those who wanted to work within
       society to ameliorate social injustices. To the activists, their
       social activism was a way of witnessing for peace and demon-
       strating the commandment to love their neighbors as them-
       selves.

199   Huxman, Susan Schultz. "Mennonite Rhetoric in World War I:
       Keeping the Faith." *Mennonite Life* 43(September 1988): 15-
       20.

       Mennonite rhetoric during World War I tried to maintain the
       strength and integrity of their nonresistant faith. Mennonite
       tracts containing passages of scripture and the Dordrecht Con-
       fession of Faith of 1632 supported the sincerity and lengthy
       history of their opposition to war. Their publications focused on
       their distinctiveness and high moral standards, and they rein-
       forced the belief that Mennonites were supposed to live for the
       coming world. Their magazines and newspapers tried to foster

strong self-identification by pointing out the dangers of compromise with militarism, since compromise was equated with selling out, sin, and jeopardizing beliefs. Mennonite editors welcomed the opportunity the war provided to support charities not connected to the military effort, but they sought to downplay the significance of the conflict by relegating war news to the back pages. As an instance of editorial down-playing, when America entered the war *The Mennonite* covered it with a two-column article on page four next to a three-column piece advocating more physical exercises for Mennonite preachers, so that they would deliver better sermons.

200   Juhnke, James C. "Kansas Mennonites During the Spanish-American War." *Mennonite Life* 26(April 1971): 70-72.

Kansas Mennonites, troubled in 1898 by the demands of citizenship versus their historic position of nonresistance, issued a report which expressed support for arbitration to avoid the Spanish-American War and praise for President McKinley's supposed attempts to avoid it. They adopted an apologetic tone about their unwillingness to serve in the army because they perceived that, for most Americans, a willingness to fight for one's country validated citizenship, and they wanted to be good citizens. A major Mennonite newspaper took a passive, neutral position regarding the war, but the brutal American repression of the Filipino resistance movement which followed the U.S. victory prompted some criticism of the nation's imperialism from Mennonite circles. William Jennings Bryan ran on a peace platform during the election campaign of 1900, which provoked debate among Kansas Mennonites. The lack of a noticeable peace vote in Kansas suggests that they were primarily interested in their growing commitment to American citizenship, and they wanted to maintain a good image to protect their exemption from conscription, which never became necessary due to the brevity of the war.

201   Juhnke, James C. "Mennonite Benevolence and Civic Identity: The Post-War Compromise." *Mennonite Life* 25(January 1970): 34-37.

Some writers have argued that the sources of Mennonite altruism are found exclusively in the spiritual heritage of their Anabaptist faith. However, strong outbursts of American Mennonite benevolence have coincided with periods of war and patriotism: during the Spanish-American War Mennonites formed

an emergency famine relief mission to India; in 1917 they gave
so generously to relief programs that church officials had to
work to find appropriate ways to disburse the money; during the
Second World War their relief programs functioned in an
outstanding fashion. The fact that Mennonite benevolence has
peaked during periods of intense nationalism suggests that they
have a strong desire to be as worthy of citizenship as anyone else,
even though they cannot join other Americans in fighting a war.
They feel their pacifism is seen as a blemish on their citizenship,
which prompts them to sacrifice in the best way they can--by
supporting benevolent causes. American Mennonite benevolence is thus a unique product of their own heritage and existing
patterns of American altruism. Their altruistic spirit is a product
of pacifism and militaristic nationalism.

202   Juhnke, James C. "Mennonite Benevolence and Revitalization
       in the Wake of World War I." *Mennonite Quarterly Review*
       60(January 1986): 15-30.

       World War I and its aftermath prompted new forms of
benevolence among American Mennonites. Because of the
wartime rise in farm prices, rural Mennonites had surplus
money; as a result they responded generously to financial
appeals from their mission boards and charities. This charitable
trend, combined with the famine in the Soviet Union and pleas
by Soviet Mennonites for relief assistance, led for the first time
to a spirit of interdenominational Mennonite cooperation in
foreign assistance and the founding of the Mennonite Central
Committee. However, the foreign relief effort allowed the
control of conservative Mennonite elders to be questioned, as
exemplified by the story of two Mennonite women who dutifully
wore their bonnets when they met church officials before
departing for MCC relief work in Europe but who, half-way
across the Atlantic, ceremoniously threw them overboard. MCC
relief work represented a renewal of the historic tradition of
benevolence which was deeply rooted in the Mennonite faith; it
earned them respectability, demonstrated their patriotism, and
displayed their willingness to serve their country peacefully.

203   Juhnke, James C. "Mennonite Progressives and World War I."
       Mennonite Life 41(December 1986): 14-16.

       After the turn of the century, the American Mennonite col-
leges began to employ young progressive thinkers who had
abandoned the strict dualism, authoritarianism, and parochial-

ism of the older conservatives and wanted Mennonites to accept the ideals of democracy. Accepting the belief that World War I would make the world safe for democracy, many supported the military effort and relegated nonresistance to secondary status. However, much as they may have wanted the allies to win the war, they were curiously ambivalent about becoming personally involved in the fighting. When young Mennonite draftees wrote to the presidents of Goshen and Bluffton colleges asking their counsel regarding conscientious objection, the college officials responded without providing advice on pacifism--and they emphasized the importance of defeating the Kaiser. The president of Bluffton sent a copy of his letter, along with the inquiry, to the draftees' camp commander, thereby appearing to show more support for the military than for Mennonite beliefs. After the war, as a result of their attitudes, the progressive wing of the Mennonite colleges was discredited and most of the progressives had to resign.

204   Juhnke, James C. "Mennonites and Ambivalent Civil Religion in World War I." *Mennonite Quarterly Review* 65(April 1991): 160-168.

World War I prompted the General Conference Mennonites to withdraw from the Federal Council of Churches because they felt that the Council supported the spirit of war too strongly. This decision reaffirmed their conservative roots and their separation from the American mainstream, and it was seconded by the other Mennonite groups. The attitude of the mainstream churches was based on the history of American civil religion which defined America, depending on the point of view, as a peaceful nation which only went to war temporarily and with noble purposes, or as an aggressive country molded by the revolution and later wars. Thus the American religious establishment could easily support President Wilson's call to fight what he defined as an idealistic war. After the war the American Relief Administration headed by Herbert Hoover provided the fledgling Mennonite Central Committee with an opportunity to carry out relief work in the Soviet Union, which gave it legitimacy and an opportunity to flourish.

205   Juhnke, James C. "Mennonites in World War I." *Mennonite Life* 45(December 1990): 25-28.

When the United States entered World War I and imposed the draft, Secretary of War Newton Baker denied that it was a form of involuntary conscription--every right-thinking American would volunteer because of the justice of their country's call, he felt. While the draft law provided exemptions for members of the peace churches, the War Department required all inductees from those groups to report to training camps, where they would presumably catch the patriotic spirit and voluntarily join the army. This put the draftees into the position of defending their beliefs against officers and soldiers, and many suffered physical beatings, humiliation, harassment, and intimidation as a result. Ultimately, some conscientious objectors were allowed to serve in agricultural assignments if they refused noncombatant roles in the military. After the war the new Mennonite Central Committee worked with the American Relief Administration to feed 75,000 Russian people during the 1922-23 famine--a small portion of the total relief program but important for the Mennonites in fostering their own internal unity and in gaining respect from outsiders.

206   Juhnke, James C. "Mob Violence and Kansas Mennonites in 1918." *Kansas Historical Quarterly* 43(Autumn 1977): 334-350.

During the liberty loan drive of April 1918, patriotic mobs in several areas of Kansas decided to force Mennonites to buy liberty bonds which would support the war. One mob of masked men surrounded a farm house, cut the telephone wires, then tarred and feathered the farmer's son when he refused to buy the bonds. Two days later he bought some. The mob visited another Mennonite family three different times from April through June, each time increasing the violence until they broke down and bought bonds to save their lives. Another mob visited the home of a Mennonite minister and nailed an American flag on the front of his house. When he sensed the crowd was still angry, he urged them to join him in singing "America." The crowd of patriots was abashed when he was the only one who knew and could forcefully sing all four verses. They shuffled their feet nervously and drove away. Many incidents of violence were only mildly reproved by the press and government leaders, which poisoned relations with the German-Americans for decades.

207   Juhnke, Roger. "The Perils of Conscientious Objection: An Oral History Study of a 1944 Event." *Mennonite Life* 34(September 1979): 4-9.

In August 1944 a group of potential inductees into the army harassed and beat six conscientious objectors during a bus ride across Kansas for medical examinations at Fort Leavenworth. The trouble started when one of the C.O.s responded to the sarcasm of the inductees by leveling aggressive charges of "murderers" at men who were already fighting in Europe. This prompted the physical harassment and beatings, which lasted until they neared Leavenworth. The abusers tried repeatedly to force the six to renounce their pacifism, which they would not do. The C.O.s did not complain that evening, but doctors who noticed their cuts and bruises the next day alerted an officer who broke the story open. Later, the C.O.s refused to file charges; the county attorneys brought charges against the eight ring leaders, though the magistrate only gave them light fines. Though the men were almost all only 18 years old and lacked effective adult supervision on the bus, the incident reflects the tensions and animosities which confronted Mennonites during the war period.

208   Kauffman, J. Howard. "Dilemmas of Christian Pacifism Within a Historic Peace Church." *Sociological Analysis* 49(Winter 1989): 368-385.

In response to a survey of attitudes toward war, politics, and social issues, 71 percent out of 3,591 Mennonites said they would accept alternative service, 10 percent indicated they would accept noncombatant service in the military, and only 5 percent were willing to accept regular military service. These statements represent a significant rise in Mennonite opposition to military service since the Second World War, when 45 percent of drafted men went into alternative service, 15 percent into noncombatant military service, and 40 percent served in the armed forces. Those responding were more ambivalence in their justifications of specific wars, however, regardless of whether they would fight personally. Three-quarters of the respondents felt that their members should vote, almost 66 percent believed they should be free to hold government offices, and 61 percent were willing to write letters to government officials. This increased willingness to participate in the political process signals a decline in traditional Mennonite distinctiveness, except for their adherence to pacifism. Those who participate in American and Canadian politics have a strong tendency to support conservative parties.

209   Keim, Albert N. "Service or Resistance? The Mennonite Response to Conscription in World War II." *Mennonite Quarterly Review* 52(April 1978): 141-155.

American Mennonites had such bad memories of their treatment during World War I that, as the threat of war grew during the 1930s, they started developing a new model of alternative service for conscientious objectors. At a conference in 1935 Guy Hershberger proposed an alternative service model comparable to the Civilian Conservation Corps which would be applicable in time of war. As the war grew closer in Europe, Mennonites prepared their position, in concert with the other Historic Peace Churches, which suggested that the purpose of conscientious objection was "constructive service to the needy in the spirit of Christ." It proposed service in a number of areas, such as relief for refugees, reconstruction, farm service, forestry, health service, and community work. While Mennonites strongly articulated their opposition to war but were not opposed to conscription, the Quakers, more of whom opposed conscription, provided the sophisticated leadership and lobbying in Washington in 1940-41. This was the crucial period when the Selective Service Act--with its provisions for alternative service--was being drafted by Congress, followed by the design of implementation provisions by the government agencies.

210   Klaassen, Walter. "Mennonites and War Taxes." *Pennsylvania Mennonite Heritage* 1(April 1978): 17-23.

Anabaptists believe that humans are generally sinful and not willing to be governed by God's spirit. Therefore, governments, whether benevolent or malevolent, are instituted by God. However, since governments are irrevocably linked to coercion, killing, violence, law, and vengeance, they are outside the realm of Christ; so true Christians cannot participate in their functions. But they have to be obeyed except when they directly contradict the will of God. Anabaptists have accepted the need to pay taxes, though sometimes with ambiguous feelings when they know that the money will be used to support warfare. Mennonites initially refused to pay war taxes during the American Revolution because they felt the rebellious colonial governments were illegitimate, but they eventually recognized the political changes and paid them. In the Civil War, most Mennonites on both sides were exempted from the army if they paid fees, a requirement that did not conflict with their historical tendency to compromise with governments. In World War I they were pressured to purchase liberty bonds to help finance the war effort, and again some protested and resisted but most bought them under duress.

211   Krahn, Cornelius, J. Winfield Fretz, and Robert Kreider. "Altruism in Mennonite Life." In *Forms and Techniques of Altruistic and Spiritual Growth*, edited by Pitirim A. Sorokin, 309-328. Boston: Beacon Press, 1954.

Altruism among Mennonites is based primarily on their conceptions of their faith and themselves. Their historical literature is filled with references to suffering for Christ's sake, a theme which forms a sense of mission based on the fellowship of saints. Also, there is a strong consciousness of the challenges of the Sermon on the Mount and other New Testament writings to have a faith based on good works. At the local level, Mennonite communities are based on Christian altruism, particularly on the regular, spontaneous mutual assistance which occurs whenever neighbors are in need, such as assistance in building barns. They support a wide range of cooperative economic groups and charitable institutions. The Mennonite Central Committee actively provides relief services all over the world. Evaluation of their programs is not really based on the numbers of people fed or the number of lives saved: it is best symbolized by the sticker placed on each case of food and each article of donated clothing which summarizes their belief about altruism: "In the name of Christ."

212   Kraybill, Ron and David Brubaker. "A Resource for Dealing with Conflict--the Mennonite Conciliation Service." *Mennonite Life* 43(March 1988): 4-7.

The history of the Mennonite Conciliation Service (MCS) began in 1975 with the suggestion that, while the Mennonite Central Committee had worked toward forming conceptions of peace and moral injunctions against war, it was not doing much to prevent conflict situations from building into violence. The proponents of the MCS suggested that it should work through local networks supported by a national office and it should intervene in situations of social strife. It would benefit Mennonites by encouraging them to deal with their own conflict situations. While some Mennonites argued that they have many instances of conflict within their own ranks, and thus questioned the establishment of a conciliation service, others felt that by focusing on their peace theology they had not paid much attention to developing the psychological and social skills for resolving conflict situations. Finally started in 1979, the MCS was formed with a charge to concentrate on two basic areas: helping Mennonites resolve interpersonal, congregational, and business conflicts before they wound up in court; and providing a ministry of conflict resolution to non-Mennonites in such areas as housing problems, racial disputes, or sit-ins.

213   Kreider, Robert. "Environmental Influences Affecting the Decisions of Mennonite Boys of Draft Age." *Mennonite Quarterly Review* 16(October 1942): 247-259, 275.

Detailed correspondence with 35 Mennonite ministers early in World War II revealed some of the environmental factors which influenced the decisions of 179 young men to chose either military service or the Civilian Public Service camps for conscientious objectors. Environmental factors in Mennonite churches which appear to strengthen the belief in nonresistance and pacifism: church maintenance of the conservative witness on nonresistance; their tendency to emphasize nonconformity from the broader society; their strong peace programs in Sunday schools; and their closeness to other congregations of their faith. The more closely the individuals associated with their churches, the more likely they were to chose the CPS camps. Factors in the home environment prompting decisions for conscientious objection include: the parents of the youth are regular church members who give their children a peace education; nonresistant values are practiced in their daily lives; and they have close families that do not place a high value on materialism. More conscientious objectors come from farm families, where traditional values are easier to maintain, than from urban professional or business environments.

214   Kreider, Robert S. "The 'Good Boys of CPS.'" *Mennonite Life* 46(September 1991): 4-11.

Mennonites assigned to Civilian Public Service camps during World War II had a reputation as being "good boys," in part because they were comfortable living in communitarian environments and they were used to hard, hand labor on farms. At Camp No. 5 in Colorado the men worked willingly to plant trees, drain wetlands, and construct irrigation systems, but they became irritated that a lot of their labor was devoted to the large, wealthy ranches in preference to the poorer ones; they also questioned the fact that they were doing ranch work, such as fencing and branding cattle, that had nothing to do with conserving soil. Soil Conservation Service officials were sometimes offensive, dictatorial, and insensitive toward the men, such as assigning them to drain an earthen dam preparatory to the construction of a military base, or allowing news photographers to come in, despite the strong aversion of many Anabaptists to being photographed (some fled across the fields when they saw the photographers coming). Despite these difficulties, the men in the camp kept a low profile and the public impression of tranquility in the camp remained.

215   Lapp, John A. "The Peace Mission of the Mennonite Central Committee." *Mennonite Quarterly Review* 44(July 1970): 281-297.

The Peace Section, a unique body within the Mennonite Central Committee, serves the peace mission of the church with three separate goals: to nurture peace convictions among Mennonites through educational programs; to support the efforts of Mennonites who remain out of military service; and to promote reconciliation and peacemaking among Christians outside the Peace Churches and in situations of conflict. During World War II the Section was the theorizing and study group for the MCC-- the intermediary for Mennonites who had concerns about the war and the draft. After the war the mandate for the section was expanded to include all issues related to the historic Mennonite stand on peace and nonresistance, such as church-state relations, racial strife, industrial relations, penal reform, poverty, and class problems. The Section studies these issues, expresses Mennonite positions in various ways, and supports a wide variety of publications, activities, and cooperative efforts. The effort to promote a common Mennonite position on peace issues prompted a 1950 "Declaration of Christian Faith and Commitment," which concluded with a statement that Mennonites "cannot compromise with war in any form." This article is part of an "MCC Anniversary Issue."

216   Lehman, James O. "Conflicting Loyalties of the Christian Citizen: Lancaster Mennonites and the Early Civil War Era." *Pennsylvania Mennonite Heritage* 7(April 1984): 2-15.

At times during the first half of the Civil War, people in Lancaster County, Pennsylvania, became quite tense about

Mennonite nonresistance. The debate may have been started by news that the Moravians, a peaceful people during the Revolutionary War, appeared to support the war. Shortly thereafter, vitriolic newspaper columns and editorials started criticizing, and defending, Mennonites for their pacifism--and attacking one another for their points of view. One writer charged that an anti-Mennonite author was covetous of the fine Mennonite farms. Democratic papers charged that since the rural Mennonite districts had voted Republican, they were therefore hypocrites for supporting the party that took the nation to war without being willing to fight in it. Attacks on the Mennonites in the press died down, then rose again in 1862 during discussions on a state draft law. One newspaper said that since Mennonites "have acquired wealth in abundance beyond a parallel in the country, will they not respond to the call of such a kind mother [the government]?" Two months later the same paper acknowledged Mennonite contributions of blankets for drafted men.

217   Lehman, James O. "Duties of the Mennonite Citizen: Controversy in the Lancaster Press Late in the Civil War." *Pennsylvania Mennonite Heritage* 7(July 1984): 5-21.

Mennonites in Lancaster County were put under a lot of stress in 1863 and 1864 when Confederate armed forces entered the State and the federal draft laws were passed. Provisions of the 1864 draft law which appeared to favor the Mennonites, such as the possibility of alternative service, were virulently attacked by the major Democratic newspaper in Lancaster County. It argued that Mennonites acted with extreme inconsistency by voting overwhelmingly for the Republicans, the party that supported the Civil War, yet they refused to serve in the military. An examination of the voting record throughout the County from 1861 through 1864 shows that, indeed, the Mennonite and Amish vote, which was roughly split between the parties in 1861, became strongly Republican thereafter--and the newspaper attacks made very little difference. Evidently the Mennonites had little sympathy with the South, since it was clearly in rebellion with the legitimately constituted government; they associated the Democratic party with urban problems they didn't care about; and they felt they could most easily convince their neighbors they were good citizens by voting for the Republicans.

218   Lehman, James O. "The Mennonites of Maryland During the
       Revolutionary War." *Mennonite Quarterly Review* 50(July
       1976): 200-229.

       A modest number of Mennonite families, perhaps 50, lived in
       the frontier areas of Frederick and Washington counties, Mary-
       land, during the American Revolution, cut off from the numer-
       ous Mennonites in Pennsylvania but just as troubled by the
       frontier residents with their spirit of patriotism. Although they
       did not keep records themselves, there are clues that indicate
       they suffered harsh treatment from the interim patriot govern-
       ments established in those areas since they would not consent to
       serve in the armed forces. Following directives from Annapolis,
       fines were repeatedly imposed by the interim county govern-
       ments and paid by Mennonites. In December 1776, with the
       patriot cause under General Washington going badly, the Com-
       mittee of Observation in Washington County assessed more
       fines and decided to compel the Mennonites to march off with
       the militia to give noncombatant assistance to the troops. The
       Committee directed that a stone stable be converted into an
       additional jail to house the suspected Tory supporters. The
       situation relaxed when many members of the Committee left
       office in January 1777.

219   Martens, Hildegard M. "Accommodation and Withdrawal: The
       Response of Mennonites in Canada to World War II." *Social
       History* 7(November 1974): 306-327.

       Canadian government policies toward Mennonites during
       World War I were confused. Some Mennonites had been
       promised exemption from military service when they immi-
       grated while others had not; local interpretations of federal
       government policies differed; and Mennonites varied as to
       whether or not they would accept alternative service under
       military supervision. They were troubled by the hostility of
       many Canadians--Methodist ministers in Saskatchewan re-
       ferred to them as the "Mennonite menace." These problems
       continued as World War II approached. In September 1940
       Canadian Quakers tried to establish a national, noncombatant
       service, so they were asked to join Brethren, Amish and Men-
       nonite denominations in forming a Conference of Historic Peace
       Churches. This group established a more unified relationship
       with the Canadian government than had existed 25 years before.
       It obtained approval for an Alternative Service in civilian
       camps; persuaded the government to allow buyers of Victory

Loans to affix special stickers certifying that the funds would only be used for relief work; and worked to resolve a variety of other problems related to coping with conditions in a country at war.

220   Meyer, Jacob C. "Reflections of a Conscientious Objector in World War I." *Mennonite Quarterly Review* 41 (January 1967): 79-96.

A day-by-day account of a Mennonite draftee's life as a conscientious objector in army camps from late July 1918, through the end of the year. His positive approach toward his fellow C.O.s and toward the officers in the camps, combined with his education, quickly placed him in a leadership position. The account, reconstructed from his letters and a cryptic diary, gives straightforward explanations of specific aspects of his pacifist beliefs, such as why he would not wear a uniform. It also reveals his thinking about issues that he had not yet resolved, such as whether standing at attention was a civil courtesy or a military order. These comments are all recorded within the context of daily life in army camps, where he read and wrote letters for illiterate men to their families and girlfriends, formed Bible study classes, did office work, and so on. He remarks several times on the feeling of being abandoned by his church, which had formed a Relief Commission that he felt did nothing for the drafted Mennonite men.

221   Neufeld, Tom Yoder. "Varieties of Contemporary Mennonite Peace Witness: From Passivism to Pacifism, from Nonresistance to Resistance." *Conrad Grebel Review* 10 (Fall 1992): 243-257.

The belief of some Mennonites in the "just war" theory was demonstrated by the fact that half of the eligible Mennonites fought in World Wars I and II. However, nonresistance has been the central feature of Mennonite thinking throughout their history. True followers of Jesus simply do not retaliate or defend themselves against aggression. Some of the nonresistant Mennonites are happy that others are willing to establish states and use whatever force and violence are necessary to preserve and promote them--after all, the state simply reflects God's will. Other believers in nonresistance are not so happy about such a dualism. They see nothing legitimate about the violence of the state, which cannot be God's will. Mennonite peace activists reject these lines of thinking: what's good for believing Christians is appropriate for all. God's revealed will is for peaceful-ness and justice for everyone. Their activist peacemaking is intimately grounded in faithfulness to Christ's commands, but it also recognizes and embraces concerns for the violence implicit in imperial power, unequal gender relationships, environmental degradation, economic inequality, and political oppression.

222   Nisly, Hope. "Witness to the Way of Peace: The Vietnam War and the Evolving Mennonite View of Their Relationship to the State." *Maryland Historian* 20(Spring/Summer 1989): 7-23.

Mennonite response to the Vietnam War was affected by the fact that they had supported missionaries there since 1954. These missionaries told their churches how the U.S. war effort was harming the Vietnamese, who in turn felt that the missionaries had some complicity in the war. While Mennonites perceived a growing need to address the American political leadership on problems of social justice and peace, any involvement with the government remained controversial. In a spirit of compromise in 1966, they decided to contact the government whenever its actions were unjust as long as the issue was essential to Mennonite interests. In 1968 they established an office in Washington that would observe and report on developments, monitor peace issues, and facilitate presentations by constituent groups to government officials. Consistent with their beliefs, the Washington office was to focus on the Mennonite people and not on the government. They believed that their nonresistant peace position would be unique in Washington, and Mennonite individuals and groups, before making their witness to the government, would benefit from its information and guidance.

223   Peterson, David. "Ready for War: Oregon Mennonites from Versailles to Pearl Harbor." *Mennonite Quarterly Review* 64(July 1990): 209-229.

After the First World War, Oregon (Old) Mennonite congregations were confronted with changing social values due to increased mobility, outside ideas, and the economic necessity of obtaining jobs off the farm. These new ideas challenged their traditional separation from society and distinctiveness as a people. During the interwar period they found themselves divided into conservative and liberal factions which disagreed over the extent of permissible outside, secular influences. While liberal congregations welcomed some outside contacts, conservatives did not as much. Conservative churches remained closer to the traditional practices, though they did adopt some of the beliefs and practices of the fundamentalists in their surrounding communities. When the U.S. entered the Second World War, only 55 percent of the draftees in the liberal congregations participated in Civilian Public Service while 45 percent served in the military; 84 percent of the conservatives chose the Civilian Public Service. The conservatives were able to retain traditional nonresistant peace values due to their greater distinctiveness, nonconformity, and strict group discipline.

224   Redekop, Calvin. *Mennonite Society*. Baltimore: Johns Hopkins University Press, 1989.

The Mennonite movement is best characterized as a utopian social/religious system whose members take a firm stand about peace, refuse to swear oaths, and believe in being separate from the rest of the world. The conservative application of Christian ethics is the predominant aspect of their belief. Numerous schisms have divided Mennonites into many separate branches, but individual congregations provide a great deal of mutual aid via disaster-relief societies, insurance organizations, and cooperative rural activities. Most Mennonite conferences cooperate in supporting the Mennonite Central Committee (MCC), a worldwide relief and service organization that expresses the ethos of Mennonite congregations and exemplifies their feeling for providing service to others. The MCC serves as a symbol of Mennonite identity, important as a means of holding people in the faith together who otherwise might become alienated by the narrow, parochial nature of individual congregations. Redekop provides a broad discussion and analysis of Mennonite beliefs, community structures, social organizations, personality, aesthetics, family life, education, economics, relations with the state, missions, service, and contemporary stresses within their movement.

225   Rushby, William F. and John C. Thrush. "Mennonites and Social Compassion: The Rokeach Hypothesis Reconsidered." *Review of Religious Research* 15(Fall 1973): 16-28.

The results of a study at Goshen College demonstrated that Mennonite students held highly orthodox Christian values, ranking salvation as their highest value; but they were quite low in what the author calls "establishment-mindedness"--support for the economic and political status quo. He found that they held views which were socially very compassionate, and when the liberal political biases were removed from the questions which Rokeach had used in an earlier survey, the Mennonites answered with even more compassion. The results suggest that Mennonites are skeptical of answers to social injustice that rely on the government, but they strongly support social change nonetheless. The earlier study by Rokeach, which linked conservative Christian orthodox religiosity with prejudice, bigotry and dogmatism is refuted by this study; while Mennonites are not strongly establishment-minded, they show a positive correlation between the strength of their orthodox beliefs and their compassionate feelings about social and economic justice.

226   Stahl, John Daniel. "Conflict, Conscience, and Community in Selected Mennonite Children's Stories." *Mennonite Quarterly Review* 55(January 1981): 62-74.

Mennonite children's literature from the decade of the 1950s focuses on the theme of not retaliating in conflict situations. These stories seek to instill in young Mennonite readers the importance of the individual having a loving relation to the group. One book consists of eighteen stories based on the archetypal martyrs of Anabaptist history, though while some stories have heroes who suffer for their beliefs, others have more positive orientations. One story, for instance, is a moralistic folktale about a preacher who discovered a gang of men stealing the thatch off his roof: when he invited them in for a meal, they were embarrassed by his kindness, went out and repaired the damage, and left. In another novel the theme of altruistic love is presented both on political and personal levels. A third work concentrates on a Mennonite youngster learning about the meaning of nonresistance. The three works exhibit warm family bonds, emphasize ideals of forgiveness, self-denial, and non-retaliation, and delve into the minority status of Mennonites, which sometimes requires them to suffer for their faith and their belief in peace.

227   Stucky, Gregory J. "Fighting Against War: The Mennonite *Vorwaerts* from 1914 to 1919." *Kansas Historical Quarterly* 38(Summer 1972): 169-186.

The *Vorwaerts*, a Mennonite newspaper published in Hillsboro, Kansas, reflected the dilemma of a pacifism which insisted that conflicts are an inevitable result of sin and ungodliness in the world. The paper took a pro-German stance until the United States entered the war in 1917, and thereafter it cautiously but courageously argued the Mennonite position. It remarked cynically on the first issuance of Liberty Bonds that they served the interests of patriots like Rockefeller and Morgan who could prominently purchase multimillion-dollar bonds and save on their taxes. Judiciously, the newspaper carried the pages of English-language pro-war and pro-bond advertisements submitted by the government, but continued to print their own opinions in German which their subscribers could read. It had the courage to publish the account of mob violence against a Mennonite man who was publicly willing to give thousands of dollars to support the Red Cross but not one cent to support the war effort, and it was forthright in its arguments against irrational anti-German feelings.

228   Suderman, Elmer F. "The Mennonite Community and the Pacifist Character in American Literature." *Mennonite Life* 34(March 1979): 8-15.

Several American works of literature examine the ways that war, along with the violent attitudes it fosters, impinges on peaceful Mennonite communities and characters. In one novel, the pacifist community becomes confused in the face of surrounding war, as pacifism doesn't hold the people together. Pacifism seems as futile as war. Another novel focuses not on the evil of Hitler's Germany but on the evil within the characters in the peaceful community--pacifism is not an easy answer. In others, the characters are concerned only about superficial issues, or the stories point to the hatred and violence that can erupt anywhere, even in pacifist communities under pressure. These works describe pacifist communities which are more concerned with keeping themselves out of war than they are with ending violence in the world. The literature captures the dilemma of pacifists living in a world which views pacifism as unrealistic, but it fails to offer a defining vision of peace, an ethos where love and nonresistance would promote satisfying human relationships, or an overriding concept of how virtue and wisdom apply in a peaceful society.

229   Suter, Linda. "Dogma and Deed: The Peace Position in Mennonite Fiction, 1914-1945." *Mennonite Quarterly Review* 65(January 1991): 69-91.

The works of eight novelists illustrate and interpret the different ways Mennonites in the Soviet Union coped with their peace traditions during the First World War and the Russian Revolution. One novel portrays Mennonites as insulated and snobbish toward their Russian neighbors, while another depicts the waste and horrors of the period--peace witness not as abstract philosophizing but as direct protest against atrocities. Another focuses on the inner peace that can result from suffering--the moments of peaceful beauty that occur in spite of inhumanity, ugliness, and despair which give people courage to go on. Another probes such issues as alternative service, the horrors of war, and the dilemma of confronting the world versus retreating into closed communities. Others delve into the dissolution of the Mennonite peace principles in the face of the revolution, with characters viewing nonresistance as a surrender to evil and "an irrelevant Christian ideal." These novelists synthesize the Russian Mennonite struggles during the revolutionary period and focus on the contradictions between the abstractions of peace and the real horrors of war and revolution.

230   Teichroew, Allan. "Mennonites and the Conscription Trap." *Mennonite Life* 30(September 1975): 10-13.

American Mennonites reacted to the approach of World War I by lobbying the President and other government officials to convince them of the sincerity of their nonresistant beliefs and their patriotism. Presuming they would qualify for noncombatant service under the Selective Service Act, Mennonite leaders urged their young men to register for the draft as required by the law, arguing that they should accept the dictates of the state unless they posed a conflict with the teachings of Christ. In addition, they were convinced that President Wilson would include them in a noncombatant category. However, government officials, wanting to minimize the number of conscientious objectors, planned to send as many potential C.O.s into military training as possible, an experience which would, they hoped, transform them into good soldiers. The vague hopes and expectations of the Mennonite leaders during the summer of 1917 paralyzed them from taking any stronger action; as a result, the young Mennonite men who were drafted that summer were sent to military camps to be trained for combat along with all other draftees.

231   Teichroew, Allan. "World War I and the Mennonite Migration to Canada to Avoid the Draft." *Mennonite Quarterly Review* 45(July 1971): 219-249.

When the American conscription act was passed in 1917, midwest Mennonite leaders were cautiously hopeful about the sincerity of the government's promise to honor their nonresistance. Despite the fact that most were children of immigrants, they did not openly consider, at first, emigrating to avoid the American draft. As time went on, however, the open border, the welcoming attitude of the Canadian government, and the support of other Mennonites prompted an increasing flow northward--perhaps up to 800 in all. When conditions for alternative service became known in June 1918, instead of stemming the tide the emigration seemed to increase, perhaps due to the increasing hostility that Mennonite draftees and civilians were suffering. On their return to their congregations after the war, some of the draft evaders were greeted with scorn and abuse-- one man was pelted with a volley of rotten eggs by his own church--but most returned with no problems. While the motivations of the draft evaders were inconsistent, one attribute they all shared was a complete unwillingness to be involved in any way in the American military machine.

232   Thiessen, Irmgard. "Values and Personality Characteristics of Mennonites in Manitoba." *Mennonite Quarterly Review* 40(January 1966): 48-61.

A study of the personality traits and cultural values of Canadian Mennonites using five psychological measures. One of the results of the study showed that the Mennonites placed a stronger value on their religious concepts than the control group of non-Mennonites. In answer to sentence completion tests such as, "My personal goal in life is ..." the Mennonites frequently provided religious answers such as "to live to the glory of God," while the control group often answered with more secular replies, such as "to get rich." In another phase of the study, the author showed the two groups various pictures and asked them to write a story suggested by each. The results indicated that the Mennonites wrote as many stories which included violence as the control group. The conclusion was that Mennonites have as many aggressive tendencies as the rest of the population; they just don't act them out.

233   Toews, J. B. "Nonresistance Reexamined: Why Did Menno-
       nites Leave Russia in 1874?" *Mennonite Life* 29(Mid-Year
       1974): 8-13.

       The nonresistance of Russian Mennonites in the 1870's was
       an integral part of their totally closed society, in which they lived
       apart from the Russians, only spoke German, and had complete
       religious freedom and exemption from military service. While
       their belief in nonresistance prompted them to avoid outsiders
       rather than make an active commitment to fostering peace, they
       did provide some relief services to Russian troops during the
       Crimean War and the Russo-Turkish War. However, when the
       government proposed universal military conscription, they felt
       highly threatened. Some decided they could compromise with
       the government, which was willing to establish programs of
       alternative service, but others preferred to emigrate to the United
       States and Canada. Another factor prodding migration to North
       America was land hunger for their expanding population.
       Russian law prevented them from subdividing their farms, so the
       farm owners became increasingly affluent while those without
       property became poorer, a division that had produced bitterness
       between the groups. Mennonites who migrated to North America
       had to live on individual farms and they gradually became more
       connected with the outside world.

234   Toews, John B., editor and translator. "Nonresistance and
       Migration in the 1870's: Two Personal Views." *Mennonite Life*
       41(June 1986): 9-15.

       Russian Mennonites in the 1870s thought of their pacifism and
       nonresistance in terms of exemption from military service--
       guaranteed by the Czars since 1800--plus the cultural and
       religious milieu of their settlements. Diary extracts by Dietrich
       Gaeddert and Jacob Epp from 1870 through 1876 indicate the
       tensions in the Mennonite communities when it became known
       that the former privilege of military exemption was going to be
       revoked. Delegations to St. Petersburg, the visit of an emissary
       from the Czar, and delegations to the United States and Canada
       to ascertain the conditions for immigration all promoted hopes
       and tensions among the Mennonites. Epp particularly focuses on
       preserving their religious lifestyle, with the repeated theme that
       the troubles are a result of the Mennonite people falling away
       from their faith. If the people would repent from their ways and
       return to their Savior, the thunderstorms ahead would not
       overwhelm them. Contradictory opinions about the discussions

with the government and reports from America divided the people, with some communities selling everything to emigrate but others deciding to accept the alternative service options allowed by the Czar.

235   Toews, Paul. "The Impact of Alternative Service on the American Mennonite World: A Critical Evaluation." *Mennonite Quarterly Review* 66(October 1992): 615-627.

At the beginning of World War II, Mennonite leaders were quite optimistic about the establishment of an alternative service to the draft, the Civilian Public Service system. They were grateful for the establishment of the system, and optimistic that the CPS camps would serve as models of peaceful, harmonious communities. They felt that the Mennonite experience, their idealism and commitment to nonresistance, offered an alternative to warfare, a new view of patriotism, an example for the entire nation to follow. Mennonites changed from inwardly focused fundamentalists who were wary of one another to people who had a renewed commitment to their basic values but were looking outward for dialogues with other peace churches. Before the war, Mennonite outreach and service was confined to helping other Mennonites; after the war their concerns were much broader. Their voluntary service programs, which started as an outgrowth of CPS activities and continued under the auspices of the Mennonite Central Committee, were worldwide in scope. The CPS and voluntary service programs allowed the Mennonites to remain theologically conservative at the same time they were becoming socially activist.

236   Toews, Paul. "The Long Weekend or the Short Week: Mennonite Peace Theology, 1925-1944." *Mennonite Quarterly Review* 60(January 1986): 38-57.

By 1900 the problems of Mennonites in earlier war periods were mostly forgotten. The onset of World War I, unlike earlier wars, fostered among Americans a highly intolerant attitude toward peace resisters and conscientious objectors, who were treated more severely in the United States than in Germany, France or Great Britain. Several hundred conscientious objectors were sentenced to prison and 17 were sentenced to death for refusing to join the crusade to make the world safe for democracy. After the war, the existence of modernizing influences and the flourishing secular peace movement challenged Mennonite self-concepts of uniqueness. The Peace Problems Committee, among others, led Mennonites to reach out more actively with a positive message that nonresistance should lead to the prevention of war. Some leaders were highly critical of these initiatives, denouncing the involvement of Mennonites with government agencies, peace groups, and other peace churches and arguing that Christians should not try to stop war but should prepare for the second coming of Christ. By 1940 Mennonites had redefined nonresistance to include outreach to society and interaction with the American political system.

237   Toews, Paul. "'Will a New Day Dawn from This?' Mennonite Pacifist People and the Good War." *Mennonite Life* 45(December 1990): 16-24.

Both before and during World War II, Mennonites and the other peace churches worked closely with the American government to provide a Civilian Public Service (CPS) system which was unique in American history. A spirit of accommodation for conscientious objectors was prompted by memories of the conscription system in World War I, which caused many Mennonites to be abused. In 1940 the Burke-Wadsworth bill, and a subsequent executive order, established the alternative service program that the Mennonites had been working for. While a small number of conscientious objectors would serve in civilian government agencies, the rest would serve in camps administered by the National Service Board for Religious Objectors and directly supervised by the churches. Mennonites were euphoric about the CPS system since they could now prove their good citizenship, serve their country peacefully, and provide a witness to the duties and obligations Christians have toward others. The CPS experience, however, posed a conundrum for Mennonites since it prompted them to provide social service for society at large, an idea which differed from their historic orientation toward improving themselves as Christians.

238   Ulle, Robert F. "Pacifists, Paxton, and Politics: Colonial Pennsylvania, 1763-1768." *Pennsylvania Mennonite Heritage* 1(October 1978): 18-21.

In December 1763 the Indian residents of Lancaster County, Pennsylvania, were massacred by a gang of white frontiersmen known as the "Paxton Boys." While American public opinion quickly condemned this mob violence, within a few months it had become the touchstone for significant political divisions within the colony. To some contemporary observers the oppressed frontier inhabitants were insufficiently protected from Indian depredations by the pacifist ruling class in the older communities. A better analysis is that the division followed religious lines: the dominant political group, the Quakers, who had controlled the colony since they founded it, were supported by the other pacifist peoples, the Mennonites, Moravians and Schwenkfelders; they were opposed by High Church English, German Lutherans and Reformed, and the Scotch-Irish Presbyterians. Quakers and Mennonites also lived in the same frontier areas as the Presbyterians, and they suffered from Indian attacks the same as they did. The Mennonite belief in nonresistant love inspired them to regard the Indians as their friends no matter what happened, which prompted their political support for the Quakers.

239   Weaver, J. Denny. "Mennonites: Theology, Peace and Identity." *Conrad Grebel Review* 6(Spring 1988): 119-145.

Erosion of the German culture among American Mennonites over the past 100 years has weakened their distinctiveness as well. As a result, their thinking about theology and religious issues has tended to be from the perspective of outsiders, particularly fundamentalists, despite the fact that the fundamentalist theology is alien to their tradition. In contemporary America, with their cultural uniqueness mostly lost, urban Mennonites still find a sense of community, though they have a problem identifying just what it is that distinguishes them as Mennonites; why are they different if their former German culture has been lost? During this transition period, Mennonites need to focus more explicitly on their unique values, which were previously accepted implicitly and intuitively. Weaver defines this uniqueness by combining three cornerstones of a Mennonite view of their distinctive faith: Christocentrism, the belief that Mennonites ground their faith in the life of Jesus; the communal imperative for the followers of Jesus; and the nonresistant, nonviolent basis of society, which completely rejects lethal violence.

Montagnais-Naskapi

The Montagnais-Naskapi, Algonquian-speaking American Indians living north of the St. Lawrence River on the Labrador Peninsula of Canada, have traditionally been a hunting, gathering, trapping, and trading people, though today they supplement these activities with seasonal wage employment. They were in regular contact with the French fur traders and missionaries since they met the explorer Samuel de Champlain in 1603. Although they historically fought some wars with neighboring peoples, particularly the Iroquois, they preferred timid external relations. They were a nomadic people whose way of life depended on peaceful trade and an attitude of sharing food in emergencies. They number over 12,000 today.[11]

240   Anderson, Karen. "Commodity Exchange and Subordination: Montagnais-Naskapi and Huron Women, 1600-1650." *Signs* 11(Autumn 1985): 48-62.

In the early period of French-Indian contact, the Montagnais-Naskapi had no political organization, no one with authority, and no requirement to obey a chief unless they individually chose to; decisions were reached by all adults. Gentleness and apathy were their highest virtues; men and women were equal in terms of initiating sex relations, choosing a marriage partner, and controlling their own work activities. Women controlled the household, the distribution of provisions, and the times when camps should be moved. The Jesuits induced some of the Montagnais-Naskapi to settle in a town near Quebec where they were protected by French soldiers, taught settled agriculture, and given land to farm. They were induced to accept Christianity, and in the process the women became subject for the first time to the authority of the men, losing their equal status, freedom to make their own choices, and self-determination. The Huron, by contrast, though also affected by contact with the French fur traders and missionaries, did not lose their social structure, and their women retained more of their traditional equality.

241   Leacock, Eleanor. "The Montagnais-Naskapi Band." In *Contributions to Anthropology: Band Societies. Proceedings of the Conference on Band Organization, Ottawa, August 30 to September 2, 1965*, edited by David Damas, 1-17. Ottawa: The National Museums of Canada, 1969.

The primary cooperative feature of Montagnais-Naskapi society was their sharing of food in emergencies. Because life was so difficult, and starvation a constant possibility, food was shared in a spontaneous, unstructured, unregulated fashion; there was no expectation that it would be reciprocated, and individuals could always choose how much to share. A man who had very little to spare would share with his bitter enemy if the other was in danger of starving. The sharing was done in times of need and was not a regular method of distributing game. The Indians' attitude was, and still is, to never even question the imperative of helping another in need. One man was asked by the author if his gifts of food to needy neighbors meant he would have to curtail his own trapping season and return to the trading post early--and was he at all annoyed by this inconvenience? The man lost his patience with the author and explained, "Suppose now, not give them flour, lard--just dead inside." He felt that the very question was inhuman.

242   Lips, Julius E. "Naskapi Law." *Transactions of the American Philosophical Society* 37(1947): 379-492.

The primary duty of the Montagnais-Naskapi chief was to maintain peace within his band, with other bands, and with the whites. However, many disputes or potential disputes were settled directly, without appealing to the chiefs. Part of the reason was the fact that individual families were isolated in the forest in the winters, so it was more effective to settle problems directly. For instance, when a man realized that another was poaching beavers in his hunting territory, he might confront the other directly, explain that he was depending on the beavers himself, and ask for half of the pelts. The other, claiming he didn't realize they were his, would immediately hand them over and promise not to kill anything else in his territory. Of course in many cases the chiefs did become involved in problems of poaching or other crimes. The Montagnais-Naskapi did not deny their guilt--they felt that everyone already knew the truth anyway, denial was pointless, and public opinion had already reached a verdict. The ultimate penalty for people who refused to conform to the public order was expulsion from the band, which led to starvation.

243   Lips, Julius E. "Public Opinion and Mutual Assistance among the Montagnais-Naskapi." *American Anthropologist* 39(April-June 1937): 222-228.

The Montagnais-Naskapi maintain peace, one of their fundamental goals, through the force of public opinion. When the people get together in spring at the fur trading post, public opinion is an important factor in settling disputes, differences, and interpersonal rights. It is normally not used as a corrective measure against the occasional violator of group norms--stealing goods, burning someone's tent, or trespassing--but the habitual offender may be censured by the people which would result in him being exiled. Normally, public opinion serves to prevent rather than to punish, to support vital principles such as the law of mutual assistance. If a passing stranger is starving, he can take what he needs to survive. If a family in the forest is ill or starving, they will put up sign posts asking for assistance. Anyone passing by will help immediately, even if the requestor is an enemy, since to fail to do so might put him and his family in peril at some point in the future when they need help and others would remember their stinginess.

244   Speck, Frank G. "Ethical Attributes of the Labrador Indians." *American Anthropologist* 35(October-December 1933): 559-594.

The cooperative, harmonious Montagnais-Naskapi society is based on their ethical attributes, habits of personal behavior, and rational, utilitarian approach to human conduct. They treat their elderly kindly and are extremely affectionate and tolerant toward their children, who are constantly caressed and kissed by their parents and never punished. They place no value on competition since spontaneous cooperation is one of their foremost principles; they are always truthful when they have to give impartial or factual information; they are highly altruistic concerning the welfare of others; and they generously give away food, clothing or property as needed--they are not obsessed by materialism as are the white people in Labrador. People who seriously violate their social standards are ostracized. They do not commit revenge for offenses against them. The author does not know of a single instance of their taking vengeance on anyone, including the white traders who openly exploit them. If they are exploited or abused badly enough, they sulk or retreat back into the forest. Crimes of violence are virtually unknown, except in cases attributable to drunkenness.

Moravians

While the word "Moravian" is used for the people of Moravia, a part of the Czech Republic, in this section it refers to the members of a Protestant denomination--the Moravian Church. Established as a faith by the followers of Jan Hus in the 15th century, they were persecuted for over 150 years until they were completely defeated in a battle with Catholic armies in 1620. Survivors went underground in Moravia, adopting pacifism as a tenet of their beliefs. In the early 18th century they adopted a communal lifestyle and founded settlements in Pennsylvania and North Carolina. The successful Moravian communes sent out missionaries to work with the Indians, and they also promoted good relations with neighboring European colonists. They maintained their pacifism during the trials of the American Revolutionary War. However, they gradually modified and abandoned their communal social structure during the late 18th and early 19th centuries as new generations increasingly adopted the ways of the dominant society. When the Civil War erupted, in order to prove themselves as good Americans they enthusiastically volunteered for military service. Today there are about 500,000 Moravians world-wide, 50,000 of whom live in the United States.[12]

245   Ettinger, Amos A. "Nazareth--An American Theocracy." *Transactions of the Moravian Historical Society* 14(1947): 24-39.

Nazareth, Pennsylvania, during the 18th century was a Moravian theocracy. Faced with spreading revolutionary fervor in the 1770s, they tried to hold aloof from participation in the military, but county authorities accompanied by soldiers began to collect fines from every male between 16 and 50 who had not drilled for service. Some of the younger Moravians started attending the drills in order to avoid the continuing fines. As the century closed the church continued to control the villagers, telling them how to vote for the new Congress and arranging marriages by lot. In 1799, however, Nazareth was shocked when a man admitted that he had proposed to a widow, whom he had loved quietly for a couple of years, and she had accepted his proposal. The horrified elders denied them their request to allow a marriage, and they were ordered out of the village when they were married anyway by a justice of the peace. A General Synod in 1818 began to liberalize the church, marking the beginning of the town of Nazareth's transformation into a modern, secular community.

246   Forell, George Wolfgang. "The Moravian Missions among the Delawares in Ohio During the Revolutionary War." *Transactions of the Moravian Historical Society* 23(1977): 41-60.

The reluctance of the Delaware Indians in the frontier areas of western Pennsylvania and Ohio to become involved in the American Revolutionary War may have been due to the peaceful influence of the Moravian missionaries who worked among them. For instance, one of the Indian leaders who had decided to support the British side, Captain Pipe, made a very conciliatory speech at Detroit to the commander of the fort in favor of the Moravian missionaries. When the British leader tried to accuse the missionaries of treason, Pipe responded that he and the other chiefs were more guilty than the missionaries. The author concludes that the missionaries considered the Indians to be morally noble people--more so than many of the Europeans--because of their ''peaceable, sociable, obliging, charitable, and hospitable'' natures, as one wrote. The failure of peaceful relations on the frontier was not due to the influence of the missionaries on the Indians; rather it was due to the lack of Christianity among the white settlers.

247   Gilbert, Daniel R. ''Bethlehem and the American Revolution.'' *Transactions of the Moravian Historical Society* 23(1977): 17-40.

During the French and Indian War, Moravians in Bethlehem, Pennsylvania, fortified their town and prepared for a defensive conflict, though they were urged to not injure attackers if at all possible. They held an ambiguous relationship to the war effort during the American Revolution: the church fostered a policy of non-involvement and discouraged discussions of issues, but it assisted the revolutionary cause when required to do so. The church counseled against bearing arms, although some men went into the military, many paid others to serve for them, and some went to prison because they would not do either. Because of the strategic inland location of Bethlehem, troops were quartered in the community on several occasions, posing considerable disturbance to the inhabitants. Church buildings were used as a major hospital for the Continental Army from 1776-1778: army personnel and Moravians cared for up to 700 wounded and sick soldiers at one time. While the Moravians were not happy with their role of supporting the army, as one of their leaders said, ''we did not have the courage to refuse.''

248   Mainwaring, W. Thomas. ''Communal Ideals, Worldly Concerns, and the Moravians of North Carolina, 1753-1772.'' *Communal Societies* 6(1986): 138-162.

In 1752 Moravians established a new community, Bethabara, on a large tract of land in North Carolina. The commune was closely knit, with ownership of goods in common; they felt distinctive and separate from other settlers, but not isolated since they developed crafts and trade with outsiders. They believed in pacifism and achieving salvation by loving God. Residents of the community were grouped into seven choirs (social groupings), who lived together: boys, girls, unmarried males, unmarried females, married couples, widows and widowers. Casual contacts between unmarried men and women were forbidden: marriage partners were proposed by the elders and ratified by lot. But dissatisfaction grew about the lack of private property. In 1770 they began moving to Salem, a new town which did not have a communal economy. Other aspects of the early Moravian community persisted longer: the system of lots and living by choirs lasted into the early 19th century; in 1856 they began allowing non-Moravians to live in Salem; and they gave up pacifism in 1861 when their young men marched off to fight for the Confederate cause.

249   Myers, Richmond E. "The Moravian Church and the Civil War." *Transactions of the Moravian Historical Society* 20(1964): 226-248.

Although Moravians in 1740 had been as strongly opposed to bearing arms as the Quakers, by 1860 their attitude had completely changed. At the onset of the Civil War, the church actively supported patriotism; for instance, a church synod at Lititz, Pennsylvania, in May 1861 passed a resolution expressing its "hearty support" for all measures taken by the federal government in upholding the constitution. Outsiders noted the special zeal which characterized Moravian support for the government and the high number of enlistments of soldiers from their communities. Before the Battle of Gettysburg, the Moravians at Lititz and students at Moravian College in Bethlehem actively joined in preparing a defense against the invading southern army. The reason for the change of attitude was primarily due to the fact that the second- and third-generation Moravians were no longer living in separate communities as some of their forebears had, and they no longer held their values. They were as much involved with voting, sharing Fourth of July celebrations, and enjoying the privileges of citizenship as other members of their communities.

250   Spangenberg, August Gottlieb and Andrew Anthony Lawatsch. "The Moravians and the Indians During the French and Indian War." *Transactions of the Moravian Historical Society* 22(1969): 1-13.

An account of Moravian experiences in the Seven Years' War written by their leaders during the period. Despite their belief in peace, August Spangenberg convinced the Moravians at Bethlehem, Pennsylvania, to fortify their town with a stockade and to post armed guards. He reasoned that the guards would frighten off Indians from attacking, and besides it was better to kill a thief, murderer or wolf that threatened one's house than endanger the family. During the war the Moravians welcomed refugees from frontier violence into their towns: at one point Bethlehem, Nazareth, and nearby villages housed 640 refugees, while over 100 children of refugees were counted at the fortified Moravian town of Bethabara, North Carolina. At the end of the war both the Indian nations and the English administrators wanted to have their peace conference in Bethlehem, since both sides had such high confidence in the Moravians, but the authors convinced the authorities that such an event would be too traumatic for their town, so the conference was arranged for the county seat of Easton instead.

251   Weinlick, John R. "The Moravians and the American Revolution." *Transactions of the Moravian Historical Society* 23 (1977): 1-16.

During the Revolutionary War, American Moravians differed in their feelings about pacifism as well as their hopes about which side would win the conflict. Instead of having an absolute view of pacifism, they were most strongly committed to evangelism. Many of the congregations, located in communities that did not fall to the British, were forced to provide service and resources to the colonial cause, while those in occupied New York and Philadelphia had to assist the British troops briefly. Moravian buildings and homes were used for military storage or as hospitals, and Moravian men who resisted the Test Act, designed to force people to affirm their loyalty to the patriot cause, were imprisoned and treated badly if local officials wanted to harass them. The firmly pacifist stances of the so-called settlement congregations in the North--Bethlehem, Nazareth, Lititz, and Hope--became less stringent as the war dragged on; congregations in other communities had more leeway to choose between pacifism and accommodation to military service. At the end of the war, Moravians accepted the American victory overwhelmingly.

Nayaka

The Nayaka, numbering about 1,400 people in 1981, live on the forested western slopes of the Nilgiri Hills in the Indian state of Kerala, near the southern end of the Western Ghats. They subsist on gathering wild roots, fruits, and nuts, fishing, and some hunting and trapping; they take short-term, casual jobs and trade forest products for necessary goods. They have virtually no settled agriculture or animal husbandry. Conflicts are rare, since they live as families relatively autonomously from one another, avoiding both competition and cooperation with others.

252   Bird, Nurit. "The Kurumbas of the Nilgiris: An Ethnographic Myth?" *Modern Asian Studies* 21(February 1987): 173-189.

Early travelers' accounts of the Kurumbas have been criticized by modern anthropologists as inaccurate and vague, but the author's perceptions about the Nayaka, a Kurumba sub-group, tend to support observations in the travel accounts. Individual Nayaka groups operate independently with little concern for others, except their non-Nayaka neighbors. If someone moves out of his local group, his whereabouts will be lost and even his close relatives will forget him. They have no concept of a common Nayaka territory and no myths that explain their origin as a people. Families have little direct social intercourse with others: their closest interpersonal relationships are between spouses; husbands and wives are each other's closest, and perhaps their only, friends. The Nayaka are highly relaxed about their activities, sitting about much of the day, heading for the forest or the market as their mood suggests, interrupting themselves when an alternative is presented. The security of their resources allows them to not depend on outsiders; employers pay them in advance for services or products expected in return--a pattern of indebtedness that prompts repayment. A considerably expanded version of this paper appeared under the title "An Introduction to the Naikens: The People and the Ethnographic Myth," by Nurit Bird-David in *Blue Mountains: The Ethnography and Biogeography of a South Indian Region*, edited by Paul Hockings (Delhi: Oxford University Press, 1989), 249-280.

253   Bird-David, Nurit. "Beyond 'The Hunting and Gathering Mode of Subsistence': Culture-Sensitive Observations on the Nayaka and Other Modern Hunter-Gatherers." *Man* n.s. 27(March 1992): 19-44.

Modern hunter-gatherers, including the Nayaka, generally engage to some extent in additional subsistence activities such as cultivation, keeping livestock, trade, and working for wages. Their perspective toward those activities frequently differs from their neighboring peoples: they see their relationship with the natural environment in terms of give and take, much as they do their relations with their human associates; they see themselves as fitting in to a cosmic order of sharing; they are particularly attuned to local nuances of the environment and its changes; they feel flexible and trusting in the provision of their needs from the natural environment, though they recognize that the availability of resources varies so they have to provide for contingencies; and they have a resource bias as opposed to the activity bias of production societies. The Nayaka have had various opportunities to engage in wage labor on a plantation or for a timber company, plus numerous opportunities to gather products for sale. They continue to spend any income quickly on food and other consumption items, and maintain their independence for hunting and gathering in the forest whenever they wish.

254   Bird-David, Nurit. "Nayaka." In *Encyclopedia of World Cultures, Volume III, South Asia*, edited by Paul Hockings, 194-196. Boston: G. K. Hall, 1992.

Nayaka living in the same settlement refer to one another with kinship terms, but they do not cooperate--or compete--in work activities; furthermore, they do not share their harvests or exchange gifts. They are friendly toward one another, but they live as self-contained conjugal families--husband, wife and small children. When separations between spouses occur, they do so during the early years of a marriage; once a marriage survives beyond that, it normally endures for life. Small children are indulged greatly, rarely punished or scolded, and live with their parents or older siblings most of the time. At about age 10 they start to drift away, visiting friends for increasingly long periods until they become economically autonomous. Since they highly value personal autonomy, they do not interfere with others or even gossip about one another. They avoid conflicts by not dealing with one another--neither cooperating nor competing--and by moving away from a settlement if a potential conflict situation arises.

255   Bird-David, Nurit. "Single Persons and Social Cohesion in a Hunter-Gatherer Society." In *Dimensions of Social Life: Essays in Honor of David G. Mandelbaum*, edited by Paul Hockings, 151-165. Berlin: De Gruyter, 1987.

Except for spouses and their own young children, the Nayaka feel *nachika*, shyness, toward all others, including close relatives. By contrast, relations between spouses are extremely close: they are each other's best friends. They work together in subsistence food gathering, collecting products for sale, trading in the market, caring for children, and carrying their young children while they walk. Single individuals help hold Nayaka society together. They normally live in well-defined, separate portions of the huts of unrelated conjugal couples, contributing toward their economic welfare but sleeping and eating separately. These arrangements may last from a few days to several months before the single people move to other families. The single people assist families in various gathering activities, and they normally socialize at the fires of other couples in the evenings. Thus, the social cohesion of the Nayaka is strengthened, above the level of the married couples who keep to themselves, by the shifting single people. These singles foster economic cooperation, provide linking information through their socializing, and assist the group to come to consensus decisions.

256   Bird-David, Nurit. "The Giving Environment: Another Perspective on the Economic System of Gatherer-Hunters." *Current Anthropology* 31(April 1990): 189-196.

The Nayaka view the natural environment and the forest as a giving system within which the spirits exist like benevolent parents. As an outgrowth of this belief, they view themselves as sons and daughters of the forest, and each other as siblings. Their system of giving parallels that of close siblings--they give objects and food without calculation or expectation of reciprocity. The use of objects is openly requested, and the consequent gifts are expected. They highly value the process of giving objects freely, which are passed on from person to person, symbolizing the closeness among them. The author contrasts the Nayaka with other agricultural peoples who view the spirits as ancestors and themselves as clans: as a consequence those peoples have developed calculated, reciprocal giving relationships.

257   Bird-David, Nurit H. "Hunter-Gatherers and Other People: a Re-examination." In *Hunters and Gatherers 1: History, Evolution and Social Change*, edited by Tim Ingold, David Riches, and James Woodburn, 17-30. Oxford: Berg, 1988.

The Nayaka are able to incorporate elements of the economic and social lives of neighboring peoples into their own way of life, which serves to strengthen it. Among themselves, they consider their spouses to be their best friends, spending much of their leisure time with them; but they are inhibited about having social interactions with their kin, particularly close relatives. They address one another using formal kinship terms. When they do share large game meat, they are careful to divide it precisely in order to minimize economic dependency and personal obligations. They highly value personal independence, autonomy from their kin, and equality. These relationships form a contrast with their relations with non-Nayaka. Those are marked by economic inequality and interdependence, personal obligations and contractual indebtedness, and the social attachments of unequals. The Nayaka often form personal friendships with the non-Nayaka, and they may appeal to them to intervene when they have problems that their own lack of an authority structure cannot resolve. Nayaka relations with outsiders complement their own relationships, and both, functioning in conjunction, foster individual well-being and an effective social system.

Nubians

In 1902 a dam was built across the Nile River at Aswan, in southern Egypt, flooding the river-front agricultural lands of the Nubian people closest to the dam and forcing the villages to move to higher, and less fertile, ground. The dam was raised in 1912 and still higher in 1933, destroying the best agricultural lands of the Nubians south to the border with Sudan. With most of Egyptian Nubia desolate by 1960, announcement of the construction of the High Dam, which would totally inundate the valley south of Aswan, prompted major world attention on saving the ancient Nubian monuments. World public opinion was less aroused about the fact that 50,000 Nubian people in Egypt and an equal number in Sudan would have to be resettled to the north and south of the huge reservoir. A "salvage ethnography" effort was made to record and describe the remnants of the ancient Nubian culture that was still alive in the old villages before the resettlement would start in 1963-64. Robert A. Fernea's book [261] describes the peaceful strategies of the pre-resettlement Nubians, and other works amplify the themes of that book and describe the cultural, social and religious practices that fostered Nubian peacefulness.

258   Callender, Charles. "The Mehennab: A Kenuz Tribe." In
       *Contemporary Egyptian Nubia: A Symposium of the Social
       Research Center, American University in Cairo, Volume II,*

edited by Robert A. Fernea, 181-217. New Haven: Human Relations Area Files, 1966.

A description of the tribal structure, kinship, social groupings, administration, rituals, territoriality, and leadership in the northern section of Egyptian Nubia. Leadership in the major lineages, the foremost divisions of the tribe, is held by men who handle the financial and ritual activities of the lineage and take care of the distribution of tribal property, other than land. The lineage head is responsible for maintaining peace and order and resolving conflicts both within his group and with outsiders. He handles minor disputes informally, without fines and publicity. While villages have watchmen with minor police powers, crimes are committed only occasionally, and those are usually handled within the lineages. Major problems are reviewed publicly by the heads of the lineages, who determine the guilt, if any, of the parties to the problem and their fines.

259   El Zein, Abdel Hamid. "Socio-Economic Implications of the Water-Wheel in Adendan, Nubia." In *Contemporary Egyptian Nubia: A Symposium of the Social Research Center, American University in Cairo, Volume II*, edited by Robert A. Fernea, 298-322. New Haven: Human Relations Area Files, 1966.

The land irrigated by the Nubian water-wheel was divided into 24 equal parts called *karats*. The builder-owners of the wheel, or their heirs, shared the labor of operation--and received a share of the water--in proportion to the number of *karats* of land they owned in the irrigation area. Since the work of operating the wheel couldn't be fragmented, their system allowed only the 24 shares of water to run to 24 *karats* of land, so families were effectively prevented from subdividing their property into smaller parcels. In case of disputes among heirs, the village elders would advise a family to give the *karat* to one family member to farm, with the others entitled to a share of the produce. The water-wheel system also fostered the regulation of land ownership since the amount of land a man could own was determined by how much he was able to actually cultivate himself. The water-wheel system thus inhibited subdivisions of the land, prompted village unity and stability, and fostered a cooperative social system with relatively stable and equitable distribution of resources.

260   Fernea, Robert A. "Integrating Factors in a Non-corporate Community." In *Contemporary Egyptian Nubia: A Symposium*

of the Social Research Center, American University in Cairo, Volume II, edited by Robert A. Fernea, 260-287. New Haven: Human Relations Area Files, 1966.

Nubians place a high value on resolving village disputes within the community, frequently through the intervention of respected third parties. When a public quarrel arises, such as a fight between two unrelated children which brings supportive mothers out onto the street followed by other kinsmen shouting insults, neutral bystanders will always intervene to end the conflict and restore peace. Serious conflicts are discussed after the Friday prayers in the mosque by the men of the congregation. Peaceful conflict resolution is supported by community values and by the networks of reciprocal relationships which bind people to their kin and non-kin alike. These relationships form the basis of Nubian economic and social life. Cooperation among farmers is grounded on fixed agreements; at weddings and funerals, relatives and fellow villagers attend and provide assistance because of past obligations. If someone ignored his reciprocal obligation to attend a funeral, he would become a censured outcast in the village. While everyone has networks of ties, they are careful about entering into new reciprocal relationships since they would then be obligated to repay them.

261   Fernea, Robert A. *Nubians in Egypt: Peaceful People*. Austin: University of Texas Press, 1973.

Fernea's book was the result of an ethnographic survey of the Nubian people before their country was inundated by the Aswan High Dam in the 1960s. The author focuses on the factors that contributed to the peacefulness of the Nubians, especially how they share the food and other produce from major village resources such as cows, palm trees, and the complex water-wheels that irrigated their fields near the Nile River. He explains how the extended family relationships, defined by the fractional shares that people owned of those village resources, contributed to economic well-being and social harmony. He discusses the Nubian ethic of getting involved in the disputes of others--their belief in resolving disputes publicly. Their widespread system of gift-exchanges, he feels, mitigates tensions not only between families and social groups, but also between older and younger generations. Evident throughout the book is the attitude of the Nubians toward themselves: they strongly believe that they are a peaceful people who are able to resolve conflicts effectively. The text of the book has been reprinted, along with some other material, in *Nubian Ethnographies*, by Elizabeth Warnock Fernea and Robert A. Fernea (Prospect Heights, IL: Waveland Press, 1991).

262 Fernea, Robert A. and John G. Kennedy. "Initial Adaptations to Resettlement: A New Life for Egyptian Nubians." *Current Anthropology* 7(June 1966): 349-354.

After the Nubian people were resettled north of the Aswan Dam in 1963, the sudden availability of modern conveniences, such as pumped water and transportation, gave them more leisure time, which created opportunities for expanding their social interactions and unifying their new communities. Social problems such as drinking and gambling also increased, however. Family relationships and ceremonial patterns were changed by several factors, including the fact that communities were arranged very differently in New Nubia, distances were reduced between peoples, and transportation was more widely available. Open social structures and reciprocal relations had been vital aspects of the ceremonial occasions among families and neighbors in the villages of Old Nubia, where distances determined who could and could not attend. In New Nubia the compactness of the communities and the presence of transportation allows everyone to attend every ceremony, which has prompted the Nubians to modify the social aspects of their traditional ceremonies to fit the new circumstances. While the unified move of the Nubian people to a new area has produced greater awareness of their ethnic heritage, it has also given them the ability to participate more fully in the life of the Egyptian nation, which they appreciate.

263 Kennedy, John G. "Nubian Zar Ceremonies as Psychotherapy." *Human Organization* 26(Winter 1967): 185-194.

The Nubians hold their zar ceremonies as a means of coping with the evil spirits which they believe cause their illnesses. They think that evil demons are attracted to people who have guilt feelings about their strongly held peaceful, nonviolent values, but they blame the spirits and not the individuals for the mental illnesses. They resort to the zar healing only as a last resort, after charms, exorcisms, herbs, and perhaps even Western doctors have failed. The ceremony is normally held for seven consecutive days in a large room with the windows closed amid an intense atmosphere of incense, music and dancing. The heat provokes the demons to jump from the body. Particular songs will prompt individuals into dancing before they finally fall into exhaustion at the center of the room. Often the spirit must be tempted to leave the prostrate persons with gifts from the relatives. Healing takes place in an atmosphere of strong faith by the patient, an intense feeling of support from the group, and a cultural context rich with the symbolism of dress, music, dancing, cleanliness, purity, and significant numbers. Reprinted as chapter 10 in *Nubian Ceremonial Life: Studies in Islamic Syncretism and Cultural Change*, edited by John G. Kennedy (Berkeley: University of California Press, 1978), p.203-223.

Onge

The Onge (also referred to as Onges) are one of the last remaining Andamanese Negrito peoples who inhabit Little Andaman Island, located at the southern end of the Andaman archipelago in the Bay of Bengal. When the government of India, which administers the islands, opened Little Andaman to settlement by refugees in the 1960s, the Onge became a tiny minority of the island's population, unable to practice their former nomadic hunting and gathering livelihood any longer. They are now supported entirely through government handouts. The 1981 census recorded 33 Onge out of 7,209 inhabitants on the island. Their former peaceful forest existence was described by Lidio Cipriani; other writings supplement his works.

264   Cipriani, Lidio. "Report on a Survey of the Little Andaman During 1951-53." *Bulletin of the Department of Anthropology (India)* 2(January 1953): 61-82.
    Until the recent past visitors to Little Andaman Island found the Onges to be quite hostile toward outsiders, though the author found them to be very friendly, happy, peaceful, and free of quarreling during his four-month visit in 1952 and 1953. For instance, their marriage ceremony consists simply of the groom leading the bride by the hand to his bed, but if, in case of an arranged marriage, she is not willing, she simply disappears into the forest for a while to signal her refusal. When this happens, everyone remains indifferent and silent about the issue. The Onges do not like to provoke anger. They believe that the forest spirits will be offended if they see that the people have collected wild yams. To prevent anger by the spirits, they trick them by cutting off most of each yam but replanting a bit of the root with the stem and leaves, thus effectively deceiving them. As an added benefit, the plants regrow--their superstitious belief prevents the supply of yams from being decimated by overuse.

265   Cipriani, Lidio. *The Andaman Islanders*. New York: Praeger, 1966.

The Onges are normally very helpful and friendly toward one another. One Onges man was accidentally bitten by a poisonous snake while climbing a tall tree in search of honey. After the author saved his life with injections of antiserum, his wife went fishing and hunting, normally a man's work, and the rest of the community provided him and his family with food. Minor squabbles blow over quickly, though when more serious disputes occur, such as controversies about the division of game, a camp may divide briefly into factions. Even then, however, the factions remain close, the dispute is resolved quickly, and the reconciliations, filled with tearful embraces, may continue for days. When they are angry, the Onges never raise their voices--disagreements are handled with a dignified silence. The Onges groups avoid disputes over territory since they have common understandings of their territorial boundaries.

266   Danda, Dipali G. "Little Andaman and the Onge." *Human Science* 36(March 1987): 66-91.

Between 1967 and 1979 thousands of outsiders were settled on Little Andaman Island and the Onges were resettled into two villages on the island where they perform some plantation labor and collect welfare supplies. Although they do not have to hunt or forage for food any longer, and many other aspects of their culture and daily lives are totally changed, some of their customs remain. While they now have a greater sense of individual ownership, they still cooperate in construction activities such as building a canoe or a hut, and they hunt cooperatively. The communal kitchens of the past have been replaced by individual cooking facilities. Married couples are very affectionate and care for their infants constantly. The government agency has chosen a couple of men to be leaders and has indicated that they do not need to do the same manual work as the others, a new concept for the Onges. While the women appear to be in good spirits, the men seem to be listless since there is little purpose to their lives.

Orang Asli

The Malay phrase "Orang Asli" (original people) is applied to peoples living in Peninsular Malaysia who were formerly called "aborigines." Anthropologists have classified these peoples into three different groupings based, primarily, on physical characteristics: the Negritos, the Proto-Malays, and the Senoi. The Semai, Temiar, and Chewong (see those sections for information) are all Senoi peoples, and the Batek (also a separate section) are Negritos. A census of the Orang Asli in 1969 recorded 53,000 people, of whom the Senoi were the most numerous--nearly half of the total. The Orang Asli live in almost all of the states of the Malay Peninsula, though they comprise less than one percent of the total population of the country. As of 1975 about 60 percent of the Orang Asli were considered to be forest-dwelling peoples living on swidden agriculture, hunting, and gathering; the rest were simply rural peoples. However, Clayton Robarchek reported in 1989 [379] that the Malaysian government is in the process of resettling the Semai and all of the other Orang Asli into permanent villages, and it is forcing them to take up market-related activities and join the economic mainstream of the country. They are also being pressured to adopt Islam. These changes free the natural resources of the forests for exploitation.

267   Endicott, K. "The Effects of Slave Raiding on the Aborigines of the Malay Peninsula." In *Slavery, Bondage and Dependency in Southeast Asia*, edited by Anthony Reid, 216-245. St Lucia and New York: University of Queensland Press, 1983.

The history of Malay slavery during the 19th century against the Orang Asli continues to have a profound effect on the aboriginal peoples. Their stories of slave raids are an important aspect of their worldview, which concentrates on a fear of strangers, particularly Malays. This fear of strangers is used as a threat to prevent misbehavior by their children, since adults do not like to punish them. The distinctive feature of the Orang Asli, their peaceful, nonaggressive, passive natures, can be directly traced to their formerly being the objects of violent slave raids. Most of the groups learned that flight into the forests meant the possibility of survival, while fighting was generally hopeless; an inferior, passive, supplicating manner in the presence of the Malays represented safety, while the appearance of aggressiveness brought injury or death. Some were protected by the Malay traders, who were concerned about any interruptions by slave raiders on their profits from their monopolistic, exploitative trading practices. One group, the Temiars, couldn't flee their settled villages, so they lived in defensive longhouses and learned to fight for their freedom.

268   Schebesta, Paul. *Among the Forest Dwarfs of Malaya.* Kuala Lumpur: Oxford University Press, 1973. Reprint of the 1928 edition.

An account of the author's travels among the Orang Asli, primarily various groups of Negritos. He indicates that the people live without any sense of tribal organization or higher authority than the family groups. While spouses are normally quite affectionate, if the affection wanes the marriage is dissolved; once children are born that rarely happens. They are quite devoted to their children: mothers prefer to put ornaments on children before themselves, and fathers will take care of them in the absence of their mothers. Adults do not hit children and are never cruel or aggressive; murder is unknown. According to the author, the natural environment of the Malay Peninsula--dense forests--is responsible for Negrito gentleness, timidity and silence. The forest stifles superficiality, pride, and a lust for possessions, and it fosters loyalty to traditions, happiness, and a peace of heart. Their belief that it is a sin against their god to torment or make fun of helpless captive animals contributes to their gentleness. Sins such as mocking animals are expiated whenever a thunderstorm approaches by the transgressor making a leg-cut and sacrificing some blood to appease the storm god.

Paliyan

The Paliyan live in the Palni Hills, and other nearby ranges, at the southern end of India's Western Ghats on the border of Kerala and Tamil Nadu states. The 7,000 people (as of 1981) subsist as nomadic gatherers, as occasional workers on hillside plantations, and by doing sporadic labor for contractors and farmers in the valleys. They avoid cooperation, competition, and all signs of overt aggression.[13]

269   Gardner, Peter M. "Ascribed Austerity: A Tribal Path to Purity." *Man* n.s. 17(September 1982): 462-469.

While the Paliyan consider themselves autonomous from their Tamil neighbors, the latter regard them to be just a specialized part of their own society. The Tamils view the Paliyan as unpredictable gatherers of yams and recluses who live off the forest, unreliable workers but gentle, harmless, guileless, and trusting people nonetheless. To the Tamils they appear to be free of the normal social constraints of society, when in fact they are highly self-restrained. The obvious austerity of the Paliyan lifestyle convinces their neighbors that they are spiritually pure. Because of these perceptions, the Hindus include the Paliyan in religious rituals which would normally be closed to impure outsiders, such as serving as the keepers of shrines, assisting with offerings to forest deities, and helping at temple rites.

270   Gardner, Peter M. "Bicultural Oscillation as a Long-Term Adaptation to Cultural Frontiers: Cases and Questions." *Human Ecology* 13(December 1985): 411-432.

Whenever violence occurs or even threatens, the Paliyan quickly retreat from their villages at the edge of the Tamil world into a nomadic life in the forest. If one family suddenly feels threatened by a menacing-looking stranger, it may rapidly gather its few belongings and leave; the rest of the village, seeing their haste to depart, may follow suit without knowing what the problem is--as if a general alarm had been sounded. Their return may take several years, a tentative, gradual process based on their sense of the peacefulness at the edge of the forest. The ones living in proximity to the Tamil neighbors adopt their customs, though they view their own cultural environment as moral, proper and correct--as culture--and that of the Tamils as a profitable and rewarding situation. Factors that affect their decisions where to live include their anarchism; the lack of importance they place on consensus, authority, specialization, or contracts; and the highly egalitarian relations they maintain between the sexes and between persons of differing ages.

271   Gardner, Peter M. "Paliyan Social Structure." In *Contributions to Anthropology: Band Societies. Proceedings of the Conference on Band Organization, Ottawa, August 30 to September 2, 1965*, edited by David Damas, 153-171. Ottawa: The National Museums of Canada, 1969.

Many elements of Paliyan social structure are covered, such as the discussion about their nuclear families, which normally form the basic, cooperative social units of their society. As with all Paliyan, married people prefer to be self-sufficient, individualistic, and socially anarchistic, so married people sometimes do not share their food with one another for months. Paliyan dislike competition since they feel it leads to social disharmony and threatens the self-reliance and egalitarianism which they highly value. However, they require catharses from the tensions that arise when the needs of individuals and groups conflict with the rules against aggression and dependency. They enjoy the violent films of their Tamil neighbors, and they dream of situations of their having power. They relieve tensions through make-believe fighting and through parodying the worship of their gods.

272   Gardner, Peter M. "Pragmatic Meanings of Possession in
      Paliyan Shamanism." *Anthropos* 86(1991): 367-384.
         Shamanism is an active part of daily Paliyan life. Their gods,
      called *samis*, are frequently called to provide individual diagno-
      sis and healing, advice about stressful situations, and solutions
      to problems of subsistence. Several men or women will clap and
      sing with increasing tempo until one or more of the *samis* come
      and possess the bodies of participants in order to provide the
      ritualized advice and healing sought by the humans. People
      humble themselves before them, curl up at their feet, exaggerate
      their disabilities, and seek their parental protection. These
      relationships of dependency contrast with normal Paliyan inter-
      personal behavior, in which individuals act independently and
      autonomously, retreat from injuries or affronts, and avoid any
      hint of overbearing attitudes toward others. Interacting with the
      samis as much or as little as they individually need, Paliyan
      escape momentarily from their adult social codes; in a society
      where everyone has equal knowledge and authority, they find
      sami judgment and wisdom to be helpful. Shamans, like every-
      one else, must be self-effacing; they derive no special recogni-
      tion or authority from being possessed by the *samis*.

273   Gardner, Peter M. "Pressures for Tamil Propriety in Paliyan
      Social Organization." In *Hunters and Gatherers 1: History,
      Evolution and Social Change*, edited by Tim Ingold, David
      Riches and James Woodburn, 91-105. Oxford: Berg, 1988.
         A Paliyan settlement located for 150 to 200 years at the base
      of a forested mountain range has absorbed some of the culture
      of the surrounding Tamil peoples of the plains and retained some
      of the cultural traits of the other Paliyan peoples who live in the
      mountains. The settlement Paliyan continue to follow the
      pattern of their forest relatives of having nuclear or slightly
      extended families, in contrast to the large, virilocal families of
      the Tamils. The settlement Paliyan husband-wife relationships
      follow patterns comparable to those of the forest Paliyan in most
      regards--complete equality between the sexes, frequent displays
      of mutual marital enjoyment, interpersonal respect, dignity and
      independence of action, equality of property rights, and rights to
      divorce. In Tamil society, by contrast, males dominate females,
      older people have authority over younger ones, and wives are
      circumspect in their social relations. Several incidents of men
      dominating women, however, indicate that social asymmetry

~ may be developing. The settlement Paliyans follow the standards of their Tamil neighbors to some extent in terms of their remarriage patterns.

274 Gardner, Peter M. "Symmetric Respect and Memorate Knowledge: The Structure and Ecology of Individualistic Culture." *Southwestern Journal of Anthropology* 22(Winter 1966): 389-415.

The Paliyan have a highly individualistic society which does not value cooperation but which also places a strong prohibition on competition and violence. Their highly indulged infants spend most of their time in direct physical contact with their mothers, who nurse them whenever they express the slightest need. When Paliyan children are weaned they undergo a traumatic period since they may receive their first mild punishments and the mothers will cease responding immediately to the children's demands for attention. Their frequent periods of anger and tantrums may last until they are about five years old, when they will begin to play quietly. When they play games, particularly games adopted from neighboring peoples, they exhibit neither competition nor cooperation. Adults are economically and socially independent from one another, except within nuclear families. Even in emergencies, sharing only extends to primary kin--parents and grown children, or siblings. Kinship groups larger than the nuclear family do not exist.

275 Gardner, Peter M. "The Paliyans." In *Hunters and Gatherers Today: A Socioeconomic Study of Eleven Such Cultures in the Twentieth Century*, edited by M. G. Bicchieri, 404-447. New York: Holt, Rinehart and Winston, 1972.

Five progressively used mechanisms help the Paliyan maintain order and resolve conflicts. The first is self-restraint: the repression of anger and hostile feelings. In order to achieve this, they avoid consuming alcohol, which they feel would make them aggressive. They also dissipate anger by applying to their foreheads *sirupani pu*, or "laughing flower." The second mechanism is to redirect feelings of aggression through dreams, fantasies, and violent films. A third is used when conflict does arise: the headman will intervene and attempt to conciliate through joking or soothing. If this fails, the parties to the dispute must separate. A grandparent or other relative may take a child if a parent becomes angry, and spouses separate when they quarrel. A whole community will depart if a dispute occurs with another. At each level, it is the injured person or group which feels the obligation to withdraw, to avoid the danger of retaliation. The fifth mechanism which prompts circumspect behavior is supernatural--the fear of revenge through sorcery.

Piaroa

There are about 7,000 Piaroa, an American Indian people, who lived before 1970 in the forests along the tributaries to the Middle Orinoco River in Venezuela. Since 1970 they have been encouraged to settle in larger communities further down the river. Joanna Overing studied them in 1968 and 1977, and her writings explain the aspects of their beliefs that foster their peacefulness.

276   Overing Kaplan, Joanna. "Dualisms as an Expression of Difference and Danger: Marriage Exchange and Reciprocity among the Piaroa of Venezuela." In *Marriage Practices in Lowland South America*, edited by Kenneth M. Kensinger, 127-155. Urbana: University of Illinois Press, 1984.

Piaroa social structure is geared to achieving safety by masking differences, particularly within the communal household. In their creation myth, Wahari the Tapir, creator of sky, land, and the Piaroa, constantly battles with his father-in-law, Kuemoi the Anaconda, creator of crocodiles, vultures, and poisonous snakes, because Wahari did not give anything to Kuemoi in return for his wife, not even a child. The myth points out the instability and peril in unequal relationships, particularly within families. The Piaroa control the danger of inequalities and differences by marrying within their local groups so that kinship ties normally pre-exist the marriage. Their word *chawaruwang*, kinsman, signifies the inclusiveness of their relationships: among all Piaroa; among persons with whom one interacts peacefully (friends); among kin with whom one has regular relations; and in the most restricted sense among the extended family which lives in the same household. Marriage within the group is the basis for Piaroa social organization, a counterweight to the dangers inherent in human differences, the antidote to their suspicions about human social nature.

277   Overing Kaplan, Joanna. *The Piaroa, a People of the Orinoco Basin: A Study in Kinship and Marriage*. Oxford: Clarendon Press, 1975.

The most salient characteristic of the Piaroa is their peacefulness. Armed conflict between territories is unthinkable: a Piaroa
who killed another man would, they believe, die by defecating
his insides. Their ideal of masculinity is one of control and
tranquility rather than fighting, hunting, or working. Despite
their opposition to combat, their society survived several hundred years of slave raiding during the 17th and 18th centuries.
Piaroa leaders must exemplify these peaceful ideals, setting a
standard that will foster the tranquility of the people. However,
the leaders of the large Piaroa houses and the more powerful
leaders of the territories are quite competitive in seeking and
maintaining their own political power. The territorial leader is
respected for his knowledge of the magic and sorcery which will
protect his people from natural and supernatural forces. He
increases his territory and power through his skill at making
effective marriage alliances. These marriages will link him and
members of his house (his kin) with the relatives of other
potentially powerful people. The book focuses on the kinship
structures of the Piaroa, which form the basis for their social
system and their political structures. The author of this book may
also be listed in library catalogs under Kaplan, Joanna Overing.

278   Overing, Joanna. "Images of Cannibalism, Death and Domination in a 'Non-Violent' Society." In *The Anthropology of
Violence*, edited by David Riches, 86-101. Oxford: Blackwell,
1986.

Piaroa communities are almost totally free of physical violence, the open expression of anger, and tangible aggression.
They place a high value on personal moderation, tranquility,
equality, and individual autonomy. They feel that competition
over resources and the power to transform resources into human
goods is the primary force producing human violence: their
political process rejects competition and the ownership of
resources, since that would end in cannibalism. They believe
that natural resources, and the cultural ability to transform them
into human food, are owned by the gods--no individual human
may own them since that would allow coercion and violence.
They see the disease and death they suffer as resulting from
extreme violence from unknown peoples, and they actively use
sorcery for retaliation and as protection. They also suffer from
the violence of their mythic past. The shaman, through his
chanting every night, is able to prepare liquids which the people
consume the next morning to keep them safe for another day. As

the teacher of their ethical values, the shaman sets the example for humility and proper manners.

279   Overing, Joanna. "Personal Autonomy and the Domestication of the Self in Piaroa Society." In *Acquiring Culture: Cross Cultural Studies in Child Development*, edited by Gustav Jahoda and I. M. Lewis, 169-192. London: Croom Helm, 1988.

The Piaroa maintain their peacefulness by the use of healing therapy rather than by imposing authority systems, civil laws or criminal laws. Their ideology completely forbids any physical coercion or violence. They feel they have abolished the use of coercion by eliminating the ownership of material resources and the control over other people's labor. No one can order another to do something, since sovereignty is held by the gods. Humans may tap into the powers of the gods to utilize resources, but no one owns the resources. Since Piaroa children have no models for violent or coercive behavior, and they are never punished physically, their play is robust but free of expressions of anger. The only expression of anger by children or adults is through silence. Children are instructed by the shamans in the virtues of their society, such as tranquility, and told about the deficiencies of social values that promote individuals, such as personal industry, talent, ambition, and courage. The shamans teach about their mythology, which elaborates on these morals.

280   Overing, Joanna. "Styles of Manhood: An Amazonian Contrast in Tranquillity and Violence." In *Societies at Peace: Anthropological Perspectives*, edited by Signe Howell and Roy Willis, 79-99. London: Routledge, 1989.

The Piaroa believe that the good life consists of tranquility and harmony. Their territory is almost completely free of physical violence, expressions of anger, and displays of violent excess. They are quite strongly egalitarian and supportive of individual autonomy for men and women. They think the ideal meal is composed of meat and manioc bread, the product of a man's hunting and a woman's garden. There is no ownership of land, no supervision of one person's labors by another. The produce of the forest is shared by all the members of the multi-family house, though the products from gardens are owned individually by the people who grew them. While the concept of a collective will is foreign to them, the Piaroa highly value social skills and the ability to live together in a community. The function of the community, as an institution, is to prevent relationships of domination from developing. The shaman teaches children lessons in social morality, such as the harm caused by vanity, jealousy, arrogance, dishonesty, cruelty, malice and ferocity; he also teaches the importance of mastering the emotions.

281   Overing, Joanna. "The Aesthetics of Production: the Sense of Community among the Cubeo and Piaroa." *Dialectical Anthropology* 14(1989): 159-175.

In mythic times the creator god of the Piaroa was evil, mad, and physically ugly, deriving his capabilities from hallucinogenic poisons. This affected all the other creative gods, leaving the forces of production--gardening, hunting, and fishing--infused with competition, violence, greed, arrogance, and lust, and poisoning peaceful relations within and between communities. Those productive, but poisonous, forces were cast out into space where they are kept in crystal boxes by another set of gods. The beads worn by the Piaroa represent those boxes plus the productive forces and poisons within each person. The productive forces have to be kept under control: the healing song is potentially the breath of the jaguar; the beads of life contain poison. The powers of the moon, controlled by the shamans, allow them to clean the forces of production and make moral, virtuous decisions. Thus, the ability of individuals to maintain harmony with others forms the essence of beauty; aesthetics focuses on resisting a return to the mythic period of violence; social life insists on individuals living peacefully together as an antidote to those past excesses.

282   Overing, Joanna. "There Is No End of Evil: The Guilty Innocents and Their Fallible God." In *The Anthropology of Evil*, edited by David Parkin, 244-278. Oxford: Basil Blackwell, 1985.

The Piaroa system of ethics is based on the view that human nature is composed of wild desire and poisonous knowledge. Both are overcome through personal will--humans learn personal restraint in order to achieve happiness and tranquility. Humanity is not innately aggressive, good or evil; rather, people learn aggression by allowing knowledge to poison their will and hence their passions. At the age of six or seven, children learn the virtues of restraint, respect for others, avoiding quarrels, leading a tranquil life, being responsible for their own actions, and controlling jealousy, dishonesty, vanity, and cruelty. The Piaroa stress control over malice and arrogance, which particularly disrupt peacefulness. They are taught that emotions and desires must be mastered, a process that allows responsibility and free will to develop. A free will to respect others, the desired result of consciousness, is highly desirable. They compare moral goodness with cleanliness, beauty, restraint, and moderate moonlight; evil is associated with dirt, madness, excesses, ugliness, and fierce sunlight. They perceive nature as neutral, tame and stable, while human culture is wild and poisonous.

Quakers

The Society of Friends, or Quakers, was formed by followers of the English mystic George Fox in the middle of the 17th century. Quakers believed in the "Inner Light"--that God continued to speak to followers through the divine spirit--as well as in the authority of the Bible. They adopted a simple lifestyle and organized their church into hierarchical units called monthly meetings, quarterly meetings, and yearly meetings. Their silent worship services were held without clergy. A prominent Quaker leader later in the 17th century, William Penn, was allowed to found a colony named after himself--Pennsylvania. The colonial legislature was controlled by Quakers for three-quarters of a century, and a substantial amount of historical literature deals with the conflicts Quakers felt between the needs of ruling a political body and their uncompromising beliefs in peacefulness. Their beliefs in peace prompted them to become leaders of various social movements, such as anti-slavery in the 18th and early 19th centuries; in the 20th century they have become world leaders in relief work and social justice movements. This section includes only a small selection of the literature on Quaker relief and social activism. There are over 100,000 Quakers living in the United States and Canada.[14]

283   Bacon, Margaret H. "Friends and the 1876 Centennial: Dilemmas, Controversies, and Opportunities." *Quaker History* 66(Spring 1977): 41-50.

        Friends were undecided how much to support the Philadelphia Centennial Exhibition in 1876, since it commemorated a bloody war in which they had not fought 100 years before--the same reasoning they had used for not joining Fourth of July celebrations. One writer in a Quaker magazine urged Friends to not even visit the exhibition since the show of patriotism would include displays of weaponry and glorification of the nation's bloody history. Friends were also concerned about the alcohol, displays of fashion, and the self-congratulatory nature of the exhibition.

Orthodox Friends joined many other Protestant denominations in pressuring Exhibition Commissioners to close on Sundays, but since that discriminated against working-class people, who only had Sundays free, Hicksite Friends joined Catholics and Unitarians in opposing the closing. The women's rights movement, which had a number of Quaker women in leadership positions, tried to peacefully advance its cause by presenting a Declaration of Women's Rights at the reading of the Declaration of Independence on July Fourth. This evidently embarrassed most Friends, who disliked appearing to be extremists and hesitated joining in public protests, even for worthwhile causes.

284   Bailey, Sydney D. "Non-official Mediation in Disputes: Reflections on Quaker Experience." *International Affairs* 61(Spring 1985): 205-222.

Since the Second World War prominent American Quakers have frequently been called upon by presidents and prime ministers to serve as mediators in areas of major international crisis, such as the Middle East, East and West Germany, India and Pakistan, the Biafra War in Nigeria, Southern Rhodesia/Zimbabwe, and Northern Ireland. International Quaker mediation started when United Nations Secretary General Trygve Lie appointed Clarence E. Pickett, Executive Secretary of the American Friends Service Committee, to reconcile Arabs and Jews in 1948 when the state of Israel was formed. Despite attempted governmental manipulation, these Friends may have been influential in some cases in reaching peaceful settlements, such as their role in helping bring about an end to the Biafra War. As good mediators, they have had to avoid the limelight; the governments and politicians on both sides of the conflicts need to claim the credit for the successes reached. Thus, on the whole, mediation has been an unofficial, unheralded, but important spin-off benefit of the internationally known Quaker penchant for peaceful resolution of conflict.

285   Benjamin, Philip S. "Gentlemen Reformers in the Quaker City, 1870-1912." *Political Science Quarterly* 85(March 1970): 61-79.

A number of prosperous Philadelphia Quaker bankers and merchants led efforts to reform the city's corrupt Republican machine from 1870 to 1912 without much success. The Quaker reformers adhered firmly to the Republican party, which had abolished slavery and promoted peace with the Indians, so they could not effectively challenge the city's Republican bosses nor could they support Democrats. Also, most accepted Quaker injunctions against direct involvement in politics. Their sense of moral responsibility and civic duty led these potential leaders to become involved, but only at the intellectual and polite level. One Quaker who served 16 years on the city council was often the sole opponent to corrupt contracts and special appropriations, though he was always polite and genteel in his comments. The reforming Committee of 100 followed Quaker influence even to the point of making decisions by consensus. Except for one success in electing a reformer for mayor in 1880, their attempts to reform politics failed because they lacked political sagacity, were unwilling to work outside the Republican party, and remained aloof from political organization.

286   Benjamin, Philip S. *The Philadelphia Quakers in the Industrial Age, 1865-1920.* Philadelphia: Temple University Press, 1976.

During the decades after the Civil War, Quakers tended to ignore the massive problems of the era, to stick to established patterns of philanthropy, and, with an attitude of distrust for the recipients of their benevolence, to impose their own social values on the poor. In the schools which they opened for the Freedmen in the South they tried to curb the Blacks' expressions of emotion, love of music, and artistic expression. When President Grant placed them in charge of the Indian reservations in Nebraska and Kansas, their practical education programs emphasized changing Indian clothing styles, social roles, and work habits. Although they began to grow away from their superiority attitude toward Asians by the 1880s, when a Quaker man of Japanese ancestry married the daughter of a prominent white Philadelphia Quaker family it caused a tremendous strain in the Arch Street Meeting in 1890. They supported an immigrant group of Doukhobors from Russia at the end of the century, but their support dried up when the refugees continued living communally rather than adopting the proper individual homes as the Quakers advocated.

287   Brock, Peter. *Pioneers of the Peaceable Kingdom.* Princeton, NJ: Princeton University Press, 1968.

The history of Quaker pacifism in North America from the colonial period to the First World War begins with the uncompromising refusal by Quakers to participate in any type of colonial military service and the resulting beatings, imprisonment, and confiscation of property which they suffered. In Pennsylvania, the Quaker colony, some Friends questioned the political expediency of their involvement in a government which provided arms for police officers and which included capital punishment in the law code. During the American Revolution, while Quakers prominently refused to pay any kind of war taxes, they also quietly discussed their opposition to war with their friends and neighbors and provided relief supplies to Quakers in other cities who were suffering from the war. As a result of the war, Quakers became more disciplined, more uniform in their beliefs, more sensitive to the suffering of humanity, but to some extent more narrow spiritually and culturally. During the Civil War many Quakers were drafted, others enlisted, and all who served in the military faced a deeply divided Society when they returned to civilian life. This volume consists of some of the chapters that appeared in the author's larger work *Pacifism in the United States: From the Colonial Era to the First World War* (Princeton: Princeton University Press, 1968).

288   Brock, Peter. "The Peace Testimony in 'A Garden Enclosed.'" *Quaker History* 54(Autumn 1965): 67-80.

Though Quakers withdrew in many ways from active participation in American society after the American Revolution, they continued to discuss various peace issues such as whether to pay taxes if they knew part of the money was being used for military purposes. But they played a limited role in the peace societies that developed outside their church after 1815, even though those groups studied the history of the Friends and gave them credit for their inspiration. Quakers viewed them as worldly and acted condescendingly toward them. They were particularly hostile toward the New England Non-Resistance Society, a group which opposed all involvement with governments in the belief that they are all tainted with the blood of state-supported violence. A minority of Quakers also held anti-state views, but most supported the highly conservative, sectarian Friends who were absolutely hostile to the radical nonresistance movement and the abolitionists who were associated with it. The Friends could not tolerate their opposition to human government, strong language, or militant tactics, which they felt were incompatible with Quaker quietism and acceptance of government.

289   Brock, Peter. *The Quaker Peace Testimony, 1660 to 1914.* York, England: Sessions Book Trust, 1990.

An historical summary of Quaker pacifism in England, America, Canada, Norway, Ireland, France, Prussia, Australia and New Zealand which concentrates on the relationships of Friends with established governments, their affiliations with other pacifist groups, and their patterns of conscientious objection. At first George Fox was primarily opposed to fighting, but this concept was broadened in 1660 to a prohibition of combat by all Quakers. Subsequently the Society opposed any involvement with the military, rejected arguments in favor of self defense, and began questioning related issues. For instance, the book charts the development of Quaker attitudes toward paying taxes which support warfare. Initially they accepted Christ's injunction to "render unto Caesar" and paid all taxes demanded by governments. These ideas were modified in America during the Revolutionary War by some meetings which decided to support the resistance of members who refused to pay war taxes. However, the more radical idea of not paying that portion of general taxes which was devoted to military purposes--which resulted in distraint of personal property--was practiced by some Quakers but not approved by the Society.

290   Bronner, Edwin B. "The Quakers and Non-Violence in Pennsylvania." *Pennsylvania History* 35(January 1968): 1-22.

William Penn incorporated Quaker idealism in the founding of his colony. Examples of idealistic laws included guarantees of religious freedom, a modest use of police power, and, for crimes involving Indians and whites, jury trials with half of the jurors from each race. At first the Quaker assembly refused to agree with the British governors to swear oaths, to impose capital punishment, or to provide financial support for the military--but ultimately they had to compromise. In order to be allowed to continue their practice of affirming (rather than swearing oaths), the government forced them to accept many additional justifications for executions. In line with their belief in pacifism, the Quaker assembly used a variety of techniques to stall appropriating money for the military, but they did compromise and repeatedly appropriated the money. In 1756, six Quakers resigned their seats, unable to compromise any longer. These events do not prove that they lost the strength of their pacifist ideals, however: in one monthly meeting, only 5 out of 250 members were questioned about their peace testimonies between 1754 and 1757.

291   Brutz, Judith L. and Bron B. Ingoldsby. "Conflict Resolution in Quaker Families." *Journal of Marriage and the Family* 46(February 1984): 21-26.

The 130 men and 158 women in the Lake Erie Yearly Meeting who responded to a survey indicated that they held strongly pacifist beliefs; they also were involved in a surprisingly high incidence of family violence--the same or slightly higher than a comparable national survey. While the Quaker respondents did not report as much severe violence between spouses or from parents to children as the national sample, severe sibling violence among the Quakers was even greater than the national sample. The authors suggest possible explanations for this puzzling data: 78 percent of the respondents were converts, and while they had embraced a belief in nonviolence they may have been raised in families where more violent patterns prevailed; it may be easier to work for peaceful international relations and justice at the community level than to promote nonviolent, peaceful family patterns; the effort to foster pacifism may produce pressures that the respondents vent in their family relations; and, finally, the data may be skewed because Quakers may be more honest than Americans in general in reporting their family violence.

292   Brutz, Judith L. and Craig M. Allen. "Religious Commitment, Peace Activism, and Marital Violence in Quaker Families." *Journal of Marriage and the Family* 48(August 1986): 491-502.

Results of a survey of family violence among Quakers, reported in general terms in [291], are described in detail. The survey questioned husbands and wives about their religious commitment (extent of participation in church activities), their peace activism, and the number of their violent acts toward family members during the previous year. Analysis of the data showed that reduced levels of violence tended to be associated, not necessarily with religious affiliation, but with higher levels of religious commitment, and that the nonviolent nature of Quaker beliefs was a significant factor in that commitment. Women who were active in peace work were less violent than those who weren't, but husbands active in peace work also reported higher levels of family violence, whether or not they also were committed to church work. It is possible that peace activism fosters a conflict between the nonviolent beliefs of Quakers and the traditional socializing of American males to be aggressive, while the nonaggressive socializing of American females may simply enhance their Quaker beliefs about violence and fit in well with peace activism.

293   Carroll, Kenneth L. "A Look at the 'Quaker Revival of 1756.'" *Quaker History* 65(Autumn 1976): 63-80.

Historians of 18th-century American Quakerism have concluded that the political crisis in Pennsylvania in 1756--when Quaker members of the colonial assembly were forced to confront the fact that they were part of a government that was at war--had a formative effect on the revival of the Quaker faith in America. In fact, the seeds of religious revival started growing, to a greater or lesser degree, in Quaker meetings in England, Ireland, and America well before 1756. The beginnings of zeal for revival, reform, and discipline may be traced to England decades earlier, and it was shared on both sides of the ocean by the prominent American Quakers who traveled to Britain, and vice versa. This reawakening in all parts of the Quaker community allowed the Friends in Pennsylvania to effectively deal with the events of 1756, and it strengthened them for the even greater struggles to come during the American Revolution.

294   Collett, Wallace T. "'Let Us Try What Love Will Do': The Story of the American Friends Service Committee." *Mennonite Life* 38(March 1983): 12-18.

Since 1917 the American Friends Service Committee has been involved in a wide range of service activities in the United States and abroad, including assistance for the poor during the depression, relief for refugees and other victims of war, reconstruction and community development programs, and support for social justice, literacy, equal housing, equal employment, school desegregation, migrant farm workers, and so on. In recent decades, the AFSC has largely shifted its role from crisis relief to facilitating development projects that might help to prevent crises. In the early 1970s, minority staff members began to challenge the underlying racism, as they perceived it, in the white, middle class, liberal AFSC establishment. The Committee struggled for answers--one person observed, "there were some uneasy times, some deep searching for guidance"--before establishing an affirmative action program to promote the end of sexism and racism in the organization. Summarizing the history of the AFSC, the author describes the work of the group as "concerned with the world as it is and as it ought to be ... the practice of our faith."

295   Conwill, Joseph D. "Back to the Land: Pennsylvania's New Deal Era Communities." *Pennsylvania Heritage* 10(Summer 1984): 12-17.

During the depression the American Friends Service Committee founded a unique rural community homestead project in southwestern Pennsylvania. In 1933 the new Division of Subsistence Homesteads in the United States Department of the Interior began assembling land and selling lots to form a community in Westmoreland County. The AFSC was involved because of massive unemployment in the coal mines and their experience in working with unemployed miners. When the government started to retrench in 1936, the Friends decided to establish another community, Penn-Craft, in neighboring Fayette County. The purpose of the two communities was to resettle unemployed miners in homes that had enough land around them--several acres each--so they could virtually feed themselves from their own gardens. Community enterprises would provide some cash income and a co-op store would sell consumer goods cheaply. Critics derided these two communities as anachronisms that sought to resurrect a Jeffersonian agrarian ideal, but the Friends argued they simply wanted to cushion the effects of industrial depression by giving people the ability to feed themselves without renouncing the benefits of industrialism.

296   Curtis, Peter H. "A Place of Peace in a World of War: The Scattergood Refugee Hostel, 1939-1943." *Palimpsest* 65(March/April 1984): 42-52.

During the early years of the Second World War, when people were fleeing the European continent from Nazi persecution, American Friends began extending their relief services to the refugees. Iowa Quakers proposed to the American Friends Service Committee that they might be able to help Europeans who did make it into the country with the transition to American life. They suggested that the facilities of the Scattergood School near West Branch, Iowa, should be turned into a temporary boarding facility for the European immigrants until they could make arrangements for jobs and permanent settlement. When the Europeans began arriving in 1939, the Quakers organized farm work, language instruction, and acculturation activities to ease them into their new country. By the end of 1942 the influx of refugees had died out and the project was ended the following year.

297   Cutler, Lee. "Lawrie Tatum and the Kiowa Agency, 1869-1873." *Arizona and the West* 13(Autumn 1971): 221-244.

In July 1869 Lawrie Tatum, a Quaker from Iowa, assumed responsibility for the Kiowa-Comanche reservation in southwestern Oklahoma. Tatum's attitude was that a policy of friendship and fair, peaceful administration should convince the Indians to stop their raids and become farmers. The Kiowas, however, were warriors who gained prestige by successfully raiding other Indian or white settlements, and they had no interest in settling down. As Indian raids continued, Tatum began to lose his faith in the effectiveness of his peaceful policies. He was pressed on one side by his superior, also a Quaker, who was safely removed from the scene and continued to urge a practice of kindness and mercy, and on the other by the contempt of the Kiowa for his perceived weakness. Several Kiowa leaders were captured after a raid, tried and sentenced in a Texas court, but their impending release from prison in 1872 prompted him to resign. Despite some successes, Tatum's administration was basically a failure since he couldn't resolve the dichotomy between the Quaker culture of peace and a Kiowa culture based on raiding, killing, and war.

298   Drake, Thomas E. *Quakers and Slavery in America.* Gloucester, MA: Peter Smith, 1965. Reprint of the 1950 edition.

American Quakers prepared a petition in 1790 to end the slave trade, and despite its failure they continued agitating about the issue until 1808 when the Constitution ended the trade. After that they exhibited their hostility toward slavery by boycotting the products of slave labor on the southern plantations, particularly cotton, rice, and sugar. Some anti-slavery Quakers helped runaway slaves on the Underground Railroad while others assisted freed Blacks. In the 1830s the American anti-slavery movement developed a rabid, crusading spirit that provoked strong sectional hostilities. While some Friends sympathized with this spirit, other more conservative Quakers, usually from urban, mercantile backgrounds, tried to be quieter and more accommodating. The dissension between these two groups prompted 2,000 Quakers in Indiana in 1842 to form their own

Yearly Meeting on strongly abolitionist principles, which inspired other meetings to reexamine their policies as well. As the sectional divisions in the nation became stronger, and as the nation seemed to be drifting toward war, most Quakers, with an overwhelming conviction of the importance of avoiding violence, backed into quieter stands.

299   Frost, Jerry W. "As the Twig Is Bent: Quaker Ideas of Childhood." *Quaker History* 60(Autumn 1971): 67-87.

Quaker attitudes toward children and the way they should be raised changed considerably about 1760. While there is very little direct evidence of how they actually raised children in the earlier colonial period, it is clear that they viewed infants and children as small adults. They sheltered children from the evils of the world as much as possible, a caution motivated by their acceptance of original sin and by a fear for the future of their faith, which could only be perpetuated by successfully raising their children. They believed that parents were to love their children without pampering and never to punish when angry, since anger only begets anger in the child. After 1760 they began to place more emphasis on the innocence of children and less on their innate sinfulness derived from the fall of Adam. They developed a more sentimental attitude toward children, who were viewed as lively spirits--sweet little beings who should be educated to the beauties of creation and the happiness derived from being good. Surviving letters reveal sentimental attitudes of fathers and mothers who were both engaged in raising their children.

300   Gentry, Martha E. "Consensus as a Form of Decision Making." *Journal of Sociology and Social Welfare* 9(June 1982): 233-244.

Quaker meetings represent successful examples of consensus-style decision making, though the Friends base their consensus on everyone receiving the spirit of God rather than on people seeking a common human agreement. While individual differences may foster possible frictions, Quakers employ several techniques to help mediate conflicts: they punctuate meetings with periods of silence so that everyone can consider their own views and those of others; they try to set aside self-serving viewpoints during these periods of seeking the inner light; committees may be formed to gather more facts; and issues can be postponed for future discussions at later meetings. Individual disagreements founded on personal biases, ambitions, or pride will be discounted, but they will be respected if based on honest examinations of facts. Members are all expected to speak in the meetings, and if a meeting appears to come to a consensus about an issue, the clerk will record the decision; everyone will then assent to the minute, the clerk's written record. A normal outcome of the consensus decision is that everyone supports any resulting actions that are taken.

301   Hess, Dale. *A Brief Background to the Quaker Peace Testimony.* Toorak, Australia: Victoria Regional Meeting, The Religious Society of Friends, 1992.

Summarizes the history of pacifism in the Christian Church from biblical times through the articulation of the Quaker peace testimony by Fox and others in 1661. In some cases the different pacifist groups of Christians clearly influenced later Christians, while in other cases such connections may not have existed. The pamphlet is based on secondary sources; the author recommends important books on the history of the Quakers, the Anabaptists, and pacifism in general.

302   Illick, Joseph E. "'Some of Our Best Indians Are Friends ...' Quaker Attitudes and Actions Regarding the Western Indians During the Grant Administration." *Western Historical Quarterly* 2(July 1971): 283-294.

Friends approached President-elect Grant in January 1869 about fostering peaceful relations with the Indians of the West. He responded in April with his Peace Policy toward the Indians, and Congress supported his program with two million dollars. The president appointed Friends as superintendents over the Nebraska and the Kansas/Oklahoma Indians; the superintendents in turn appointed Quaker Indian agents. While many white Americans of the period wanted to exterminate the Indians, Quakers believed in training them for farm work and educating their children in the agricultural/mechanical ways of white culture. In his first annual report to Congress, Grant explained that he had asked the Friends to be involved with administering Indian affairs because of "their opposition to all strife, violence, and war," and, he concluded, "the result has proven most satisfactory." Their involvement did not last much beyond the Grant administration due to problems with white land hunger on the frontier and the desire of Congress to have control over patronage appointments for the Indian posts. The Quakers continued working with the Indians outside the government.

303   James, Sydney V. *A People among Peoples: Quaker Benevo- lence in Eighteenth-Century America*. Cambridge: Harvard University Press, 1963.

The 18th century was a crucial time for the development of the American Quaker community. The author describes the change in their attitudes toward non-Quakers during that period, from being centered on their own affairs, to a very outreaching, altruistic outlook. His basic analysis is that they were put under stress by a variety of factors: the failure of their ability to directly or indirectly influence government decisions, particularly in Pennsylvania; their growing alienation from the practice of slavery; their opposition to government Indian policies, espe- cially that of Pennsylvania; and their complete opposition to the Indian Wars and the American Revolutionary War. They re- solved these problems in several ways: by gradually eliminating slavery from their midst, in a step-by-step process that preserved the solidarity of the group, some of whom initially were slave owners; by forming various charitable outreach organizations and institutions that gave them a sense of moral accomplishment without the problems of holding the reins of government; by sending missionaries to help Indian peoples on the frontier settle into a farming economy. Their outreaching charitable efforts gave them the opportunity to project their altruism by example and win the approval of the non-Quaker society around them.

304   Jones, Lester M. *Quakers in Action: Recent Humanitarian and Reform Activities of the American Quakers*. New York: Macmil- lan, 1929.

The American Friends Service Committee began in 1917 with an initial budget of $115,000 to support relief workers in France in distributing food and supplies, repairing damaged farm machinery, and rebuilding ruined villages. After the war they moved into relief work in Germany where, by 1921, they were feeding over 1,000,000 people at 8,364 feeding stations in 1,640 German communities. Along with the English Friends, the AFSC provided relief in Austria, Poland, and, starting in mid- 1920, they assisted with famine relief in Eastern Russia. Be- tween September 1920 and June 1921, out of 650,000 people in the Russian county of Buzuluk where the English and Ameri- cans were working, 403,500 people, nearly two-thirds of the population, were fed by the Quakers. The AFSC also assisted the families of miners in Appalachia during coal strikes of the 1920s because conditions of near starvation were so severe. As the AFSC wrote to the protesting mine owners, "For a period of 250 years [Quakers] have held that love and good-will, not war and hatred, will bring about better world conditions."

305   Jorns, Auguste. *The Quakers as Pioneers in Social Work.* Montclair, NJ: Patterson Smith, 1969.

Early Quaker leaders in England had a strong desire to eliminate poverty. Their methods for accomplishing this aim were to organize charity better and, a longer-range goal, to eliminate the vast inequities between the upper and lower classes. Prohibiting extravagance in clothing and amusements was a means to that end. While all Quakers were expected to work hard and support themselves, those who couldn't were allowed to apply for help from the Monthly Meeting. The non-Quaker poor could apply also. There, public discussion of the individual application was normal--a humiliating procedure designed to keep people from seeking funds lightly--though in certain cases the need could be handled quietly by committee. During the 18th and 19th centuries Quakers were continually in the forefront of social service. They actively tried to find work for unemployed Quakers, either with other Friends or in the larger society, and they sought to establish home spinning industries for the unemployed. They also pioneered in other humanitarian fields--the abolition of slavery, educational development, prison reform, control of alcoholism, public health, and care of the insane.

306   Kashatus, William C., III. "A Quaker Testimony to the American Revolution." *Pennsylvania Heritage* 16(Spring 1990): 18-23.

During the American Revolution, 1,276 patriotic Quakers who supported the revolutionary cause in one way or another paid for their beliefs by being disowned by the Society of Friends--some for serving in the military, others for paying taxes and fines, still others for diverse deviations from Quaker pacifist beliefs such as swearing loyalty oaths. The Free Quaker Meeting was founded by Friends who had been disowned, though some of its leaders appeared to be motivated by other considerations than religious beliefs. In fact, these founders based their beliefs on what they felt were the original precepts of Quakerism. They strongly denied the right of a meeting to disown other Quakers for their beliefs: the primary tenet of the faith was that each person had to respond to the inner light, the word of God which came to everyone. The belief in pacifism, they felt, was secondary, and no one should be disowned for not accepting it. The significance of the Free Quakers was their challenge to the Society of Friends about accepting the Inner Light versus a uniform belief in pacifism.

307   Kennedy, Thomas C. "Fighting about Peace: The No-Conscription Fellowship and the British Friends' Service Committee, 1915-1919." *Quaker History* 69(Spring 1980): 3-22.

The No-Conscription Fellowship (NCF) a British pacifist organization during World War I, and the Friends Service Committee (FSC), also formed at the time, were able to cooperate well early in the war: Quakers served among the NCF leadership, and the FSC took positions that supported pacifists outside their church. Problems arose between the groups when the British draft law of 1916 was passed, since the FSC was totally opposed to the provisions for alternative services: it believed that the only valid responses to militarism were refusing to assist the war effort, arguing publicly against war, and silently suffering state persecution. The NCF, reflecting its membership, was not as absolutist and argued that individuals should follow their consciences. When the NCF began actively publicizing instances of prison brutality against some of the imprisoned conscientious objectors, the Friends felt that they were becoming simply a "society for prevention of cruelty to C.O.s," as one Quaker said, and they began to distance themselves even further from them. The result of these quarrels was a weakening of the overall pacifist movement during the war.

308   Ketcham, Ralph L. "Conscience, War, and Politics in Pennsylvania, 1755-1757." *William and Mary Quarterly* 20(July 1963): 416-439.

The idealism of the Quaker pacifists who dominated the Pennsylvania Assembly during the first years of the French and Indian War was repeatedly tested and tempered by the imperial struggle between France and England and the political struggles in the colony. When Braddock was defeated in 1755 and the Indians started attacking the Pennsylvania frontier settlements, ending 75 years of peaceful relations, the Quaker Assembly passed, for the first time, a tax and an authorization measure for raising an armed force to protect the settlers. The dramatic resignations and retirements of thirteen Quakers from the Assembly in 1756 as a protest against the increasing war efforts did not mark their retirement from politics: rather, it signaled a strategic retreat. Quakers retained considerable political influence and power, and they made these compromises in the Assembly as attempts to maintain that influence. The resignations were also prompted by a desire to preserve the religious vitality of the Society of Friends in the face of the stresses produced by war.

309 Knee, Stuart E. "The Quaker Petition of 1790: A Challenge to Democracy in Early America." *Slavery and Abolition* 6(September 1985): 151-159.

William Henry Smith, a historian of slavery, wrote that "the Society of Friends led all other denominations in the employment of moral influence for the eradication of slavery." In 1790 the Quakers became major actors in the anti-slavery movement when they introduced a petition in Congress via a supportive Pennsylvania congressman to abolish the slave trade long before the 1808 date mandated by the Constitution. Debate in Congress split along sectional lines, North versus South, with arguments articulated that would be repeated many times over the next 70 years. After the arguing and name-calling had ended, Congress compromised with a statement that limited itself with regard to the slavery issue. The importance was the raising, for the first time, of that major, divisive issue.

310 Kohrman, Allan. "Respectable Pacifists: Quaker Response to World War I." *Quaker History* 75(Spring 1986): 35-53.

Quakers were quite unprepared for the First World War. Despite their historic opposition to conflict they did not have an active plan to respond to war conditions, nor did they have a strategy for ameliorating the social and economic conditions which lead to conflicts. Their major problem was dealing with the excessive militarism and anti-German feelings that developed in the U.S. and which threatened any peace testimony. The American Friends Service Committee was created to provide an alternative to military service for Quakers faced with the draft; it would also provide visible demonstrations that they were active, patriotic citizens. Some of the Quaker groups, especially the more evangelical ones that resembled the mainline Protestants in style of worship, produced large numbers of servicemen from their ranks and little support for the AFSC. In some Quaker circles the desire to fit in with the general public opinion about the war--and indeed, the obvious sympathy of the overwhelming number of Quakers toward the war effort--restricted the ability of outspoken Friends to witness for peace.

311   Lermack, Paul. "Peace Bonds and Criminal Justice in Colonial Philadelphia." *Pennsylvania Magazine of History and Biography* 100(April 1976): 173-190.

A significant Quaker innovation in colonial Pennsylvania's court system was the peace bond, a sum of money imposed by a magistrate to prevent the anticipated continuation of disturbances or crimes, particularly slander, threatening behavior, and the use of abusive language. An early record of a peace bond occurred in 1680 when two neighbors, whose fighting had reached the stage of slander and assault, both were required to post bonds of 40 English pounds to ensure their peacefulness for a stated period of time. The bonds in frontier Pennsylvania were flexible, though often quite high--more than people could easily pay--so they had to pledge their possessions and the sureties of others, who then took a strong interest in making sure that the bonded person would not continue to commit the troublesome behavior. As Philadelphia grew larger after 1700 and crimes began increasing, the courts became more professional and the public started demanding more punishments for criminals. The humane criminal code of William Penn was steadily modified by the legislature until it had as many harsh punishments as England had.

312   Marietta, Jack D. "Conscience, the Quaker Community, and the French and Indian War." *Pennsylvania Magazine of History and Biography* 95(January 1971): 3-27.

The pacifism of the 18th-century American Quakers focused on the prohibition of interpersonal violence and ignored potentially complex issues such as state taxation for supporting warfare. During the crisis of the French and Indian War from 1754 through 1758, three separate Quaker factions strongly disagreed with one another on how to deal with such underlying ethical issues: the Quaker assemblymen in the Pennsylvania government, who had no problem with supporting the just wars of the colony; the dissidents in the Philadelphia Yearly Meeting who increasingly became uncomfortable with paying taxes to support their government's warfare; and the London Friends who sought to manipulate the American Quakers for their own ends. When a property tax for supporting the war was passed in 1756, Quakers outside the Assembly protested its payment.

They were, in effect, repudiating the counsel of George Fox, who had advised Quakers to support their legitimate government, even in wartime. In the Philadelphia Quaker meetings, however, neither the reformers nor the members in the Assembly would push for a showdown, preferring to wait for consensus to develop in their meetings.

313   Marietta, Jack D. "Wealth, War and Religion: The Perfecting of Quaker Asceticism 1740-1783." *Church History* 43(June 1974): 230-241.

While some Quakers realized that the desire for wealth contradicted Christian values, nothing interfered with their accumulation of property. During the French and Indian War and the American Revolution, reformers began to criticize their extensive wealth, arguing that it was inconsistent with Quaker pacifism and caused such other social evils as slavery, drunkenness, usury, and overwork. John Woolman blamed selfishness and wealth as the cause of war, which in turn caused impoverishment and misery. The reformers claimed that the acquisition of wealth was the antithesis of Christianity since it pushed God farther away from the individual--though few wealthy Friends cared enough to give up their own fortunes. During the Revolution, Quakers refused to pay war taxes, which were contrary to their pacifist beliefs; patriotic critics responded that those who derived benefits from society should help pay to defend it, especially if they wouldn't fight themselves. Quaker properties were seized by government agents in lieu of tax payments. Anthony Benezet saw these seizures of property as a proof of the sincerity of Quaker pacifism and a boost to the Society.

314   Maurer, Marvin. "Quakers in Politics: Israel, P.L.O. and Social Revolution." *Midstream* 23(November 1977): 36-44.

Analyzes the support for the Palestinians by the American Friends Service Committee and its apparent hostility toward Israel. The AFSC sponsored a conference in 1977 in the Washington area in a public attempt to build harmony and understanding between the Palestinian cause and the Israeli cause. The author maintains that the pretense of neutrality at the public level was abandoned at the working group level, where the biases in favor of the Palestine Liberation Organization and against Israel came across clearly. Quakers began meetings with declarations about their humanitarian goals and their beliefs that mutual trust and meaningful exchange could reach across conflicting ideologies; but the constant focus was on Israeli repression of Palestinians and not on Arab repressions of other Arabs. The author concludes that AFSC support for communist regimes and their "commitment to, and even their adulation for, third world dictatorships, helps explain their support for the P.L.O...."

315 Mekeel, Arthur J. "The Relation of the Quakers to the American Revolution." *Quaker History* 65(Spring 1976): 3-18.

During the 1760s, Quakers provided leadership among Philadelphia merchants in their struggle with the British government over the new tax levies. Friends were hoping to moderate the protest movement, to prevent it from becoming too radical, which would further sour relations with the government. But when a ship, the *Charming Polly*, arrived at the city in July 1769, the tax issue was so heated that a mob threatened violence to prevent the cargo from being unloaded. Although the ship left, the incident, with its threat of violence, prompted Quakers to withdraw any further support from the resistance movement, a resolve that was strengthened by the Boston Tea Party in late 1773. In 1774 and 1776, Quakers issued statements which indicated their indebtedness to the King for their liberties, reminded Americans that it was God who established governments, and blamed the current problems on people falling away from true righteousness. These documents were bitterly condemned by the patriots. During the war, Quakers in Pennsylvania were treated far more harshly than they were in the other states for their refusal to respond to the draft laws.

316 Munroe, Robert L. and Ruth H. Munroe. "Weber's Protestant Ethic Revisited: An African Case." *Journal of Psychology* 120(September 1986): 447-455.

Research was conducted on secondary-school students among the Abaluyia people of Western Kenya, many of whom were converted to the Quaker faith by missionaries. Questionnaires were administered to 172 students from Quaker families and 270 from non-Quaker families to determine their attitudes toward achievement, problem solving, and status. In general, the results only modestly supported the Weber thesis--that the Protestant ethic influences attitudes toward achievement. Responses to questions showed that Quaker influence was discernible, though modest and not always consistent: for instance, Quaker youngsters had received less physical punishment from their parents than the non-Quakers, but both groups had received equal amounts of parental love. The cultural values of the Abaluyia as well as those of the Quakers evidently played a significant role in forming student attitudes. Students recognized that the Quaker value of hard work and success did not necessarily translate into higher status in Abaluyia society. The Quakers did report less anxiety symptoms than the others, a result that might be due to their orientation to achievement.

317   Nash, Gary B. "Poverty and Poor Relief in Pre-Revolutionary Philadelphia." *William and Mary Quarterly* 33(January 1976): 3-30.

In the 1760s Philadelphia's Quaker merchants, concerned about the increase in paupers due to the economic downturn and the threatened tax burden on the city, proposed the formation of a privately managed almshouse. When the idea was approved by the Assembly in 1766, the "Bettering House," as it was called, was built just outside the city as a place where the poor could live and work to earn their support. The name indicates the moral expectation of the institution, since it was assumed that the requirement of the institution would be to either improve the poor--teach them to work--or at least to keep them away from the city. The Quaker supporters actually raised less than 20 percent of the budget of the institution, the rest coming from taxes and loans. But growth in the number of poor persisted and the Quaker managers found that, despite their efforts, care for the needy in the city continued to deteriorate. The cures they had promised a decade earlier had not worked--poverty appeared to be a permanent part of the economic system of the city.

318   Neely, Sharlotte. "The Quaker Era of Cherokee Indian Education, 1880-1892." *Appalachian Journal* 2(Summer 1975): 314-322.

In 1881 the North Carolina Yearly Meeting and the Western Yearly Meeting began supporting schools run by Quakers, with additional support from the federal government, for the Cherokee Indians in the mountains of western North Carolina. By 1885 seven schools were in operation. The Quakers oriented their instruction to practical subjects--agriculture for the boys and housekeeping for the girls--though they included religious instruction also. Their ideals of nonviolence and equality of the sexes were put into effect in the schools: discipline was evidently not violent and enrollment of boys and girls was nearly equal. Relations between the Cherokees and the Quakers who founded and ran the schools were apparently quite good until the end of the decade, when an authoritarian superintendent provoked controversy and unhappiness. To end the strife, the Friends turned the operation of the schools over to the federal government in 1892.

319   Nelson, Jacquelyn S. *Indiana Quakers Confront the Civil War.* Indianapolis: Indiana Historical Society, 1991.

Although historians have maintained that relatively few Quakers served in the army during the Civil War because of their opposition to fighting, the author found through her research that 1,212 enlisted or were drafted into the Union army in Indiana. These 1,212 Friends represented between 21 and 27 percent of the Quaker males between the ages of 15 and 49, a much higher figure than previous estimates. In some areas enough Friends volunteered to fight that several "Quaker companies" were formed, and in some counties more Quakers enlisted in the army than listed themselves on the registers as being "conscientiously opposed to bearing arms." Letters and diaries by Quakers who served in the army indicate they felt patriotic toward their country, they believed they were serving God, and they thought that the war was right and just. Indiana Quakers who were firm in their conscientious objection to fighting in the Civil War suffered very little for their beliefs. Most meetings were quite tolerant of different individual reactions to the draft by members; many men paid the commutation fees, while others, after 1864, accepted a noncombatant service.

320   Nelson, Jacquelyn S. "Military and Civilian Support of the Civil War by the Society of Friends in Indiana." *Quaker History* 76(Spring 1987): 50-61.

Many Friends in Indiana actively supported the Union cause in the Civil War. Of the state's approximately 4,000 to 5,000 male Quakers in 1861 between the ages of 15 and 49, about 1,200 (21 to 27 percent) decided to fight in the army. In some counties, the number of Quakers in uniform exceeded the number who requested conscientious status, and throughout the state only a small number who fought were disowned by their monthly meetings. One meeting explicitly decided not to punish their men who joined the army, since they believed that the soldiers were just obeying the dictates of their consciences. Their letters showed they initially enjoyed camp life and military discipline, though they were soon exposed to death, disease, hunger and hardship. Some became inured to the horrors of war and expressed enjoyment for the sounds and sights of battle. On the home front, many Quakers, even those opposed to fighting, responded to patriotic calls for citizen support by donating supplies, volunteering for the Indiana Sanitary Commission, and selling or even giving their horses to the government.

321   Pickett, Clarence E. *For More Than Bread: An Autobiographical Account of Twenty-Two Years' Work with the American Friends Service Committee.* Boston: Little, Brown, 1953.

During the early period of the depression, the American Friends Service Committee focused its attention on crises in the United States. The author, the executive secretary of AFSC, explains how his organization, composed of many conservative Quaker businessmen, overcame reservations about providing relief for a community without food or resources during a 1929 strike. In addition to extensive relief efforts, the AFSC established and provided continuing assistance, guidance, connections and commitment to a demonstration community development project, a skilled furniture-making industry in the Morgantown area. In Europe, the Quaker presence was maintained not for evangelizing but for representing "the cohesive quality in human life," as the author writes. During the late 1930s and the 1940s, in addition to resuming relief services, the AFSC provided assistance for the refugees or would-be refugees from Nazi terror. In 1947 the AFSC spent its half of the Nobel Peace Prize money, $25,000, to buy streptomycin, a medicine then available in quantity only in the U.S., to send into the Soviet Union to help treat Russian children with tuberculosis.

322   Radbill, Kenneth A. "The Ordeal of Elizabeth Drinker." *Pennsylvania History* 47(April 1980): 147-172.

The journal of Elizabeth Drinker reveals the traumas that the pacifist Quakers in Philadelphia endured during the American Revolution; it also shows the closeness of the family and the inner strength of the writer. Suspected by the Pennsylvania government of having pro-British sympathies, a number of Quakers, including Elizabeth's husband Henry, a successful merchant and manufacturer, were arrested in the autumn of 1777 and taken into custody in Virginia. Mrs. Drinker's journal, the contents of which are described in detail, conveys not only her distress about her husband's welfare and her concern about the

British occupation of the city but also the traditional acts of Quaker charity toward the needy and the wounded men on both sides of the conflict. Constant pressure by Quaker lobbyists on the Pennsylvania government finally resulted in the exiles' release in April 1778, followed soon after, in June, by the British evacuation of the city. Henry's return did not end the trials of the Drinker family, however. In October 1781 mobs celebrating the victory at Yorktown decided to attack and vandalize the homes of Quakers, including the Drinkers'.

323   Rauch, Julia B. "Quakers and the Founding of the Philadelphia Society for Organizing Charitable Relief and Repressing Mendicancy." *Pennsylvania Magazine of History and Biography* 98(October 1974): 438-455.

During the decades after the Civil War, Quakers had a very strong commitment to charity. In Philadelphia, which had fewer than 5,000 Quakers in 1881--0.6 percent of the population--they supported many soup kitchens and helped organize the charities in the city along "scientific lines," part of a nationwide effort known as the charity organization society movement. The Society for Organizing Charity (SOC), founded in Philadelphia in 1879, epitomized the attitudes of the wealthy people during that era: if only the poor would work as hard as they did, they wouldn't be paupers. The prosperous Quakers viewed poverty as caused by a lack of proper moral values, not by the economic and social structures of society. Charities were reformed and eligibility requirements for relief were tightened by the SOC, in part with an attitude of antipathy to the poor. Once the SOC was formed, Quakers formed 19.8 percent of the directors and 29.4 percent of the "friendly visitors," the upper-class people who visited the poor and tried to give them a vision of a better way to live.

324   Rempel, Richard A. "British Quakers and the South African War." *Quaker History* 64(Autumn 1975): 75-95.

British Quakers were divided in their pacifism when the Boer War broke out. Though the Society of Friends was the only faith that was actively identified with the anti-war movement, some of their prominent members, such as the president of the Peace Society, supported the war. As a result, Quakers responded weakly by simply appealing for peace. War opponents who did speak out were increasingly attacked by pro-war mobs whose violence was incited by the patriotic press during the winter and spring of 1899/1900. The government did nothing to condemn the violence. After the election in October 1900, Quakers took a different approach in their opposition to the war. They began investigating and exposing the government's brutal treatment of Boers in concentration camps, particularly the deaths of children and the burning of Boer farms; the publicity they generated had a considerable impact on British public opinion. They also went to South Africa as nurses and to distribute relief supplies through a Friends South African Relief Committee. The war prompted some Quakers to recognize the immorality of imperialism.

325   Saunders, Malcolm. "Peace Dissent in the Australian Colonies: 1788-1900." *Journal of the Royal Australian Historical Society* 74(December 1988): 179-200.

British involvement in the Crimean War of 1854-56 and the Sudan expedition of 1885 prompted Australians to form groups opposed to those wars. Pacifist societies not connected to specific wars were formed in Adelaide in 1860 and Sydney in 1864, though neither endured long. In 1885 a touring Quaker gave lectures which prompted local Friends to start forming peace societies not connected with opposition to any particular war. They only lasted a short time. In 1888-89 another English Quaker spoke to large audiences promoting activist peace organizations, and once again the Australian Quakers helped found local peace societies. As before, the societies lasted only a few months to a couple of years. One positive result of these efforts was that Quakers began coming out of their isolation and making efforts to transform their own peace discussion groups into active organizations. The failure of these 19th-century groups was due to their lack of unity, a lack of Australian leadership, and the lack of interest by Australians since they had been at peace, except for their attacks on the Aborigines, since the beginning of settlements by the whites.

326   Sloan, David. "'A Time of Sifting and Winnowing': The Paxton Riots and Quaker Non-Violence in Pennsylvania." *Quaker History* 66(Spring 1977): 3-22.

When the Paxton Boys, an armed group of frontiersmen, marched on Philadelphia in 1764, over 100 Quakers, including many youths, took up arms to defend the city. Though the crisis was settled by arbitration, a large number of Friends had clearly abandoned their beliefs in nonviolence. Since Quakerism was based on faith rather than intellectualism, it could only be demonstrated to skeptics through the actions of individuals and by the consistency of group practices. Unity was especially important during times of great stress, when Quakers could demonstrate the strength of their faith and not retreat from their principles. During the two following years of soul-searching, only four of the 140 deviants who had taken up arms admitted their errors; the rest, as the concluding report said, relied on themselves rather than their God for protection, and they thereby weakened the Society in its time of danger. These protracted examinations of Quaker principles of nonviolence, while they did not result in a purging of members, did prepare the Society for its ordeals and crises a decade later when the Revolutionary War began.

327   Sowle, Patrick. "The Quaker Conscript in Confederate North Carolina." *Quaker History* 56(Autumn 1967): 90-105.

The North Carolina legislature in 1861 granted an exemption from military service for conscientious objectors, including the 2,000 Quakers in the state, but the following year the Confederate Government passed a conscription law that did not allow any exemptions. Later in the year the law was modified to permit exemptions if C.O.s hired substitutes or paid a $500 exemption tax. Quakers officially condemned the tax but indicated a spirit of understanding toward those of their members who decided to pay. Most paid; some fled or went into hiding because their consciences would not allow them to pay; about 50 openly refused to flee or compromise and were persecuted severely. The punishments and tortures they suffered--some ingenious in their inhumanity--exemplified the frustration and dislike for them by the Confederate military people. "War Quakers" who joined the church after the war started were suspected of having phony motives for their conscientious objections, and those who refused to compromise were tortured as much as the other Quakers. More of the recent converts refused to purchase exemptions than the other Friends.

328   Taylor, George Rogers. "Nantucket Oil Merchants & the American Revolution." *Massachusetts Review* 18(Autumn 1977): 581-606.

The major merchants and whaling princes of Nantucket Island during the Revolutionary War were Quakers whose neutrality may have been inspired partly by their pacifist faith; but it was especially motivated by their desire to keep and build their wealth. Three of the leaders had strong British sympathies and apparently carried on treasonous relations with England during the war. A fourth merchant supported the patriot cause. When a Loyalist fleet invaded the island in April 1779, the sailors seized most of the patriot's property, apparently in collusion with the Tory faction, though the patriot merchant was not able to prove it in a subsequent trial. At the end of the war the three Tory merchants moved their whaling operations to escape the hostility of Massachusetts: to Nova Scotia, Britain, Bermuda, and France. When war resumed between Britain and France a decade later, the whaling merchants could sail under whichever flag was convenient--just so they could maintain their neutrality and pursue their business interests. One eventually returned to New Bedford when memories of his Tory record had faded, reassembled his fleets, and further increased his fortunes.

329   Tiedemann, Joseph S. "Queens County, New York Quakers in the American Revolution: Loyalists or Neutrals?" *Historical Magazine of the Protestant Episcopal Church* 52(September 1983): 215-227.

In the New York Yearly Meeting during the American Revolution, over 90 percent of the Quakers successfully maintained their pacifist beliefs; only 6.5 percent had to be disciplined for violations such as fighting or paying military taxes. Quaker pacifism was often misunderstood by patriots, who presumed that since they wouldn't fight and since they respected established civil authority, they must be Tories. While the percentage of Quakers in Queens County who declared themselves to be neutralists in 1775 was 86.3 percent, far higher than the 60.3 percent of the whole population, the proportion who declared their sympathies for either Whigs or Tories was nearly the same as in the general population. Quakers living in towns with a lot of Friends were quite likely to declare themselves neutrals, implying that their commitment to pacifism was assisted by peer pressure. Also, in towns with higher numbers of Friends there were greater percentages of declared neutrals in the general population, implying that Quaker pacifist beliefs, when maintained by a large enough group, may have significantly influenced the values of the community at large.

330   Tolles, Frederick B. "Nonviolent Contact: The Quakers and the Indians." *Proceedings of the American Philosophical Society* 107(April 1963): 93-101.

In contrast to the violence which normally characterizes contacts between peoples of different cultures or traditions, relationships between Quakers and American Indians have been completely peaceful for 300 years. The Quakers have been motivated by love, respect, friendship, and a desire for mutual understanding. William Penn was careful to be totally fair in his dealings with the Indians, but, perhaps of even greater importance, he had a basic attitude of respect toward them. He was interested in their religious rites which, while not Christian, represented to him alternative ways of finding truths. In the 1760s John Woolman, a Quaker, traveled and lived among the Indians along the frontier in order to learn from them and perhaps to assist them in finding the truth, and thirty years later Quakers from Philadelphia Yearly Meeting started working among the Indian nations of New York and Pennsylvania to teach them settled agriculture and education. From 1869 to 1879 Quakers were appointed as superintendents, agents, and school teachers among the Indian tribes of the Great Plains; according to the author, they received friendly, warm responses from the Native Americans.

331   Tolles, Frederick B. "The New-Light Quakers of Lynn and New Bedford." *New England Quarterly* 32(September 1959): 291-319.

The spreading ferment of early 19th-century liberal ideas first caused trouble in 1816 among Lynn, Massachusetts, Quakers when some members began espousing New Light doctrines. They believed that the Inner Light was a higher principle than the Bible, and that the message of Christ was subject to possible refinement. The Quaker elders in Lynn were stymied from expelling the rebels since the rule of consensus prevented any rapid censure. Passions on both sides peaked by 1822: New Light activists forced themselves into meetings, supporters of the majority bodily carried them out. With crowds gathering to witness the spectacle of Quakers fighting, a New Light activist came to another meeting wearing a sword, as he had publicly threatened to do. The sword-bearer and his cohorts were overpowered and hauled off to prison in a scene of utter pandemonium. They were subsequently convicted in a jury trial for disturbing the peace. The ideas expounded in Lynn were brought down to New Bedford where a similar drama was played out in 1823-1824, without the theatrics but with as significant a divide in the Quaker community.

332   Tully, Alan. "King George's War and the Quakers: The Defense
       Crisis of 1732-1742 in Pennsylvania Politics." *Journal of the
       Lancaster County Historical Society* 82(Michaelmas 1978):
       174-198.

       During King George's War from 1739 through 1742, Quakers
       in the Pennsylvania Assembly and the Governor, a former army
       officer, clashed over providing military support. Since the
       Assembly would not pass a militia law, the Governor issued a
       call for volunteers. But when numerous indentured servants
       volunteered in response to the call, their masters became
       inflamed; the Quakers, supporting the property rights of the
       masters, gained popularity against a seemingly tyrannical ex-
       ecutive. While the Governor and the Assembly both appealed to
       supporters in London, hostilities between the two sides contin-
       ued to increase. The Governor harassed and vilified the Assem-
       bly in public. Supporters of the Governor and the defense party
       in Philadelphia hired a mob of sailors to intimidate and disrupt
       voters at the polling place on election day, 1742, but they were
       repeatedly driven off. Quaker leaders had anticipated trouble
       and persuaded their followers to not bring arms. Finally, the
       Governor and the Assembly began to make peaceful accommo-
       dations since both sides felt threatened and frustrated, both
       wanted to get their respective agendas moving, and both realized
       the need for compromise.

333   Tully, Alan. "Politics and Peace Testimony in Mid-Eighteenth-
       Century Pennsylvania." *Canadian Review of American Studies*
       13(Fall 1982): 159-177.

       During the early stages of the French and Indian War in 1756,
       six Quaker legislators dramatically resigned from the Pennsyl-
       vania Assembly because they were unable to compromise their
       peace principles by voting for military protection. For decades
       the issue of whether their pacifist beliefs would allow Quaker
       legislators to vote money for military activities had strained the
       unity of Pennsylvania Friends, though they did appropriate
       funds when directly ordered to by the Crown. In the absence of
       direct royal orders, they had straddled the fence and done
       nothing. Debates among Quakers in the 1740s had focused on
       pacifism versus civil defense, but had avoided the central issue
       of whether Quaker legislators should support military appro-
       priations. When the French and Indian War started on the
       western frontier of Pennsylvania, they had to deal with a direct
       military crisis and not a remote war or a potential threat by a

privateer to Philadelphia. Despite this, the Quakers still wanted to continue their participation in, and control over, the Pennsylvania legislature in order to maintain William Penn's Holy Experiment. For that end, the compromises had seemed necessary.

334   Weddle, Meredith Baldwin. "Conscience or Compromise: The Meaning of the Peace Testimony in Early New England." *Quaker History* 81(Fall 1992): 73-86.

While pacifism was an essential element of the Quaker faith from the beginning, the meaning of the term changed over time. Early Quaker peacefulness was based on obedience to Christ's message to love one another and to live with an inner spirit of purity and love toward other people; the focus of their concern was on their own souls, their own actions, their own personal obedience to God's command to not be violent. The early Quakers did not think in terms of the violent actions of others. They held a range of opinions about warfare, but for most, so long as other people were doing the fighting and they themselves were not personally involved, their consciences were clear. New England Quakers were directly involved in major conflicts. During King Philip's War the governor of Rhode Island, numerous other officials, and a number of military officers were all Quakers whose direction of the fighting was never questioned by their meetings. These attitudes began to change by the 1690s, when Quakers started questioning informally the acceptance of violence in society.

335   Wellenreuther, Hermann. "The Political Dilemma of the Quakers in Pennsylvania, 1681-1748." *Pennsylvania Magazine of History and Biography* 94(April 1970): 135-172.

The peace testimony of the Quakers in the 17th century was focused on the individual Christian's responsibility not to fight, and was closely linked to a second testimony in which government was sanctioned by God, was not necessarily bound by Christian principles, and was expected to provide protection. The Quaker founders of Pennsylvania were confronted with the contradiction that they were personally obligated to act peacefully yet they had to protect the citizenry. The political crises that the Quaker Assembly had to deal with in its relationships with a succession of governors in 1693, 1709, 1711, and the 1740s were based on the political consequences of the peace testimony, framed within a context of imperial relations and the

Assembly's striving for advantage against the executive power. Until 1739 the peace testimony was balanced against the military needs of the government; after 1740, changing conditions, notably direct threats to the colony from privateers in the Delaware River, caused the Assembly leaders to compromise their pacifist beliefs in favor of the apparent need for military protection.

336   Williams, Dorothy M. "Feathers of Peace." *Quaker History* 65(Spring 1976): 32-34.

Before the battle of Saratoga in 1777, Indian raids on the white frontier settlements in New York had prompted most settlers to flee to safer areas. One day in September, after the bulk of the whites had left, an Indian war party surrounded a Quaker meeting house which contained, at that moment, a group of Friends having their weekly meeting. When the Indians looked in and saw that the whites were unarmed, they refrained from attacking them. Since one of the members of the Indian group and one of the Quakers spoke French, the two groups were able to communicate. The Indians made it clear that when they had surrounded the meeting house they had fully intended to massacre everyone in it, but the peacefulness of the meeting convinced them to not hurt anyone. One of the Quakers invited the Indians to his house and served them bread and cheese before they quietly left. Other versions of this story have been narrated in Quaker histories, but this account, according to the author, is based on the earliest known sources.

337   Wilson, E. Raymond. "Evolution of the C.O. Provisions in the 1940 Conscription Bill." *Quaker History* 64(Spring 1975): 3-15.

A few Quaker leaders, including the author, provided leadership in lobbying for conscientious objectors when Congress was considering the reimposition of the draft in 1940. These Quakers tried to get Congress to accept the idea that the depth of a man's convictions to pacifism, his conscientious objections, should be the measure of the status he was accorded in the draft system rather than his membership in a peace church. They also advocated exemptions for men whose absolutist beliefs would not allow them to cooperate even to the point of registering. They lost on both issues. Furthermore, the Quakers wanted conscientious objectors to be placed under civilian supervision, and again they lost since the alternative service system was placed under the administration of Selective Service. As a result, the American Friends Service Committee was required to work closely with the military in running the Civilian Public Service camps, which placed them in the awkward position of compromising their ideals and working to support the system of conscription.

338   Witte, William D. S. "American Quaker Pacifism and the Peace Settlement of World War I." *Bulletin of the Friends Historical Association* 46(Autumn 1957): 84-98.

A month after the outbreak of World War I, American Friends sent President Wilson a proposal for a Parliament of Nations, an idea which they had actively studied during the war years. When Wilson returned from Paris with the text of a Covenant of a League of Nations, Quaker opinions about it were divided. Proponents asserted that it represented the best document for the times, that it was a step in the right direction, and that the defects could be modified later. One writer suggested that the League was the most significant step toward an international kingdom of God since the time of Constantine. Quaker opponents of the treaty argued that it perpetuated the evils of great power domination, it did not effectively foster disarmament, and it did not represent the people of the world. By 1920, though the majority of Friends clearly favored the League, they turned their attention to their own approaches to world order: working through love as a force for individual regeneration, and relying on Christian principles of peaceful conflict resolution as the basis for international cooperation.

339   Worrall, Arthur J. "Persecution, Politics, and War: Roger Williams, Quakers, and King Philip's War." *Quaker History* 66(Autumn 1977): 73-86.

Rhode Island residents, outraged in 1672 by controversial measures taken by the colonial government to deprive them of their civil rights, elected a faction led by Quakers. It included a Quaker governor, Nicholas Easton, and Friends in the assembly. Once in control of the government, they had to face the reality of dealing with the threat of war. Warfare broke out in 1675 when the New England Indians, led by King Philip of the Wampanoags, began attacking white frontier settlements, achieving several victories. The colonists looked for scapegoats--Indians and Quakers. During the winter of 1675/76 the Massachusetts government reversed a period of gradually improving relations with the Friends by enforcing laws against them, some of whom responded with public acts of courageous defiance. The Rhode Island Quaker government was forced to compromise their principles and provide for the defense of the colony, commission military forces, and form a committee to command a fleet which would defend Newport. The war weakened the Quaker party, however, and in May 1677 the Rhode Island voters elected the anti-Quaker faction.

340   Zuber, Richard L. "Conscientious Objectors in the Confederacy: The Quakers of North Carolina." *Quaker History* 67(Spring 1978): 1-19.

Quakers in North Carolina during the Civil War were pacifists in the heart of war, anti-slavery abolitionists surrounded by slave-owners, unionists in the midst of the confederacy. But most of them did not have serious problems enduring the situation. The state was relatively liberal in its policies, in part because Quakers had been influential citizens, and it allowed them to avoid the draft by paying a $500 tax or hiring a substitute. Quakers who had been born into their faith had few problems with the local draft enforcement officers, but people who had pacifist leanings and only joined the church when the war broke out, the so-called War Quakers, were perceived as draft dodgers and forced into the army anyway. At first many Quakers refused to pay the $500 exemption tax, though over the course of time most did pay it in order to stay out of the service. Some Quakers got in trouble for harboring drafted relatives who had deserted, as well as other deserters; harboring deserters seemed to be in line with their Christian duty of opposing war.

Rural Northern Irish

In the 17th century Protestants from Scotland began migrating to Northern Ireland, where they became land-owning farmers and the Irish natives--Roman Catholics--became their workers. Irish agitation for home rule throughout the 19th century, and Protestant resistance to the idea in Northern Ireland, prompted the British to divide the island and, in 1922, create the Irish Free State (now the Republic of Ireland). The six Protestant-dominated counties in Northern Ireland remained part of the United Kingdom. In the 1960s concern by the Catholic minority in Northern Ireland about civil discrimination led to reactions, counter-reactions, and violence by extremists on both sides. British army units were assigned to Northern Ireland in 1969, and the government of the counties was directed from London starting in 1972. Since then several conferences have tried and failed to reach political compromises; sectarian violence has continued to menace both the 846,000 city dwellers and the 690,000 rural residents.[15]

341   Buckley, Anthony D. *A Gentle People: A Study of a Peaceful Community in Ulster*. Holywood, Co. Down, Northern Ireland: Ulster Folk and Transport Museum, 1982.

The tolerance and kindness that characterize Catholic-Protestant relations in the rural Upper Tullagh area of Ulster developed because of historical and geographical circumstances: historically, the Protestants relinquished their former social superiority in favor of a more egalitarian society; and geographically, the people of both faiths live closely together, without clear sectarian boundaries. Both groups take pride in defining their community as neighborly and peaceful. The people realize that church social activities could promote sectarian feelings and divide their community, so they strive to bridge them and form non-sectarian groups. Sports for young people are organized by non-sectarian sporting associations rather than by the Protestant and Catholic schools, which eliminates any chance of sectarian sports rivalry. Catholics helped raise funds to support the marching band of the local Orange Hall, and Protestants supported the Catholic reconstruction of the grounds where a saint had lived--everyone is proud of both the band and the beautified saint's grounds. The Catholic members of the Lions Club even decided to abandon drinking at their meetings in order to attract the Protestants in the community, who would only join when it became a dry club.

342   Buckley, Anthony D. "'You Only *Live* in Your Body': Peace, Exchange and the Siege Mentality in Ulster." In *Societies at Peace: Anthropological Perspectives*, edited by Signe Howell and Roy Willis, 146-162. London: Routledge, 1989.

The residents of the rural Irish community studied by Buckley in 1975-76 are proud of the peacefulness of their village. They associate peacefulness with their rural "good neighborliness," and violence with the cities where people are, as they see it, selfish and not neighborly. In this village there are no defined sectarian boundaries, which helps prevent violence. Three-quarters of the people are Catholic, but they live as neighbors with Protestants throughout the district. The minority group doesn't threaten the majority and the majority has nothing to gain by threatening the peacefulness. While the Protestants and Catholics identify with their sides in the larger Ulster scene, in the village neither wants violence so both refrain from blaming the other. They deliberately cultivate interfaith links: they join non-sectarian clubs, the clergy have close ties, and neighbors have good exchange relationships. The people are vigilant against the aggressive acts that can start to divide a society, such as hostile graffiti, which they quickly remove. In their minds, only the presence of a housing project occupied by outsiders from the cities threatens the peace.

343   Bufwack, Mary S. *Village Without Violence: An Examination of a Northern Irish Community*. Cambridge, MA.: Schenkman, 1982.

Loyalty to groups is strong in Northern Ireland, where myriads of social groups tie people together, and personal, face-to-face, regular contact builds identity and peaceful relations much more than abstract theology does. This book describes how one village in Northern Ireland, Naghera, was able to maintain peace during the early years of sectarian violence, 1969-1973, due to the fact that many people of both Protestant and Catholic faiths had lived and worked together for generations. At the level of informal relations, cooperation was the norm: Protestants supported Catholic Church social and charitable activities, Catholics supported those in the Protestant churches. An important factor in their ability to maintain peace was that they had many community economic and social organizations which cut across religious lines and served a socially integrating function. Thus the Catholic and Protestant farmers, sheep raisers, and business people united for common economic causes, and these groups promoted other social and cultural functions as well. Furthermore, they made continuous efforts to demonstrate interfaith goodwill. They did not participate in political actions that might have alienated others in their community, and the closest they were exposed to violence was the heavy-handed investigations and unprovoked arrests by the British army.

344   McFarlane, Graham. "Violence in Rural Northern Ireland: Social Scientific Models, Folk Explanations and Local Variation (?)." In *The Anthropology of Violence*, edited by David Riches, 184-203. Oxford: Basil Blackwell, 1986.

Bufwack, Buckley, and a few other social anthropologists have found that the rural Northern Irish people feel they have to make special efforts to maintain their tranquility in the midst of the surrounding violence. This article reviews the literature about these villages and shows that the model of internal harmony and peacefulness held by the villagers is accurately reflected by the anthropologists. Numerous possible sources of data errors are examined and rejected one by one. If the anthropologists play down the violence that does occur in their study areas, they do so because the people themselves play it down. The people feel the troubles are caused by a violent minority of outsiders; they normally deny that local people from the other side of the sectarian divide could be involved. Their reactions are somewhat ambiguous, however, because when violence does occur people condemn it but they also remember previous violence which may almost justify it. Their attitude of playing down violence acts as a cultural brake on its growth, and the danger to Northern Ireland is that the rural viewpoint may disintegrate.

Rural Thai

Herbert P. Phillips based his book [346] on his research in the community of Bang Chan, located in the lowland alluvial plains of Thailand about 20 miles northeast of Bangkok. His work in that community was part of a larger research effort called the Cornell Thailand project. During the census previous to his visit, that of 1956, 1,771 people were recorded in the village. The people of the Bang Chan are Theravada Buddhists and rice farmers.

345   Hanks, Lucien M., Jr., and Herbert P. Phillips. "A Young Thai from the Countryside." In *Studying Personality Cross-Cultur-ally*, edited by Bert Kaplan, 637-656. New York: Harper & Row, 1961.

The rural Thai personality is the product of accommodation to a social system that minimizes hostility and independence; it is based on friendly, but not intimate, relationships. The authors narrate the detailed life story of a young man and discuss his lack of assertiveness, decisiveness, and strength as an illustration of the Thai social and psychological processes. The young man affiliated himself with his uncle and worked in his business in order to gain, in return, his kindness, charity and benevolence. He gave up on marrying the woman he loved because of pressure from the uncle to marry a relative of his. The rural Thai social system fosters this continuing dependence of subordinates on superiors as part of a balance against personal independence. They feel friction can increase between independent, social equals; they always strive to prevent conflict in face-to-face situations by behaving with constant good humor, politeness and affability. With both social equals and unequals, any open expression of hostility would upset the reciprocal system of mutual benefits. Hostilities can only be expressed in the most circumspect fashion.

346   Phillips, Herbert P. *Thai Peasant Personality: The Patterning of Interpersonal Behavior in the Village of Bang Chan*. Berkeley: University of California Press, 1965.

The rural Thai villagers do not tolerate direct, face-to-face aggressiveness, which they control through constant good humor, friendliness, and gentleness. Their relaxed, pleasant relationships are marked by laughter, nervous giggling, and discussions of inconsequential topics. They beat around the bush and avoid serious or embarrassing conversations in order to prevent face-to-face difficulties from arising. Awkward requests or statements may be made through intermediaries. While most families are quite placid, when disagreements do occur people will leave to avoid dissension; it is better for a family to break up than to fight. At all times they show a strong sense of respect and politeness toward other villagers, which contributes to their toleration for deviant behavior, nonconformity, and individual failures, though these behavior traits tend to dampen spontaneity and genuineness. The author concludes that interpersonal aggressiveness is very weak among the Thai villagers because everyone is extremely careful not to provoke others--it is hard to get worked up over things. Since other people will not respond to a show of anger, there is little incentive for anyone to build up displays of aggressive feelings.

347   Piker, Steven. "Perspectives on the Atomistic-Type Society: Friendship to the Death in Rural Thai Society." *Human Organization* 27(Fall 1968): 200-204.

While the rural Thai villagers generally are distrustful of the intentions of others, they have a special category of friendship called friend-until-death which is quite different. These special friendships, normally between males, involve camaraderie, sharing, and complete mutual commitment. The friends may travel together, lend money to each other, or assist in ceremonies. Even though fighting in rural Thailand is rare, the friends feel they could count on one another should an emergency situation arise. Normally the special friendships are the result of men meeting while they are in a remote location; they do not usually live near one another and they see each other infrequently. Since the villagers' daily social relationships are superficial, transient, and lacking in trust, they have a psychological need to idealize these friends-until-death; they serve as a convenient fiction, an outlet for a man's dreams of having trusting, permanent relations. If the special friends did live close by, they could have frequent interactions, their idealized relationships would soon wear thin and each would realize the other was comparable to the rest of the villagers.

San

"San" is the generally accepted, more polite term for the peoples formerly known as "Bushmen," the original inhabitants of southern Africa. Even "San," while widely used by anthropologists, is not completely acceptable--the government of Botswana uses the made-up, but respectful, word "Basarwa" to refer to the San peoples in that country. The San all speak different languages which have many sounds made by clicking the tongue--the so-called, "click languages." In 1979 the San peoples were estimated at 40,400 total: 24,400 in Botswana, 11,500 in Namibia, 4,000 in Angola, and 500 others. While many of these people were primarily hunters and gatherers 50 years ago, their livelihood has steadily changed in the second half of the 20th century. Most now are wage laborers, farmers, or pastoralists. The !Kung and G/wi and are separately covered in this bibliography, but works that deal with several San peoples are included in this section. Elizabeth Marshall Thomas' popularly written account of the Marshall family expeditions to investigate the San peoples [357] brought the San, and particularly the !Kung, widespread notice.[16]

348　　Campbell, C. "Images of War: A Problem in San Rock Art Research." *World Archaeology* 18(October 1986): 255-268.

　　　　The Southern San witnessed and were involved in many battles with other peoples since the 17th century and perhaps before. The graphic depictions of conflict found in their rock art have been interpreted as realistic, historical portrayals of actual warfare, but this interpretation is challenged by a careful examination of the internal evidence in three different supposed battle scenes. These paintings seem, instead, to suggest shamanistic purposes related to the San healing practices. Actions portrayed represent the work of the shamans--figures with blood coming out of their noses, figures which point in stylized gestures, or groups of arrows that represent "arrows of sickness." The ways certain white lines, dots, and red lines are depicted on the figures also probably represent characteristics of the ritual healing performances of medicine men. Even paintings that cannot specifically be tied to healing practices may contain elements of shamanism that are not known today. Rather than explain the rock art from a Eurocentric perspective, it would be better to interpret the paintings within the cognitive system of the San themselves.

349   Cashdan, Elizabeth. "Territoriality among Human Foragers: Ecological Models and an Application to Four Bushman Groups." *Current Anthropology* 24(February 1983): 47-66.

Ecological factors and types of territorial values among four San groups provide a test case for a theoretical discussion of human territoriality. Ecological factors which allow predictions of the abundance of natural resources are annual mean rainfall, the variability of precipitation, and the differing amounts of standing water that are available to the four groups. All four San peoples control territory through access to their social groups rather than defense of perimeters. Individuals who move in with other groups ask permission to join, and if they are not wanted the groups will exclude them without hostilities. In general, San peoples with less abundant natural resources exhibit greater territoriality: the !Ko, who have the least natural resources, are the most highly territorial, exhibit a dislike of outsiders, and show little hospitality toward strangers; the G/wi, with somewhat more resources, are less territorial and have greater mobility and friendship between bands; the !Kung are highly flexible, visit widely, and are quite hospitable toward visitors; and one anthropologist has maintained that the Nharo are the least territorial of all the San groups.

350   Guenther, Mathias G. "'Not a Bushman Thing': Witchcraft among the Bushmen and Hunter-Gatherers." *Anthropos* 87(1992): 83-107.

The Nharo San, a farming people of Botswana whose poverty and disease has produced cultural disorientation, anger, and aggression, deny that they practice witchcraft, yet they do believe in a form of it. They become ill due to *kgaba*, a Tswana word meaning "bad thoughts": feelings people have within themselves which cause hatred, anger, intense ill will, and resentment to well up, poison the bearer's breath and saliva, and make him ill. As the anger boils, swallowing the saliva serves only to make the condition worse. Symptoms consist of painful joints, chest aches, and feelings of being unwell. Sick people infect others through inadvertent witchcraft--by verbal quarrels with others which pass along the disease. Treatment consists of reconciliation by the person who passed along the infection: he chews the leaves of two different plants and spits some of the resulting saliva on the ground or in the air; he may smear some directly on the victim. During this ritual he expresses his sorrow for the illness of the victim and his own lack of any remaining anger. Witchcraft among the other San groups is reviewed.

351   Guenther, Mathias Georg. "Bushman and Hunter-Gatherer Territoriality." *Zeitschrift für Ethnologie* 106(1981): 109-120.

Eibl-Eibesfeldt, an ethologist, and Heinz, an ethnologist, have argued that hunter-gatherers, especially the San, are highly territorial and aggressive--which supports the innate aggressionist school of thought. Eibl-Eibesfeldt, after brief visits among the !Ko, noticed their territoriality, the aggressiveness in their children, and the pacifist nature of their adult culture where aggression is controlled. Yet he derided ethnologists who have described comparable conditions among the !Kung, evidently because their findings disagreed with his *a priori* judgment that humans are innately aggressive. Guenther dismisses these reasons because of shortcomings in the methodology and theory of Eibl-Eibesfeldt and Heinz: the presence of crushed bones in the paleolithic record does not necessarily indicate that early men committed homicide; the early European records of the San were biased against them; territoriality among humans is vastly different from animals. He argues that territoriality follows numerous patterns which cannot accurately be simplified, and it is not necessarily synonymous with aggression. Since the !Ko live in a more difficult environment than the !Kung, their need for specific territories differs from theirs.

352   Kent, Susan. "And Justice for All: The Development of Political Centralization among Newly Sedentary Foragers." *American Anthropologist* 91(September 1989): 703-712.

The nomadic San have been able to maintain peaceful relationships by moving away from their bands and living with others whenever hostilities seem imminent. San groups that have been sedentary for a long time--over 100 years--have been able to restrict violence by having established political leaders who arbitrate disputes. Residents at the recently settled community of Kutse were in a transition stage: they had no leaders and they had difficulty in moving to other camps. Thus they had no accepted means of resolving conflicts and were plagued by frequent, alcohol-induced fights. Asked whether they had a chief, 48 percent replied that they did not have one, 30 percent said they did, and the rest didn't know--an indication of their ambivalence toward leadership. One way they are able to resolve conflicts is by moving their camps within the community or to the periphery to be as far from sources of trouble as possible. One trouble-maker, whose hostility caused a fight witnessed by the author, resolved his problems in the traditional fashion--by moving away with his family to live with relatives elsewhere.

353   Lewis-Williams, J. D. "The Economic and Social Context of Southern San Rock Art." *Current Anthropology* 23(August 1982): 429-449.

While the /Xam people, San who lived in southern South Africa, had an egalitarian, sharing society, they did have some social tensions. Since they believed that those tensions could cause illness, curing rituals and dances were held to excise the problems as well as heal the sick. /Xam rock art paintings appear to be part of this curing/healing process, perhaps done by the healers themselves. The paintings frequently portray elands (symbols of power), the icons representing the trance dances, and lines connecting those elements together. Dying elands with blood running from their noses might be connected with a line to human figures in a dance with blood running from their noses, the human nosebleed being a part of the curing ritual of the healers. The associations and metaphors in the San rock art were thus intended to prompt viewers' awareness of the trance curing, the social-healing functions of the healers, and more broadly, the San universe, their place in it, and their cooperative social relations.

354   Liddell, Christine. "The Social Interaction and Activity Patterns of Children from Two San Groups Living as Refugees on a Namibian Military Base." *Journal of Cross-Cultural Psychology* 19(September 1988): 341-360.

The author made nearly 4,000 spot observations of children's everyday activities and social interactions at a military camp in Namibia housing two different San groups, the Sekele and the Kwengo. She found significant differences between the two ethnic groups, which might be explained by the fact that the Sekele had recently been nomadic gathering/hunting people while the Kwengo had had more varied backgrounds as pastoralists and laborers. The Sekele children were more often observed to be engaged in solitary activities or simply watching others; Kwengo children interacted more frequently with older juveniles of school age. Although the activities of male children were comparable between the two groups, there were significant differences between the females. These differences in the female children may have been due to the differing roles and expectations of women, particularly the differences in their levels of cooperation in their previous modes of living; the lack of differences in the male children may have been due to the fact that men in both cultures would have interacted with considerable cooperation, whether hunting or herding.

355   Sugawara, Kazuyoshi. "Visiting Relations and Social Interactions Between Residential Groups of the Central Kalahari San: Hunter-Gatherer Camp as a Micro-Territory." *African Study Monographs* 8(February 1988): 173-211.

By 1984, 18 camps consisting of the San and Kgalagadi people were permanently settled near the !Koi!kom bore hole in the Central Kalahari Game Reserve. A study of the visiting relationships between San residents of the different camps leads to several conclusions: among adolescents, men are more active visitors than women; females restrict their visiting to members of the same linguistic group, while males will socialize with other San ethnic groups; regular visiting is often based on the existence of kinship ties; symbiotic relationships between people with complementary skills foster visiting. Giving and receiving gifts is an important objective of some of the visiting, but the San also visit simply for the enjoyment of socializing. The nature of the approaches that visitors make to a camp and the manner of their greetings with the residents define the consciousness of people as being members of particular bands. Data on approaches and greetings also support the conclusion that the traditional egalitarian social structure of the Central-Kalahari San has persisted despite the change to a sedentary lifestyle at the bore hole.

356   Tanaka, Jiro. "Social Integration of the San Society from the Viewpoint of Sexual Relationships." *African Study Monographs* 9(January 1989): 153-165.

The Central Kalahari San have very open, flexible marriage and love relationships. They frequently divorce, remarry, and have lovers in unions referred to as *zaku* relationships. While in societies with class structures men may have plural wives to symbolize their prestige and power, polygamous San relationships have no social significance. Similarly, although divorce, remarriage, and love relationships cause constant strife to interpersonal associations in other societies, the San people control any feelings of jealousy and continue living together. For instance one man and his wife lived a few meters away from the hut of another couple, the wife of which had been married to him earlier; she had left him for another man, come back to him, then left him again for the man she currently lived with. The *zaku* relationship differs from marriage in not having co-residence, but children born of any unions are cuddled and loved by the fathers, whether the biological ones or not. Another man had six wives and 13 children; he did not appear to work any harder because of his large family.

357   Thomas, Elizabeth Marshall. *The Harmless People*. New York: Knopf, 1959.

Elizabeth Marshall Thomas accompanied her father, mother (see also Lorna Marshall's writings listed in this volume), and brother on three of the family's expeditions to southern Africa in 1951, 1952-53, and 1955. Her well-written travel book describes the Kalahari Desert environment and the San peoples with whom they lived for several months, with flashbacks to their earlier experiences. She describes how the San people much prefer to flee and hide from danger rather than to fight or defend themselves--their legendary heroes are the jackals which lie and trick rather than the lions. The San go to great lengths to avoid jealousies and quarreling, and they rarely fight since their only weapons, their arrows, are deadly poisonous. However, Thomas describes the tensions that arose in a Bushmen camp when there were numerous people and not enough food, and she recounts the story of a fight that threatened to become serious until people intervened to lessen tensions. The San share everything, which is the only way they can survive in the desert environment, and the constant sharing of objects prevents resentments from developing.

358   Van der Post, Laurens, and Jane Taylor. *Testament to the Bushmen*. Harmondsworth, England: Penguin Books, 1985.

Van der Post and Taylor describe the traditional life of the San people; written for a general audience, the book contains many excellent color photographs, a chapter describing the adaptations the San are making to modern society, and a lengthy concluding chapter by van der Post expressing his admiration for these people. Taylor makes a number of observations about the peacefulness of the San: the way they distract anger in a child by affection, the way hunters share food they bring in, and related cultural information.

359   Wiessner, Polly. "Reconsidering the Behavioral Basis for Style: A Case Study among the Kalahari San." *Journal of Anthropological Archaeology* 3(September 1984): 190-234.

Attractive headbands are made by San women from purchased beads which are carefully sewed into a variety of patterns and background designs. Important for defining personal identity and interpersonal relations, these headbands are associated with beauty, plenty, festivity, and happiness, and are worn, so they say, "when one's heart soars." A major function of the headband is as an item of exchange, to be given to another after one has enjoyed it for a few months. The ideal headband consists of a major design that wanders along a background and is reminiscent of the way someone should walk quietly back to camp through the bush. To the San the effective headband evokes the modesty of the returning hunter who quietly leaves his kill at the edge of the clearing, the discretion which characterizes correct interpersonal relations. While the San are aware of the fact that material possessions can be used to manipulate people and arouse jealousy, the headbands represent much more enduring social commitments that rise above the transitory nature of reciprocal giving and the bickering it frequently produces.

360   Woodhouse, H. C. "Inter- and Intragroup Aggression Illustrated in the Rock Paintings of South Africa." *Suid-Afrikaanse Tydskrif vir Etnologie* 10(1987): 42-48.

According to Woodhouse, Irenäus Eibl-Eibesfeldt argues that statements about the absence of aggression in hunter/gatherer peoples are inaccurate and the battle scenes of San rock art in South Africa support his contention. Out of the thousands of known scenes of rock art painted by the San in prehistoric South

Africa, about twenty depict views of aggression between humans. In ten of the scenes there is no evident reason for the fighting, which involve San fighting San, San versus Blacks, and Blacks against Blacks. The fact that seven of the scenes depict cattle raids supports Eibl-Eibesfeldt's argument that competition for territory or resources is the source of aggression.

Sanpoil

The Sanpoil is a very small Indian tribe in northwestern Washington on the Columbia River, in what is now the Colville Indian Reservation. They number today approximately 1,000 people, and speak a Salishan language. They are included in this bibliography because of the details of their peacefulness in the monograph by Verne F. Ray.[17]

361   Ray, Verne F. *The Sanpoil and Nespelem: Salishan Peoples of Northeastern Washington.* Seattle: University of Washington Press, 1933.

The elderly Sanpoil informants had no memory of their people ever having been involved in war; even their mythology did not include warfare. When raiding parties descended on their villages they would not retaliate; after one village had been destroyed, the chief's comments epitomized their pacifism: "Our children are dead and our property is destroyed. We are sad. But can we bring our children to life or restore our property by killing other people? It is better not to fight. It can do no good." Factors which helped maintain their peacefulness included raising children to value peaceful relationships and focusing the duties of the chief on ensuring harmony. Also, people had the safety valve of mobility--in case of discontent, they could leave a village and live in another, where they would be entitled to the same equality and membership in the village assembly as everyone else. The Sanpoil limited their trading activity with other Native Americans in part because they felt that trade could hinder friendly relations with neighbors, which were more important to them than modest material gains.

Saulteaux

The Saulteaux are an Ojibwa-speaking American Indian people who live on hunting, trapping, and fishing supplemented by wood cutting, gathering wild rice, and guiding. They live in the southern and eastern drainage basin of Lake Winnipeg in northwestern Ontario and eastern Manitoba.

Their total population in 1978 was nearly 19,000, of which 914 lived along the Behrens River in the area which was studied by the ethnographer A. Irving Hallowell. Their outward harmony and apparently complete peacefulness masks a great deal of inner tensions and feelings of animosity for others.[18]

362   Hallowell, A. I. "The Social Function of Anxiety in a Primitive Society." *American Sociological Review* 6(December 1941): 869-881.

Fear of diseases serves to control social deviance among the Saulteaux more effectively than fear of the state or fear of punishment. They believe that illness is a penalty for committing certain proscribed sexual behaviors and aggressive actions such as theft, insults, and ridicule. The patient, uncertain about the cause of the illness and helpless to cure it, frequently turns to a native doctor. The healer encourages a confession of the disapproved conduct so the sickness can be cured. Since the sick room is always crowded, the confession becomes a public statement which will be shared with the whole community. Thus, the sexual deviancy or hostile acts of aggression are exposed to everyone--the price of healing is the shame of self-exposure. The Saulteaux believe that secrecy is part of the problem causing the disease, and publicizing it will cure the illness. Their beliefs about diseases do not completely prevent the disapproved acts from taking place, but they discourage them. Confession not only permits the individual to recover, it also serves to warn others about the consequences of the proscribed actions.

363   Hallowell, A. Irving. "Aggression in Saulteaux Society." *Psychiatry* 3(August 1940): 395-407.

To an outside observer, the Saulteaux appear to be completely peaceful: a society characterized by harmonious interpersonal relations, patience, sharing of goods, cooperation in economic production, and self-control. Suicide, murder, and warfare are unknown, theft, insults, and verbal rebukes are rare, and open displays of anger leading to physical violence are seldom witnessed. The author has never seen children fighting and knows of only a few occasions where adult couples have fought physically. However, these characteristics are a facade which masks feelings of hostility. Aggressive impulses are disposed of by the Saulteaux through gossip, behind-the-scenes maneuvering, and particularly through sorcery and magic. Sorcery allows effective attacks: it can menace a man's livelihood, harm his children, cause illness, or even kill him without any visible changes in external social relations. Frequently the suspected perpetrator of the sorcery is someone whom the sick person believes he has offended. The Saulteaux therefore have to guard against the barest hints of hostile behavior, such as mocking another person or beating another person in a dog-team race.

364   Hallowell, A. Irving. "Fear and Anxiety as Cultural and Individual Variables in a Primitive Society." *Journal of Social Psychology* 9(February 1938): 25-47.

Fear and anxiety can be caused by cultural beliefs or by individual psychological problems. The Saulteaux, for instance, have fears that can only be understood in the context of their culture. While they do not fear wolves and bears, they exhibit fear over the harmless frogs, toads, and snakes (their only species is the garter snake) in their area. These animals are identified with the mythic monsters of the past, some of which are believed to still live. One armed party was crossing Lake Winnipeg when they saw unidentified tracks on an island--they immediately took them to be the tracks of a monster frog hopping inland so they quickly fled. They are afraid of wild animals that come toward them, since the approach itself signifies sorcery, and of human cannibals wandering about preying on the unwary. In contrast to these very real (to them) dangers, individuals may have their own fears caused by personal psychological problems that are not shared by the tribe. Psychologists need to be aware of the cultural bases of beliefs that may be misinterpreted as psychotic tendencies.

365   Katz, Philip. "Cultural Differences and the Work Ethic." In *Adolescent Psychiatry: Developmental and Clinical Studies*, edited by Sherman C. Feinstein et al., 100-112. Chicago: University of Chicago Press, 1980.

The Saulteaux, along with the Cree and the Ojibwa, approach time as something here and now. If one is visiting a friend, the visit lasts until it is over--an hour, a day, many days. They value the present and don't worry about the future. The obsessive concerns of whites with material goods and the management of time cause problems with Saulteaux adolescents who focus strongly on the activities of the present. They therefore have difficulties with adhering to the work ethic, which requires them to appear on time, daily, for their jobs. Another problem they have with Western culture is their concept of private property: everything they own is shared with other members of their group. Indians who save money or hoard their acquisitions will be called, derisively, "apples" (red skin but white inside). Also, they do not openly express anger in their culture, which presents problems for adolescents who try to hold a job in white society but can't react effectively, as the whites would expect, by showing anger to racist taunts.

366   Katz, Philip. "Saulteaux-Ojibwa Adolescents: The Adolescent Process Amidst a Clash of Cultures." *Psychiatric Journal of the University of Ottawa* 4(December 1979): 315-321.

One important way the Saulteaux differ from the predominating Canadian culture is their lack of emphasis on the ownership of personal property. They believe that an individual's possessions must be shared with everyone else on the reservation, in contrast, they feel, to the selfish attitude of the whites toward personal property. Furthermore, their view of time differs from that of the whites. While they will keep an appointment, out of respect for the other person, they believe that a visit should go on as long as it needs to--hours or days--and it ends when it ends; they live for the present without much concern for the future. They also differ from whites in their attitude toward anger, an emotion that they rarely display while sober. Drunkenness is encouraged by their society, since people, when drunk, are not considered to be themselves: they can then express anger, act violently, be selfish. Adolescent Saulteaux who grow up on the reservations have difficulties coping with the clash between these cultural values and those of the larger white society.

Semai

The Semai, who numbered about 18,500 people in 1983, are the most populous Senoi tribal group among the Orang Asli peoples of Peninsular Malaysia. The eastern Semai practice (or practiced--see introduction to the "Orang Asli" section) shifting agriculture, hunting, fishing and gathering in the mountainous stream valleys of Malaysia's Perak and Pahang states. The western Semai live closer to the lowlands and the Malays, and are more acculturated with Malay ways. Robert Dentan's slender book *The Semai: A Nonviolent People of Malaya* [370] effectively established their reputation as a highly peaceful people. His subsequent works, along with the writings of Clayton Robarchek, have amplified and confirmed the themes he set out originally in 1968. Because the Semai are frequently cited as prominent examples of "peaceful peoples," the writings on them are often cited, or disputed, by those who are discussing aspects of peacefulness and violence among peoples.[19]

367 Dentan, R. K. "If There Were No Malays, Who Would the Semai Be?" *Contributions to Asian Studies* 7(1975): 50-64.

Semai identity is derived not from their ethnic group but from the people they know as individuals and the places where they live. The individual Semai identifies most closely with parents, children, and siblings, though even the ties between parents and children can be threatened by abnormal circumstances such as drunkenness. They assume that married couples form the normal human adult pattern--even adults who are single are paired with others for important public actions such as dividing up the meat from a successful hunt. Individuals can strengthen relationships to others by using the term *har*, a word meaning "both of us": instead of addressing a person one knows fairly well with the second person singular, *har* expresses an intimacy that draws people together. Semai bands express their group identification and solidarity when they symbolically close the entrances to settlements and celebrate harvest festivals by visiting each other. They have a strong identification with the land they have traditionally lived on--the place where their grandparents and parents are buried, and where they, their children and grandchildren will be buried.

368 Dentan, R. K. "Semai Response to Mental Aberration." *Bijdragen tot de Taal-, Land- en Volkenkunde* 124(1968): 135-158.

Normal Semai adults have close family relationships, though they keep their feelings and thoughts within themselves. They try never to cause difficulties for others, to harm strangers or to make people do things contrary to their own will. If attacked they will open their arms to the attacker, hoping to shame him out of his aggressiveness, or they will flee. While they are familiar with numerous types of mental aberrations, the men who fought with the British forces during the Communist insurgency of the 1950s first experienced berserk behavior. The veterans spoke freely of their experiences, expressing astonishment that they could have acted as they did. Treatment for mental aberrations by the village medical/magical expert is rendered free of charge as part of the Semai system of reciprocity: one gets back at some point from someone else the equivalent of what one has given in the past to others. The healing takes place in a "sing," a community festival in which the healer, while in a trance, tries to draw out the evil spirit that is causing the problem.

369   Dentan, Robert K. "The Response to Intellectual Impairment among the Semai." *American Journal of Mental Deficiency* 71(March 1967): 764-766.

A basic rule among the Semai is that a person should never cause difficulties for others by nagging, getting angry, or giving unwanted orders. On the other hand, they view teasing as quite acceptable, even of the mentally handicapped, since the one doing the teasing and presumably the recipient are acting in fun only. Until recently the Semai were unable to maintain people with severe mental handicaps who could not contribute to their economy, but they have been able to care for mentally deficient people who can take directions and do simple chores. The mentally handicapped are not sought out, but neither are they excluded from groups, and their behavior is tolerated. One retarded man, for instance, accidentally killed a chicken while trying to shoo it from a house; instead of bitter recriminations because of the economic loss, the family simply accepted the incident--better behavior couldn't be expected from him. The only problem the Semai have with mental deficiency is it sometimes causes aggressive or antisocial behavior; their standards of behavior do not prompt them to isolate people with intellectual impairments as Euro-Americans do.

370   Dentan, Robert Knox. *The Semai: A Nonviolent People of Malaya.* New York: Holt, Rinehart and Winston, 1968.

The Semai have a strongly nonviolent image of themselves, with each person proclaiming himself a nonviolent person, a person who does not get angry, a person who does not hit people. They divide equally all carcasses that hunters bring in and they will share food with visitors if they have any extra to spare. They have no competitive games, and their various posturing games and wrestling never involve anyone getting hurt. An interesting feature of Semai culture is that they teach their children their nonviolent approach to social relations by inculcating in them a fear of aggression along with a fear of thunderstorms. Since the young do not see aggression in their parents, and their aggressive acts toward the parents are fended off with laughter or threats, they have nothing to imitate in order to learn aggressive ways.

371 Dentan, Robert Knox. "[Response to Knauft and Otterbein]." *Current Anthropology* 29(August-October 1988): 625-629.

Responding to an earlier article and comment, Dentan describes Semai homicides in recent decades. Semai abhorrence of violence has been noted by various observers for 100 years, who have remarked on their passivity or flight in response to threats of aggression. A few suicides have been recorded, a Semai man killed a Chinese shopkeeper over a charge of cheating and seducing his wife, and another accidentally killed a hunting companion. Another account of murder is not trustworthy. One type of homicide that may have been practiced in the past was abandoning hopelessly ill people in the forest with a modest amount of food. The lack of reliable data makes it difficult to compile an accurate statistical analysis of Semai homicide rates. However, the introduction of firearms and alcohol poses a problem for maintaining their peacefulness. While some Semai still maintain that they will die before fighting against the outsiders who are taking away their lands, others are not so committed: they feel their nonviolence cannot last forever against outside aggression and the problems produced by alcohol.

372 Paul, Robert A., Donald E. Brown and Serena Nanda. "Commentaries: Responses to Robarchek and Dentan, with Replies by R. K. Dentan." *American Anthropologist* 90(June 1988): 418-423.

All three critiques take aim at an earlier article by Robarchek and Dentan [382]. Paul argues that his earlier interpretation of the data on the Semai, criticized by Robarchek and Dentan, is still born out: that humanity is innately aggressive, and the peacefulness of the Semai does not detract from his arguments. The three authors raise a variety of issues, including the effectiveness of Dentan's translation of Semai terms, the allegedly conservative nature of biological determinism, the way Semai treat animals, and, most critically, interpretations and arguments about Dentan's original passage in his book [370] in which Semai veterans were supposedly characterized as bloodthirsty killers, an image that Robarchek and Dentan sought to put to rest. Dentan replies to all three comments.

373   Robarchek, Clayton. "Motivations and Material Causes: On the Explanation of Conflict and War." In *The Anthropology of War*, edited by Jonathan Haas, 56-76. New York: Cambridge University Press, 1990.

The Semai strategies for peacefulness are based on successful resolution of conflicts without disrupting group solidarity; on individuals looking to the group for their security and nurturance; on people believing that their needs and frustrations can be dangerous; and on villagers viewing their own community as safe, secure, and good while the outer world is viewed as unsafe, hostile, and dangerous. According to Robarchek, the Semai example shows that, while human societies are affected by environmental, biological, deterministic, and materialistic factors, the ability of people to establish their own cultural patterns through their own decision making and initiative should not be overlooked. A potential conflict among the Semai which he reviews was settled because they chose to maintain their traditionally peaceful approach to their relationships.

374   Robarchek, Clayton A. "Conflict, Emotion, and Abreaction: Resolution of Conflict among the Semai Senoi." *Ethos* 7(1979): 104-123.

The Semai resolve serious conflicts with a proceeding called a *bcaraa'*, the purpose of which is to force everyone involved to settle the dispute rather than to determine if someone is guilty. Usually the facts are already well known anyway. Gathering at dusk, the men take ample time for socializing before forming a circle and discussing the importance of group solidarity, mutual dependence, and peace. Then the principals to the case give unemotional speeches presenting their viewpoints on the dispute, continuing on and on until no one has anything additional to say and all are exhausted. The headman, who has been listening to the whole proceeding, concludes matters by lecturing the parties to the dispute on correct behavior and the importance of the unity of the people. It is made clear to all that the matter has been completely settled and no one may bring it up again. The *bcaraa'* effectively removes the emotion from the parties, reconciles them, and reintegrates the whole village. It reaffirms that the group is mutually interdependent, and that correct, peaceful behavior is essential. This article was taken from a chapter in the author's dissertation [383].

375   Robarchek, Clayton A. "Frustration, Aggression, and the
       Nonviolent Semai." *American Ethnologist* 4(1977): 762-779.
          The frustration-aggression hypothesis of some psychologists,
       which describes a linear cause-and-effect relationship, needs to
       be modified. The hypothesis is that frustration causes anger,
       which causes aggression. The author describes the various
       concepts for frustration among the Semai and shows how their
       frustrations produce fear rather than anger. Their coping re-
       sponses to conditions that might produce frustrations include
       spells, charms, exorcisms, and extreme care with interpersonal
       relations--but not anger or aggression. The Semai concept of
       pehunan, for instance, which is the frustration of having an
       unfulfilled desire for things, is avoided by generosity. The
       slightest hint that something may be wanted will prompt the
       possessor to give the desired object to the other. Both people thus
       avoid danger, since the person who wants the things may suffer
       illness or injury from *pehunan* if his desire is not satisfied, and
       the person who doesn't give up his possession may be fined if
       another suffers because of his stinginess.

376   Robarchek, Clayton A. "Helplessness, Fearfulness, and
       Peacefulness: The Emotional and Motivational Contexts of
       Semai Social Relations." *Anthropological Quarterly* 59(October
       1986): 177-183.
          Using sentence-completion tests, the author was able to gain
       information about the attitudes and values of the Semai. For
       instance, to the statement "More than anything else, (s)he is
       afraid of ...," the Semai replied "becoming embroiled in a
       dispute" more frequently than their combined expressions of
       fear for tigers, spirits, and death. This fear of alienation from the
       group is a major incentive for maintaining peaceful behavior.
       Another important value revealed by this research is that when
       stressed, the Semai seek group support rather than trying to solve
       problems alone. In completing the statement, "More than
       anything else (s)he worries about ...," they said "rejection by
       his/her spouse." This exemplifies the important Semai concept
       of spouses having loving relationships, which they express by
       their word *hoo'*. This word can be translated roughly as love,
       though the connotations of protection, nurturance, cherishing,
       and support are emphasized as well. They tend to define
       "goodness" in terms of helping and nurturance, while they

define "badness" as behavior that might harm group relations, such as quarreling, anger, and fighting.

377   Robarchek, Clayton A. "Hobbesian and Rousseauan Images of Man: Autonomy and Individualism in a Peaceful Society." In *Societies at Peace: Anthropological Perspectives*, edited by Signe Howell and Roy Willis, 31-44. London: Routledge, 1989.

The most important moral imperative to the Semai is sharing food and avoiding violence. Almost all gatherings open and close with statements about the unity of the band, the importance of their interdependence, and the fact that they always help one another. They are also constantly aware of the dangers that surround them from human, natural, and supernatural forces. Thus, mutual interdependence and danger are the two major themes of the Semai world--the individual's source of security is the band. Their social structure includes a clear, but not rigid, division of labor between the sexes: there are no separate ideals for women versus men, no tasks that are strictly for one or the other. Semai individuals are extremely reluctant to yield their individual autonomy in favor of any kind of group action. Children can be told to do things, but if they refuse the matter ends there. A bridge used daily by almost every member of the band can fall into disrepair and near collapse, but everyone hates to give up precious autonomy in a collective effort to repair it.

378   Robarchek, Clayton A. "Learning to Fear: A Case Study of Emotional Conditioning." *American Ethnologist* 6(August 1979): 555-567.

The Semai show no tolerance for interpersonal violence, little affective involvement with others, and low levels of emotion except for fear. They teach their children from the time of infancy to fear violent tropical thunderstorms, which represent the anger of Ngku, the thunder spirit, who may summon his wife Nanggaa, a horned dragon living under the earth, to come up and bury the villages in landslides. As a storm approaches, the climate of fear and pandemonium grows rapidly: adults run about shouting to Ngku that they're not guilty and pounding the ground to drive Nanggaa back where she belongs. They clip pieces of their children's hair and burn them to appease the spirit. The *terlaid*, the behavior that provoked the storm, may have consisted of someone offending an animal such as a butterfly or a dragonfly--children of Ngku--by making fun of it. Parents also impart to infants their fears of strangers, who might be bogeymen that cut off people's heads. They place no cultural value on bravery. Their cultural beliefs define proper adult behavior as fearfulness, a desirable emotional condition.

379   Robarchek, Clayton A. "Primitive Warfare and the Ratomorphic Image of Mankind." *American Anthropologist* 91(December 1989): 903-920.

The ratomorphic view of mankind is the author's term for the behavioral theory that human beings deal with stimuli entirely in ratlike, mechanistic, or environmentally determined fashions. He argues, to the contrary, that humans respond to situations by making choices based on appraisals which are formed within the context of their systems of beliefs and values--their culture. He demonstrates his argument by describing the security the Semai derive from group cohesiveness, their trust for one another, their mutual dependency and nurturing behavior. He describes a *becharaa'*, an assembly they convened to resolve a serious conflict prompted by a man who had infringed on other peoples' property. At the conclusion of the assembly it seemed more important to keep group harmony than to treat the guilty party too roughly, so the *becharaa'* ended with simple admonishments to everyone not to infringe on the lands of others. To Robarchek this is an example of a group choosing to avoid violence, even though the offense committed was serious, and to reaffirm their traditional values of mutual support and unity.

380   Robarchek, Clayton A. "The Image of Nonviolence: World View of the Semai Senoi." *Federation Museums Journal* 25(1981): 103-117.

Semai responses to sentence completion tests showed that goodness and badness in people are not conceived in directly opposite ways. They think of goodness as positive nurturing behavior--helping, giving, loving, making friends--while they define badness in terms of negative affiliating behaviors--slander, gossip, ignoring advice, fighting, hitting, and stealing. These Semai values are not only cultural ideals, they are felt to be meaningful guides for individual actions which are true without question, and they are adhered to for the most part. They are accepted as important because they fit in with individual daily goals, fears, needs and wants. The Semai accept the belief that nurturance for the individual lies in the security of the band, so positive affiliation with the group is not particularly seen as a virtue--it simply makes good personal sense. Conversely, negative affiliative behavior attacks the security of the band as well as the individual. Their self-image as people who are peaceful, affiliative, dependent and nurturant does not allow aggression.

381   Robarchek, Clayton A. and Carole J. Robarchek. "Cultures of War and Peace: A Comparative Study of Waorani and Semai." In *Aggression and Peacefulness in Humans and Other Primates*, edited by James Silverberg and J. Patrick Gray, 189-213. New York: Oxford, 1992.

Until recently the Waorani of eastern Ecuador had one of the earth's most violent human societies, with a homicide rate of 60 percent. People were constantly at war and killing one another, including their own parents. The Semai, by contrast, have one of the world's most peaceful societies, with virtually no recorded violence. The authors have spent years living in both communities studying their similarities and differences in an effort to understand human peace and war. The natural environmental conditions and some of the social organizations in both societies are remarkably similar; the major difference between the two peoples is in their worldviews. The Semai see themselves as helplessly surrounded by hostile forces, both natural and supernatural, and they proceed cautiously with all their daily activities in the face of ubiquitous dangers. The Waorani realize there is danger from attacks but they are not at all terrified by the surrounding forests, which they enter alone and with confidence. The Semai see their security only in the sharing, peace and protection of their villages; the Waorani expect to be highly independent and self-reliant.

382   Robarchek, Clayton A. and Robert Knox Dentan. "Blood Drunkenness and the Bloodthirsty Semai: Unmaking Another Anthropological Myth." *American Anthropologist* 89(June 1987): 356-365.

Both authors, who have lived among the Semai more than two years each, agree that they are essentially peaceful peoples who have developed a culture that emphasizes social harmony. Dentan's book on the Semai [370], however, mentions incidents when those people were enlisted in the Malaysian armed forces fighting against a communist insurgency. They became efficient fighters, and Dentan's quote of one Semai veteran makes him sound like a bloodthirsty killer. This brief passage has been quoted widely by proponents of the view that violence and aggression are innate in human beings, and even anthropology texts have misunderstood the passage. In this article the authors explain fully the Semai veteran's comments, show how his remarks have been misunderstood by others, and discuss the fallacies of arguments by the proponents of *a priori* universal human aggressiveness--at least when those arguments are based on the Semai.

383   Robarchek, Clayton Allen. "Semai Nonviolence: A Systems Approach to Understanding." Riverside, CA: PhD Dissertation, University of California, Riverside, 1977.

Robarchek seeks to explain the social and psychological conditions that foster the nonviolent, peaceful lifestyle of the Semai people. He describes the conditions that produce their peaceful society: their personality structures, their views of themselves and their environment, their social life, their economic behavior, their religion and beliefs. After describing the physical environment, society and culture of the Semai, the author provides a detailed psychological analysis of the frustration-aggression hypothesis of human aggression and the light that the Semai case throws on it. He analyses how Semai children learn to fear strong emotion of any kind, especially anger, by being taught fears of storms and strangers. Robarchek describes the Semai method of child rearing, in which children are nurtured in a totally supportive environment for the first couple years of their lives, but then are forced to shift their dependency relationships more broadly to the village as a whole. Finally, he describes the Semai method for resolving conflicts via a judicial proceeding called a *bcaraa'*. The chapter on the *bcaraa'* appeared separately as an article [374].

Tahitians

The Tahitians, the 160,000 people who live in the Society Islands of the South Pacific, are part of French Polynesia. Politically they are citizens of France who elect a territorial assembly and representatives to the National Assembly in Paris. In the small villages people raise a variety of foods in gardens, keep animals, and fish in the lagoons. Increasingly they are raising crops for the market and buying their supplies, including their food. The capital of the Society Islands, Papeete, is on the island of Tahiti, and it is the urban center for territorial commerce, politics, tourism and communications.[20]

384   Levy, Robert I. "On Getting Angry in the Society Islands." In
       Mental Health Research in Asia and the Pacific, edited by
       William Caudill and Tsung-Yi Lin, 358-380. Honolulu: East-
       West Center Press, 1969.

       Most of the early accounts by European visitors to the Society
       Islands emphasized the peacefulness and pleasantness of the
       inhabitants, whom they said were rarely hostile, bad tempered,
       or vengeful. Crime in the Society Islands is comparatively rare--
       one island with over 3,000 inhabitants has had only two murders
       in the 20th century. The author witnessed very few physical
       fights in his village, and the ones that he did see were not violent.
       Play among children lacked noticeable fighting, and play activ-
       ity among children of the same sex included a lot of joking and
       mock aggression such as pushing, but it never became serious.
       The head teacher in two years had never seen a fight among the
       older children before, during, or after school. Tahitians do
       express hostile feelings through teasing, withdrawal, gossip,
       and, when an audience of bystanders is present, through care-
       fully controlled dramatic events that don't harm anyone. For
       instance, a man who was furious at his wife dramatically set fire
       to a pile of coconut thatching--located at a safe distance from
       their house and other buildings.

385   Levy, Robert I. "On the Nature and Functions of the Emotions:
       An Anthropological Perspective." *Social Science Information*
       21(1982): 511-528.

       The Tahitians have a number of words for some emotion
       concepts such as anger, while for others such as sadness they
       have very few words to express different meanings. Both types
       represent ways of controlling emotions--through knowing about
       them in excessive detail, or through having very little knowl-
       edge of them. While the concept of anger carries implications of
       frustration and offense to the Tahitians, the feeling of sadness
       has no external, social implications of cause. Feelings of sadness
       are expressed through physical conditions: they will say they
       feel fatigued or heavy instead. They link emotions such as fear
       and anger to the intestines, where they feel the sensations these
       emotions produce; feelings such as sadness are linked to prob-
       lems the individual has with the social environment. Tahitians
       depend on a strong emotion of enthusiasm for generating the
       energy and drive to achieve their projects. The author examines
       the nature of emotions based, in part, on these emotion concepts.

386   Levy, Robert I. "Tahitian Gentleness and Redundant Controls."
        In *Learning Non-Aggression: The Experience of Non-Literate
        Societies*, edited by Ashley Montagu, 222-235. New York:
        Oxford University Press, 1978.

        Tahitian gentleness, self-control, and lack of hostility are
        produced in part by several elements in their natural and cultural
        environments which reduce and diffuse frustrations. For in-
        stance, Tahitians believe that they have no control over nature
        or the behavior of other people. Their children are socialized by
        a large network of people rather than solely by the parents, which
        conveys the sense that social controls are caused by the whole
        community: children are powerless to rebel, subvert, or evade
        the social strictures against aggression or disturbances. While
        small children are permitted, even encouraged, to display
        aggressiveness briefly, they are discouraged from any lengthy
        displays of hostility. Tahitians feel that hostile feelings should
        be brought out into the open verbally since, if they explode into
        too much anger, that can provoke the spirits of the ancestors to
        retaliate, perhaps even kill, the angry individual. They have
        many words expressing nuances of aggression and very clear
        doctrines against it.

387   Levy, Robert I. *Tahitians: Mind and Experience in the Society
        Islands.* Chicago: University of Chicago Press, 1973.

        Tahitians are gentle people who rarely show anger, conflict,
        open hostility, or aggression. In Tahitian culture, babies up to
        age three are adored and held at the center of attention, but from
        then on an unsystematic training takes place. While a child's
        irritable behavior may be ignored, the major control technique
        is negative--threatening, gentle punishment, or shaming. Levy
        describes the Tahitians as generally disinclined to inflate their
        own individual importance--to instead deflate themselves and
        be humble. Control of anger is another important aspect of
        Tahitian peacefulness. The Tahitian language has many de-
        scriptive words for anger, which is viewed as dangerous to their
        society, but the Tahitians feel that if they hold their anger in that
        can be bad also. They feel it is best to resolve anger by coping
        with it through a number of avoidance strategies, which Levy
        describes. Since Tahitians are not personally ambitious, their
        lack of striving minimizes social situations that produce anger.

388   Thomas, David R. "Authoritarianism, Child-Rearing Practices and Ethnocentrism in Seven Pacific Islands Groups." *International Journal of Psychology* 10(1975): 235-246.

Interviews were conducted in seven different South Pacific societies with 198 mothers of young children, 18 of whom were Tahitians, in an attempt to understand the cultural variations of authoritarianism used in child rearing and how those various patterns relate to other social factors. Out of the seven cultures, Tahiti and Samoa emerged as strongly identifiable with an authoritarian pattern of child rearing, while the Cook Islanders were also classed as authoritarian but less consistently. Mothers in the other cultures were rated differently: traditional, punitive, non-permissive of aggression, and having low levels of interaction with their children. Among Tahitian and Samoan mothers, their authoritarian parenting included prohibiting aggression toward family members though not necessarily toward people outside the family, repression of children's sexual expressions, and a strict, punitive attitude. Authoritarianism appears to have a positive correlation to ethnocentric attitudes as well.

Tanka

"Tanka" is the somewhat pejorative Chinese term for the Cantonese-speaking sea fishermen of the South China coast and their families--though these people do use the term at times to refer to themselves. The Tanka may number over two million people along the coast of Guang-dong province with about 150,000 in Hong Kong. Barbara Ward (who uses the term "Tanka" in one of her articles, but in another indicates it is a pejorative term) writes about her research in the fishing village of Kau Sai--1963 population of 600--located on an island in the eastern part of Hong Kong. Although a few of the families lived on shore when she was there, most lived on their fishing boats; at the time of her writing, however, the fishermen were increasingly establishing homes for the women and children on shore so only working men would be on the boats.

389   Ward, Barbara E. "A Hong Kong Fishing Village." *Journal of Oriental Studies* 1(January 1954): 195-214.

Kau Sai is known for its honesty, peacefulness, and successful festivals--concerns of the whole village--but the social organization is quite loose. There is no recognized chief; the boat owners have complete equality and it is never possible to say who is in charge. Important matters are decided in meetings of the fishermen, and while a small number of men are clearly the leaders in terms of seniority, they may or may not take the lead in discussions. When the community prepares for its annual village festival, the people cast lots to see who will direct the proceedings: they let the god decide. This anarchism does not prepare the villagers to deal with situations involving outside government agencies or problems with land dwellers outside their community. They are normally at a disadvantage in these situations since they have little education, no organization, and a lack of self-confidence when they are away from of their element, the sea. They admit to being scared of trouble, which they define as any kind of altercation, but particularly interactions with authorities.

390   Ward, Barbara E. "Temper Tantrums in Kau Sai: Some Speculations upon their Effects." In *Socialization: The Approach from Social Anthropology*, edited by Philip Meyer, 109-125. A.S.A. Monographs 8. London: Tavistock, 1970.

Quarrels and aggression are quite rare in Kau Sai, a small, anarchistic fishing village in Hong Kong. Villagers avoid leadership roles, disapprove of any kind of verbal aggression, and feel they can gain influence and a reputation by retreating from scenes of contention. Controls against aggression, which are mostly internal, are learned in childhood through direct teaching, through being restrained whenever aggressive tendencies showed up, and especially through the failure of aggressive temper tantrums. Children between the ages of five and ten, particularly boys, go into violent temper tantrums in public because of frustrations based, in part, on the fact that Chinese adults have the habit of prodding or disturbing them to get their attention. If a small child under two and one-half is disturbed enough to cry, he or she will be comforted and nursed in response. But if adults disturb older children by messing up their games and they fly into temper tantrums, no one interferes. These lessons teach children to live peacefully with frustrations.

391   Ward, Barbara E. *Through Other Eyes: Essays in Understanding "Conscious Models"--Mostly in Hong Kong*. Hong Kong: Chinese University Press, 1985.

Twelve essays by Ward on the Chinese of Hong Kong and Southeast Asia, including the three listed separately in this section.

392   Ward, Barbara E. "Varieties of the Conscious Model: The Fishermen of South China." In *The Relevance of Models for*

Social Anthropology, 113-137. A.S.A. Monographs 1. New York: Frederick A. Praeger, 1965.

Basing her arguments on research in Kau Sai, the author modifies Levi-Strauss's "conscious model" viewpoint of the way people view their societies. She proposes three distinct models which the Chinese may have of their village social structures: the "immediate model," the social organization of their own community; the "ideological model," an idealized-Chinese-village model which is based on the influence of the traditional literati; and the "internal observers' models," the view that people have of other groups within their culture. Kau Sai has few of the expected features of the traditional Chinese village, since it has a multiplicity of families in a multi-surname community, no educated literati, no personal leadership, equality of all heads of families, no ancestor worship, no ancestral hall, and no land ownership. Although the environmental conditions in which they live--whole families living together on their fishing boats--may help produce their closely knit family structures, in their ideological model they also identify their social patterns as being a result of the fact that they are Chinese.

Temiar

Approximately 11,000 Temiar, after the Semai the next largest group of Senoi, live in Perak and Kelantan states of Peninsular Malaysia. Traditionally swidden farmers, they lived in longhouses and cultivated hill rice and tapioca as their staple crops. These were supplemented by hunting, fishing, and gathering. Their well-defined territories are high in the forested mountains of the Malay peninsula. For recent information, see the introduction to the section on the Orang Asli.

393   Roseman, Marina. "Head, Heart, Odor, and Shadow: The Structure of the Self, the Emotional World, and Ritual Performance among Senoi Temiar." *Ethos* 18(September 1990): 227-250.

The Temiars have a sociocentric society that is particularly close to the earth. Just as humans have souls in their heads and hearts, so mountains have souls in their crests and caves, and trees have souls in their leaves and roots. These souls can detach themselves from their normal places and intermingle during dreams and trance dances, though it is dangerous for the head soul to be frightened into leaving by abrupt noises or expressions of anger. Temiar rules of etiquette, social restraint, and emotional control are designed to prevent anger, physical violence, and soul loss from happening. When interpersonal problems occur, people may ask older relatives to mediate. If that fails, they will talk loudly from their own cubicles at night, describing the problems indirectly and only referring to the other individuals in the third person. When anger is stored up, it remains in the heart soul, so this kind of harangue cleans it out. Temiar performances of trance dances with their pulsing music foster healing, an intimacy with the spirits, and a reaffirmation of community ties and the uniqueness of the individuals.

394   Roseman, Marina. "The Pragmatics of Aesthetics: The Performance of Healing among the Senoi Temiar." *Social Science and Medicine* 27(1988): 811-818.

Temiars believe that the spirits of individuals, when they have been lost, captured, or transformed into an illness, can be found and restored by the powers of river, mountain or tree spirits. During healing rituals the healer sings to make contact with the appropriate natural spirit, which guides him into finding the source of the illness. The song is the emerging head soul of the singer; it points the way through the environment, links the Temiars to the land and forest, connects them with the natural spirits and restores the dislocation of the individual with the environment which has caused the illness. Bamboo-tube percussion accompanies the singing, producing pulsing sounds that imitate the calls of birds and insects, such as the barbet and the cicada. It simulates the beating of the human heart, which intensifies the feeling of longing and helps to entice the spirits to join the ceremony. The swaying dancers are associated with the wind in the foliage and the spirits of the forest. The aesthetic elements of the ceremonies are an essential link between healing spirits, humans and the natural environment.

Toraja

There are about 350,000 Toraja living in the mountains of South Sulawesi in Indonesia. They are a settled, farming people who cultivate rice, cassava, and vegetables. Though most Toraja have been converted to Christianity, enough traditional festivals, such as their funeral rites, have been retained that their communities represent important tourist destinations. The ideas of tranquility, balance, and grace which are very important on Bali are also significant among the Toraja. Several anthro-

pologists comment on the association of "coolness" with constraint and
order, and "heat" with disorder, and they discuss the unique ways the
Toraja cool their anger and hostilities.

395   Hollan, Douglas. "Emotion Work and the Value of Emotional
Equanimity among the Toraja." *Ethnology: An International
Journal of Cultural and Social Anthropology* 31 (January 1992):
45-56.

The Toraja avoid intense, dangerous emotions which might
violate acceptable behavior patterns, lead to serious physical
disorders, and disturb society; they actively try to dissipate those
feelings whenever they occur in their daily lives. For instance,
individuals experiencing heated emotions such as anger remind
themselves of the dangers of any open expressions of hostility.
Furthermore, they suppress troubling feelings or thoughts, an
approach used in one village when some boys accidentally
started a disastrous fire--the boys were not criticized or punished
since that would not replace the lost property and would only
lead to more trouble and illness for the community. Also, they
deal with some problems by reminding themselves that the gods
will compensate them for their undeserved deprivations, and
they handle others by denying that they exist. The Toraja help
other people maintain their composure through polite, respectful, conflict-avoiding skills--leaving immediately when someone seems to be heating up, or avoiding eye contact. People will
also actively try to foster reconciliation whenever they learn of
any conflict, since a rift will ruin a village.

396   Hollan, Douglas. "Indignant Suicide in the Pacific: An Example
from the Toraja Highlands of Indonesia." *Culture, Medicine
and Psychiatry* 14(September 1990): 365-379.

Since the Toraja believe that it is important to remain free of
competition and to minimize frustration, the desires of their
infants are quickly met and the needs of teenagers are usually
supported. While the latter are expected to curb their desires,
they do so because they wish to, not because of a sense of
compulsion. The Toraja value exchanges and gift giving--the
give and take of human relationships--particularly within
households where no direct, immediate returns are implied and
the relationships symbolize the concern and love among family
members. However, implicit in their reciprocal family relationships is the feeling that one must be supported by one's family
when it is really necessary. When teenagers feel slighted about

major issues, such as financial support for pursuing an education, they may respond emotionally through feelings of disappointment and hurt, and through withdrawal behavior. Normally such behavior fosters family reactions of understanding and attempts to find solutions. If family responses are too slow or insufficient, the teenagers may interpret the results as indifference and express their humiliation, anger and disappointment through attempted suicide.

397   Hollan, Douglas. "Staying 'Cool' in Toraja: Informal Strategies for the Management of Anger and Hostility in a Nonviolent Society." *Ethos* 16(March 1988): 52-72.

    This article focuses on the rational, conscious strategies used by the Toraja to control anger, which they fear since it disrupts social harmony and threatens the basis of their well-being. They view anger as shameful and improper in almost all circumstances, and they fear retribution from their ancestors and spirits if they do not remain "cool." Their strategies for avoiding and mitigating anger include: correct manners which help reduce tension-producing situations; avoidance of frustrations and desires; accepting the wealth or poverty they have with resignation; avoiding thinking about frustrations, desires, and interpersonal problems if they possibly can; and, if all else fails, trying very hard to contain feelings of anger if they do well up, since they are so dangerous and discouraged by society. When anger does occur, other people help the angry individual cool it. The author points out that the Toraja style of suppressing anger produces problems for them since they also place high value on prestige, achievement, and social status.

398   Hollan, Douglas. "The Personal Use of Dream Beliefs in the Toraja Highlands." *Ethos* 17(June 1989): 166-186.

    The Toraja take pride in their reciprocal, interdependent relationships; they highly value their custom of giving to one another, to the gods, the spirits, and departed ancestors. Yet one prominent Toraja man admitted privately, what he could not say publicly, that he had feelings of being exploited by his relatives and he resented the insinuations by others about his patronage. The dreams which he relayed to the author revealed his anxieties about his obligations to his relatives, his fear of being victimized and preyed upon by them, and the hostile relationship he had had with his deceased father. The Toraja believe that these expressions of hostility in dreams can be interpreted in a benign fashion. Their system of dream beliefs reassures the dreamer that violent dream images are not really dangerous. These beliefs encourage the dreamer to express, in dreams, feelings and fears which are contrary to the cultural values of peacefulness. They thus can cope successfully with the threatening images of the dreams and thereby are reassured about continued success in the human and supernatural environments.

399   Volkman, Toby Alice. *Feasts of Honor: Ritual and Change in the Toraja Highlands*. Urbana: University of Illinois Press, 1985.

The Toraja class system, which included nobility, common people, and slaves, has been changing during the 20th century, and with it the social relationships and rituals that express those relations have been changing as well. The focus of this book is on the continuity and changes in Toraja funerals, the major rituals of their society. During funerals, many buffalos and pigs are slaughtered and the meat divided in a process which lacks fixed rules of division. Apportioning the meat is a process that casts and recasts social relationships. People calculate how much meat they feel they should have received due to their relationships to the family of the deceased, and individuals are often flattered, or offended, by receiving what they feel is a generous--or a too-skimpy--amount. Occasionally they react to the insult of not receiving enough by showing open anger, making a scene, or even throwing some meat. Most of the time they contain and suppress their anger until some time at a future funeral they can get even with meager meat portions as a return insult.

400   Volkman, Toby Alice. "Great Performances: Toraja Cultural Identity in the 1970s." *American Ethnologist* 11(1984): 152-169.

Ritualized exchanges among the Toraja, especially at funeral ceremonies, serve to identify the place of individuals in society and to provide cultural and political links among scattered communities. Traditionally, status and social relationships determined what kinds of functions people could perform at these ceremonies and which cuts of meat they would receive when animals were sacrificed. Gifts were distributed in response to debts stretching back for generations, and these presents would weave new levels of obligations. The Toraja word *siri*--or honor, status, dignity--implies the obligation to repay gifts and create new obligations; to not do so was to incur shame, and a shamed person was no longer part of the ritual community. This sharing was ultimately based on the fundamental need for people to share food. The gift-exchange system has changed significantly in the past several decades because of tourism and the influx of money due to the employment of Toraja in outside jobs, but they are trying to hold on to their traditional values in the face of these pressures.

401   Wellenkamp, Jane C. "Fallen Leaves: Death and Grieving in Toraja." In *Coping with the Final Tragedy: Cultural Variation in Dying and Grieving*, edited by David R. Counts and Dorothy A. Counts, 113-134. Amityville, NY: Baywood, 1991.

Toraja believe that most deaths occur naturally because the person's predetermined time has come, though they also feel that some people die prematurely. Death is hastened when people live improperly or constantly become angry, and conversely people who act properly are likely to have a long life. Since intense emotional expressions can be very harmful to one's health, most grief is expressed in a controlled fashion. Immediately after the death and during the funeral, however, relatives and others who are not even close to the deceased will wail loudly, a mixture of crying, sobbing, and calling out to the deceased. Viewing the body of the dead person is a very important aspect of the mourning process for the relatives. Normally, close relatives do not feel anger about the death, though they may feel dizzy and confused. After survivors deal with their loss through the prescribed styles of grieving and wailing, they focus on their continuing relationship with the dead person's soul, which provides blessings and protection to them.

402   Wellenkamp, Jane C. "Notions of Grief and Catharsis among the Toraja." *American Ethnologist* 15(1988): 486-500.

The Toraja normally control their negative emotions, such as grief or aggression, quite carefully, fearing that if any are expressed openly they may produce a heat that will harm their health. Their word *masakke* signifies not only "cool" or "cold," but also "healthy," "safe," "content," and "blessed." For instance, when people move far away they will express their sadness but will maintain outward composure during the parting. There are a few occasions, however, when they are expected to express their emotions strongly, such as wailing during funerals, acting aggressively at kickfights held during the sowing of rice, and behaving violently while possessed during some of the rituals. All of these strong expressions of emotion are forms of catharsis: the Toraja feel that showing grief at funerals is healthy for the survivors, and the aggressive, violent behavior during kickfights and festivals is beneficial. The heat of these passions is expressed in a regulated, limited way, so that Toraja society can remain free of them the rest of the year, they believe.

403   Wellenkamp, Jane C. "Order and Disorder in Toraja Thought and Ritual." *Ethnology: An International Journal of Cultural and Social Anthropology* 27(1988): 311-326.

The Toraja world is totally ordered. They have, at all times, an accurate sense of direction, timing, orientation, detail, placement and social status. They never allow their smoke-ascending rituals, involving heat, disorder, and strife, to be mixed with the smoke-descending rituals, which entail coolness, calmness and death; even the anthropologist was instructed to keep notes on them in two separate notebooks. This sense of order is accentuated in their daily maintenance of calmness, personal stability, and smooth social relations. They avoid situations that might be upsetting: people will walk away from others when they become angry to preclude a quarrel. When Toraja do find themselves in upsetting circumstances, they will often feel confused, dizzy, and faint. Although coolness and order are most highly valued, they accept the need for occasions of disorder, passion and heat. For instance, during the *ma'maro* festivals participants become quite physically wild, and at the beginning of the rice sowing, kickfights will be held in which boys and men will team up to fight in unstructured melees.

Tristan Islanders

The small, South Atlantic island of Tristan da Cunha was settled in the early 19th century by European and American sailors and whalers who were joined by some women of partial African or Southeast Asian descent. The traditions of equality, autonomy, and interpersonal peacefulness that were established on the British colony over 150 years ago have persisted among them. As of December 1990 there were 299 Tristan Islanders, with 10 expatriates also living on the island. The economy of the Tristan Islanders was traditionally based on their sheep and cattle, garden produce, and trade with occasional passing vessels. A fishing industry was established on the island after World War II, which introduced the wage economy and attendant problems of social disruptions. When a volcano erupted on the island in October 1961 the people were all evacuated to England for nearly two years until they pressured the colonial authorities to allow them to return. During their two-year enforced sojourn in England, several scholars who had not visited the island in person were able to investigate the psychological and social makeup of the islanders.[21]

404 Keir, Gertrude. "The Psychological Assessment of the Children from the Island of Tristan da Cunha." In *Stephanos: Studies in Psychology Presented to Cyril Burt*, edited by Charlotte Banks and P. L. Broadhurst, 129-172. New York: Barnes and Noble, 1966.

When the Tristan Islanders were forced to move to Britain in 1961, they had virtually no knowledge of competition and were quite unprepared to adjust to a highly competitive society. The 40 island children who were placed in British schools were evaluated and tested to ascertain their intelligence, attitudes, personalities, and levels of educational achievement. They were rated by their teachers as being extremely low in aggressiveness, nearly as low in curiosity, with independence and competitiveness quite low as well. The only characteristic on which the teachers rated them fairly highly was in gregariousness, due not to their interacting with the British children but to their seeking the security of each other's company. A similar evaluation the second year suggests that the children were growing more curious, more independent, and, not surprisingly, more aggressive than they had been the first year. The island children had a difficult time adjusting to the large classes, they were generally very passive, and they were very shy and silent at first, a product of the taciturn culture of the adult islanders.

405 Loudon, J. B. "Private Stress and Public Ritual." *Journal of Psychosomatic Research* 10(1966): 101-108.

A Norwegian scientific expedition to Tristan da Cunha from 1937 to 1939 reported an outbreak of hysteria which affected 21 islanders. Nineteen of those people were still living in the early 1960s, twelve of whom complained of frequent headaches caused by anxiety or worry--far higher percentages of headaches than the rest of the population of islanders. A high proportion of the sufferers of the hysteria in the late 1930s and the headaches of the 1960s were the wives of the leading men of the island.

Despite the egalitarian society, these perceived leaders were the heads of households, coxswains of the boats, holders of the best jobs in the cannery, or elected members of the island council. The author concludes that among the Tristan Islanders the worry/anxiety headaches constitute an accepted form of behavior for the women who feel stresses caused by latent conflicts between the values of their homogeneous society and the leadership positions of their husbands.

406   Loudon, J. B. "Teasing and Socialization on Tristan da Cunha." In *Socialization: The Approach from Social Anthropology*, edited by Philip Mayer, 193-332. A.S.A. Monographs 8. London: Tavistock, 1970.

The Tristan Islanders think of themselves as "one big happy family." They take pride in their equality, lack of crime or strife, and their concept of "fair shares," their approach to fair relationships among people. While they constantly gossip about one another, they avoid any open appearances of conflict. Teasing, a form of aggression that masquerades as friendliness, is an important part of the socializing process--a subtle means for asserting community moral values and social control. Children are teased a lot by adults who firmly believe that they will learn patience and self-control from it. Since children are taught that lack of self-control is naughty, they are usually quiet, well mannered, and respectful of their elders, who do not hesitate to use corporal punishment if they feel it is needed. Adults tease one another a lot, both in public and in the domestic setting. Aggressive ridicule, crudeness, and strong sexual innuendos, elements of public teasing, would not be included as much in domestic teasing, which might touch on topics too sensitive for public consumption, such as racial inheritance.

407   Munch, Peter A. "Anarchy and *Anomie* in an Atomistic Community." *Man* n.s. 9(June 1974): 243-261.

After a lengthy explanation of the uses and varying interpretations of the word *anomie*--lack of norms--this article discusses the changes in the Tristan Islanders' feeling of *anomie* and their sense of value for the anarchy they have had over the past 150 years. It describes the lack of crime and the peacefulness of the previous century and then focuses particularly on the period from 1961 to 1975: the way the islanders formed a leadership structure when their community ties were threatened by the forced move to Britain in 1961; how they reverted to their traditional anarchy and *anomie* after they returned to Tristan in 1963; and how the traditional values are slowly changing under the influence of the money economy, present on the island in the form of a fish factory owned by outside interests.

408   Munch, Peter A. *Crisis in Utopia: The Ordeal of Tristan da Cunha*. New York: Crowell, 1971.

The Tristan Islanders share beliefs in the importance of their freedom, personal independence, peacefulness, courage, kindness, and generosity. They coordinate activities as precise and demanding as handling their longboats in the pounding surf with unspoken cooperation; when the helmsman does need to give directions, he speaks in a soft, humble, and dignified manner, quietly suggesting that another boatman might want to do something which might change their course a little. In 1937-1938, the author was treated with constant kindness and generosity by the islanders, who seemed to be proud and grateful to be able to help strangers, as if that gave them a sense of identity as Tristan Islanders. By 1965 the introduction of the money economy had changed their relations to outsiders, but their own economic and social relationships were still primarily based on personal, selective reciprocity. In addition to the history of the island, this popularly written book discusses the failures of British government officials in the 1960s to remove the islanders from their island homes, and, when that didn't work, to subvert their traditional ideals by forcing them to accept "modern" social values and the materialism of the Western world.

409   Munch, Peter A. "Culture and Superculture in a Displaced Community: Tristan da Cunha." *Ethnology: An International Journal of Cultural and Social Anthropology* 3(October 1964): 369-376.

This article provides a brief history of the people of Tristan da Cunha, where the first settlers in 1817 articulated the utopian ideals of the period: a complete absence of government among them, the communal ownership of property, and absolute equality. These ideals, somewhat modified over the years, became traditions in their culture and they persisted through the trying periods of the Second World War, when the island was garrisoned by the British, and the post-war period when numerous outsiders such as teachers, nurses, administrators, and chaplains were established on the island. The article describes the way the islanders were removed to Great Britain in 1961 when they were threatened by a volcanic eruption, and how they united for the first time in their history for the common purpose of convincing the British government that they wanted to return to their island. Their history demonstrates their commitment to their enduring values: nonviolence, lack of control by individuals over others, and the absence of aggression and self-assertion.

410   Munch, Peter A. "Economic Development and Conflicting Values: A Social Experiment in Tristan da Cunha." *American Anthropologist* 72(December 1970): 1300-1318.

In reviewing the economic history of Tristan da Cunha, the author focuses on the way the changing economy has affected the values of the islanders. A communal structure persisted during the trading days of the 19th century, when the island was an important stopping point for sailing vessels, but values of equality, anarchy, and personal integrity became dominant as the settlement became more isolated and adopted a subsistence economy during the age of steamships. Cooperation, shared ownership of certain resources such as cattle and fruit trees, mutual assistance on many types of projects, and gift giving became vital aspects of their economic and social structure. The introduction of a money economy after World War II, based on the wages from a new fish factory, challenged their traditional economic and social system, but the islanders were able to adapt the demands of contract labor and a money economy to their own values.

411   Munch, Peter A. *Sociology of Tristan da Cunha.* Oslo: Det Norske Videnskaps-Akademi, 1945.

The Tristan Islanders have a strong sense of self-respect and mutual helpfulness. They attach great importance to maintaining their personal dignity; to avoid losing self-control they never drink alcohol, even if offered to them by visitors. They value their independence, economic self-sufficiency, and personal freedom so much that they don't work for pay, though they will freely exchange gifts and services. All men are truly equal on Tristan: no one has authority, superiority, or influence over anyone else, though some people receive more respect, prestige, and rank than others. Their considerate, kindly behavior toward one another justly earns them a reputation as being "one of the most peace-loving people on earth." Occasionally, interpersonal hostility may reach the point where two people will stop talking to each other, but that level of tension never lasts very long. Quarrels are rare and no fights have occurred in living memory. The person who lost his temper in a quarrel would have that scar on his reputation for life, while one who diffuses tense situations with jokes gains general respect.

412   Munch, Peter A. and Charles E. Marske. "Atomism and Social Integration." *Journal of Anthropological Research* 37(Summer 1981): 158-171.

The culture of the Tristan Islanders focuses on kindness, peacefulness, consideration, and respect for the personal integrity of others. It is based on a great deal of cooperation. For instance, they own certain types of property cooperatively, such as cattle and longboats. They also enjoy cooperating on most jobs of any significance: an individual who face tasks larger than routine chores will call on others to help, though for each job he or she is likely to ask a different set of individuals for their assistance. The islanders also give gifts of extra food whenever it is available, such as from successful fishing trips or the slaughter of large animals. All of this cooperative activity is selective, symbolizing the value they place on individual relationships. People select others with whom they wish to have cooperative relationships, either kin or not, and they have many overlapping relationships; thus the peace is preserved since everyone is a friend (has a cooperative, giving relationship) of a friend of everyone else on the island.

Waura

The 200 Waura, Arawak-speaking Brazilian Indians living in the Upper Xingu National Park of Brazil's Mato Grosso, live on fishing and swidden agriculture; they also depend on outside goods such as fishhooks and steel tools. Their continued existence is being threatened by invasions from nearby ranchers and poachers. They are included in this bibliography because articles by Emilienne Ireland describe their peacefulness, in contrast to the peoples around them.

413   Ireland, Emilienne. "Cerebral Savage: The Whiteman as Symbol of Cleverness and Savagery in Waura Myth." In *Rethinking History and Myth: Indigenous South American Perspectives on the Past*, edited by Jonathan D. Hill, 157-173. Urbana: University of Illinois Press, 1988.

The Waura have a highly negative opinion of non-Indian peoples, whom they view as violent, aggressive, lacking in compassion for children, and hesitant to share material wealth with others, all of which contradict their own values. They feel white people and other outsiders are not quite human beings since they display their tempers and are stingy about sharing food. The Waura express their anxiety about relations with non-Indians through their myths, such as one dealing with the measles epidemic 100 years ago that started when outsiders first contacted them: One day a pair of spirits fell from the sky, burning the forest where they landed. They were painted as Indians but were white-skinned monsters with hairy faces and bellies. The neighboring Kustenau tribe took bits of ornaments and hair from the spirits to make fetishes, and their witchcraft became so powerful that they killed everyone in their own tribe. This Waura myth shows that the Kustenau were not exterminated due to outsiders; instead, they all died because of the collapse of their own moral values, which fostered the success of the witchcraft.

414   Ireland, Emilienne. "Neither Warriors nor Victims, the Wauja Peacefully Organize to Defend Their Land." *Cultural Survival Quarterly* 15(1991): 54-60.

In their confrontations with poachers and settlers, the Waura have remained quite peaceful so far. They view the land as the resting place of their ancestors, dwelling place of the spirits, birthplace of their children: sacred to them and to their creative spirits, their beliefs, their life. They reject warfare and violence as morally degrading, in contrast to nearby peoples who maintain warrior images. If they become violent in order to defend their lands, they feel they will cease to be Waura and will live on their own lands as strangers. They used to refer to other Indian peoples who were violent as *muteitsi*, a term of scorn and derision, themselves and other peaceful Indian peoples as *putaka*, while the white men, the most violent of all, they referred to as *kajaipa*. During the 1980s however, they have ceased using the word *muteitsi* derisively; they use it now as a generic word for Indians since they recognize their need for group identification with all of the native peoples. They recognize that they may be forced to become violent to defend their territory.

Yanadi

The economy of the 320,000 Yanadi living in India is based on gathering foods, fishing, and catching small animals such as rats whenever possible, supplemented by working for wages. The government of India decided in 1969 to relocate the Yanadi, and other residents, of the island of Sriharikota, located on the Bay of Bengal at the southern tip of Andhra Pradesh state, because the Indian Space Research Organization decided to build a rocket-launching facility there. The effect of the forced removal and resettlement on the Yanadi has been discussed by several Indian scholars.[22]

415   Agrawal, Binod C., P. C. Gurivi Reddy, and N. Sudhakar Rao. "Determinants of Cultural Adaptation in the Process of Change: A Case of Yanadi." *Man in India* 64(June 1984): 133-142.

The worldview of the Yanadi living on the Indian coastal island of Sriharikota is to live in complete harmony with god, man, and nature. This belief results in a self-reliant lifestyle which fosters equality between the sexes: at the slightest disagreement a couple may break up and form other marriages. Yanadi move about frequently in the forest, living on available work and the ubiquitous fruits and tubers. They gather only as much food as they can eat right in the forest, returning to their huts empty-handed but trusting that they will again find enough the next day. Their lifestyle has changed since 1970 when the island was taken over by the Indian Space Research Organization and they were restricted to two permanent villages. This diminished their traditional living activities, their former individualism, and their relationship with the forest. The crowding has caused problems with pollution, prevented them from food gathering at will in their immediate neighborhoods, and diminished individual privacy and independence. Since they have no group leadership, they do not know how to handle these issues.

416   Raghaviah, V. *The Yanadis*. New Delhi: Bharatiya Adimjati Sevak Sangh, 1962.

The Yanadi are a completely peaceful, nonviolent, honest people who avoid unpleasantness, provocation, drunkenness, and crime. They have no memory of warfare--it does not even figure in their mythology. Although marital relationships are characterized by tenderness, responsiveness, and mildness, Yanadi women are as free as men to shift to another partner when they feel estranged, since being divorced bears no stigma to them. Yanadis have an inferiority complex, displayed by such actions as sitting on the floor of a bus rather than on seats with other Indian passengers. According to the author, their love of peace is an inborn, tribal trait which is ingrained in their culture and is not based on a philosophy of nonresistance, much less cowardice. When the Yanadi is verbally abused, he ignores his abuser; if the verbal attack continues, he responds with a blank look and an artless smile. Only if the attack persists into physical violence does he frown, though still without retaliating. His heart-felt smile, disarming appearance, and defenseless manner, in fact, may contribute to the preservation of Yanadi culture.

417   Reddy, P. C. "The Yanadis: A Criminal Tribe of the Deccan." *Eastern Anthropologist* 1(December 1947): 3-17.

When the Yanadis settled in the plains they lost their ready access to fruits, roots, and other subsistence foods of the forest. Since they were excluded from society by the caste system, they turned to house-breaking and theft--nonviolent crime--as a major source of their livelihood. According to the author, they are almost all poor, illiterate, lazy by nature, and products of broken homes: factors that help prompt them to committing crimes. The Criminal Tribes Act is a necessary means of helping Indian society cope with tribes whose members, like the Yanadis, commit many offenses, but some aspects of the law are unjust. For instance, when a tribe in a district is labeled, under the terms of the act, a "Criminal Tribe," every registered adult male member of the tribe must report to the nearest village police official at 11 pm and again at 3 am every night for an indefinite period. Also, an accused member of a "Criminal Tribe" can be convicted of a crime simply if he is absent from his home at night.

418   Reddy, P. Sudhakara and A. Munirathnam Reddy. "The Displaced Yanadis of Sriharikota Island: A Study of Changing Interactions Between Environment and Culture." *Mankind Quarterly* 27(Summer 1987): 435-445.

When the Yanadis living on Sriharikota Island were resettled on the mainland by the Government of India in 1969, many aspects of their culture were changed. Previously they had subsisted on wage earnings supplemented by gathering of food and other products in the forests; after their move they were forced to live on the men's wages since there was little opportunity for subsistence gathering. Although husbands and wives had cooperated in food gathering, in their new situation the men, as the sole wage earners, gained more authority in the families. Barter between families became irrelevant since wages allow families to purchase necessities from stores. The inability to gather products from the forests on the mainland has undermined their former feasts, ceremonies, and ritualized gift giving. Reliance on shamans for healing has also declined and they now turn to modern medicine for their cures. Their former recreational activities--visiting friends and relatives, playing, dancing--are also in decline due to the lack of resources and time. They have lost their strong attachments to their natural environment in their new mainland villages.

Zapotec

The Zapotec Indian peoples, who numbered about 325,000 in 1988, live in the state of Oaxaca, in southern Mexico. While some speak Spanish, most speak different dialects of their own Zapotec language. The Zapotec in general are not necessarily more peaceful than other indigenous Mexican peoples, but several scholars--most notably Douglas Fry, Carl O'Nell, and John Paddock--have concentrated a lot of research effort on a cluster of Zapotec communities in the Valley of Oaxaca, some of which are exceptionally peaceful in nature. Although some towns in the valley have a "normal" amount of violence, others nearby have strong control systems that effectively preserve their peacefulness. While even the most peaceful town, dubbed "La Paz" by the scholars, which has about 2,000 people, is not totally without violence, it is very nearly so. The works by these researchers provide insights into the formation of enduring patterns of peacefulness and violence in communities that, in almost all other respects, are identical.[23]

419　Beals, Ralph L. "Gifting, Reciprocity, Savings, and Credit in Peasant Oaxaca." *Southwestern Journal of Anthropology* 26(Autumn 1970): 231-241.

　　　Most Zapotec financial needs are still taken care of by traditional gifting and reciprocity relationships, which are both social and economic in nature. "Gifting" is defined as the spontaneous giving of gifts, either goods or services, without any expectation of an equivalent return. Among the Zapotec, the workman in the field is invited to share the meal brought out to another worker by his wife, the little old lady peddler is given tortillas by people who have bought nothing from her, and strangers are given gifts of small objects or fruit while passing through villages. While reciprocity is not part of a gifting relationship, in fact there is frequently an uncalculated return-- a return favor sometime in the future, some of the recipient's time and gossip, good feelings and continuing informal expressions of friendship. On the other hand, reciprocal exchanges

among the Zapotec, referred to as *guelaguetza*, are quite for-
mal--the opposite of gifting. They require a detailed accounting
of the value of the labor and goods so that they can be correctly
balanced out by return gifts of equal value and kind.

420   Fry, Douglas P. "Intercommunity Differences in Aggression
among Zapotec Children." *Child Development* 59(August 1988):
1008-1019.

   Forty-eight children in two Zapotec communities, La Paz and
San Andres (both pseudonyms), were observed to compare the
levels of both real aggression and play aggression; the former
town is quite peaceful while people in the latter are much more
noticeably violent. Research results showed that the children in
the peaceful community were involved in less play aggression
than those of the more violent town; and during real aggressive
incidents, the children of La Paz threatened more than those of
San Andres, who tended to attack without threatening. Results
matched peoples' attitudes in both towns: in La Paz the residents
actively discouraged fighting, both real and play--children are
respectful, good, and responsible in their view; in San Andres
people expected and even condoned fighting among their
children, whom they view as naturally unruly and mischievous.
The two communities have very different patterns of violence
which they pass along from generation to generation--La Paz
children become more restrained in their behavior as they grow
older, in contrast to the children of San Andres who become
more aggressive.

421   Fry, Douglas P. "'Respect for the Rights of Others Is Peace':
Learning Aggression Versus Nonaggression among the
Zapotec." *American Anthropologist* 94(September 1992): 621-
639.

   In one Zapotec town there is a lot of violence: slapping,
punching, wife abuse, jealousy, murders. The inhabitants believe that violence is natural--fighting when drunk is normal, the
escalation of feuds and grudges into violence is acceptable,
killing a rival because of jealousy is understandable. Sometimes
aggressiveness is justified--it's human nature. Children are
raised by adults who indicate that violence is a part of life. By
contrast, in a nearby town which has much less aggressiveness,
where the inhabitants condemn the violence of the other town,
the people hold a consistent view that their community is
peaceful, that no one fights there, that they are cooperative,
never jealous, and respectful of others. Children are raised by

adults who repeat peaceful statements and act peacefully. The author's research explores the differences in the learning of aggression by young people in the differing conditions of the two communities. Environmental differences in the two communities which may have influenced their respective approaches to violence include differing exposures to outsiders, contrasting amounts of economic independence of the women, and varying quantities of land available per family for cultivation.

422   O'Nell, Carl W. "Hostility Management and the Control of Aggression in a Zapotec Community." *Aggressive Behavior* 7(1981): 351-366.

The Zapotec have a value system that approves of cooperation, respect for others, and reciprocity, and that disapproves of the expression of hostility. While they do not have a clear ethic opposing aggression, they do have cultural mechanisms for managing hostility which significantly reduce the seriousness of aggressive incidents. Community councils provide forums for airing hostilities, containing conflicts, and allowing public sentiment to be expressed about threatening incidents. Informal methods of social control are more important, however, such as the redefinition of hostility as an illness, the threat of gossip about people who cannot manage their hostilities, and, most effective of all, the process of denial. People deny any hostility in their social interactions or in their feelings toward others. When hostility does erupt into aggression, they will deny the presence of hostile feelings, which diminishes the significance of the affair, then they will understate and diminish its scope and quickly forget it. This process of denial not only reinforces their ideal--that they behave responsibly and in a cooperative fashion--it also disrupts the possibility of a chain of aggressive events taking place.

423   O'Nell, Carl W. "Nonviolence and Personality Disposition among the Zapotec: Paradox and Enigma." *Journal of Psychological Anthropology* 2(Summer 1979): 301-322.

LaPaz, a nonviolent town in Oaxaca, while not totally free of quarrels, has cultural mechanisms which prevent hostile feelings from erupting into physical violence, a contrast with more violent communities in the immediate area. An important factor in developing nonviolence in LaPaz appears to be the way children are raised. Infants experience total emotional support until the age of three, with ready access to the breast, mild socialization, and relaxed parental attitudes. This pattern of psychological dependency changes abruptly between three and five years of age when they are weaned physically and emotionally from dependence on their parents and are quickly trained to be socially dependent only. Children are socialized to be compliant, cooperative, socially dependent, and emotionally independent without being individualistic. Parents expect their children to learn respect, the highest Zapotec value, which is closely linked to interpersonal social dependency. They also use techniques such as deceit, teasing, and fear to implant social dependency in their children. Social dependency may be a more highly developed trait in LaPaz and other peaceful communities than it is in violent societies.

424   O'Nell, Carl W. "Primary and Secondary Effects of Violence Control among the Nonviolent Zapotec." *Anthropological Quarterly* 59(October 1986): 184-190.

The Zapotec of La Paz have social mechanisms which inhibit the formation of violence and limit its escalation without preventing it entirely. They place high values on respect, a word which they use as their ideal for themselves and their town; on responsibility, which they define as dependence on others and a sensitivity to the expectations of social situations; and on cooperation, which includes avoiding delicate situations in public and doing anything necessary to promote social harmony. They believe the causes of violence include various illnesses: *muina*, a mild indisposition that people feel when they are angry; *coraje*, a more advanced stage of passion where the expression of *muina* has advanced to verbal abuse or blows; and *bilis*, bile, an imbalance in the gall bladder brought on by untreated frustration or abuse. They feel that people need sympathy and treatment, not condemnation and punishment, for these afflictions. Violence control mechanisms include the fear of witchcraft and gossip, a lack of assertiveness, non-confrontational style, withdrawal from difficult situations, and the process of denying anger to prevent situations from becoming disruptive or potentially violent.

425   O'Nell, Carl W. "The Non-Violent Zapotec." In *Societies at Peace: Anthropological Perspectives*, edited by Signe Howell and Roy Willis, 117-132. London: Routledge, 1989.

In the peaceful Zapotec community of La Paz, cooperation, respect and responsibility are unobtrusive, but deeply felt, values. Supplementing those values are cultural defence mechanisms and social control mechanisms that serve to accommodate and lessen violence rather than prevent it completely. The social system of the Zapotec allows and encourages some degree of violence to occur: for instance, folk illnesses that express hostilities, and ritualized drinking that fosters mild violence. The Zapotec process of enculturating their children changes from affectively nurturant to affectively neutral at about three years of age. As children are weaned from emotional to social dependency on their parents, they learn behavior which frustrates hostilities; the frustration of their dependency, paradoxically, produces a psychological feeling of social dependency. These contradictory, ambiguous mechanisms promote a delicate balance between the needs of the self and the group. The Zapotec methods are informal and fragile, however, and they do not appear to withstand social disruptions or rapid changes very effectively.

426 O'Nell, Carl W. and Nancy D. O'Nell. "A Cross-Cultural Comparison of Aggression in Dreams: Zapotecs and Americans." *International Journal of Social Psychiatry* 23 (Spring 1977): 35-41.

An empirical study of aggression in the dreams of Zapotec males and females of all ages allows comparisons with a comparable study of American dreams and may provide information about the makeup of human aggression. The authors found that the significant decrease in aggressiveness in American dreams as people grow older was not matched by the Zapotec, a result, the authors suspect, of an unidentified cultural factor among the latter. Both Americans and Zapotec dream of being victims of aggression more frequently than they do of being aggressors. In both cultures males figure more often in aggressive dreams than females, they tend to have more aggressive dreams than females, and their dreams contain more physical aggression (compared to verbal aggression) than females. Dream aggressions are more often physical for the Zapotec than for Americans. Zapotec aggressive dreams do not vary according to sex or age as much as those of Americans. American dreams of aggressiveness involve familiar people and strangers much more than those of the Zapotec, whose dreams include a lot of aggressiveness from non-humans.

427 Paddock, John. "Studies on Antiviolent and 'Normal' Communities." *Aggressive Behavior* 1 (1975): 217-233.

Research among nearby violent and antiviolent Zapotec

communities allows many conflicting theories about factors which cause violence--such as the presence of urban crowding, ecological conditions, economic circumstances, biological inheritance, boundary disputes, outside influences, and heavy alcohol consumption--to be rejected. The antiviolent communities do differ from the violent ones in significant ways, however: they reject having their children get an education beyond the sixth grade; the young males are noticeable for their lack of emotion exhibited at important events such as major fiestas; discipline of young children is consistent and minimal, and good behavior is clearly expected; young children are taught to ignore aggression by other children or run away from it; parental correction of misbehavior is mostly done through verbal comments or occasionally a single spanking; the child is expected to appeal to authority figures such as parents in case of conflict. In the towns with a lot of violence, discipline may be more arbitrary, adults may show amusement when children misbehave or act violently, they may threaten children more, and they show noticeable approval of the children's personal achievements.

428   Paddock, John. "Values in an Antiviolent Community." *Humanitas* 12(May 1976): 183-194.

One Zapotec town has rarely experienced homicide or other major violence, despite having as much poverty, drunkenness, land shortage, and inequality as the other towns in the area. There are a lot of disputes, insults, personal quarrels, gossip, and instances of cheating in the town, and the residents are aggressively competitive in their business dealings, which concentrate wealth and power in the hands of a few people. But they are strongly opposed to actual physical conflict, and whenever a fight threatens to erupt someone always intervenes. In fact, it is just as intolerable to provoke violence as it is to create it: machismo is virtually absent in this town. During the speeches that end the quasi-judicial proceedings set up to settle disputes, community officials frequently stress the threats which quarrels pose to the community. Since violent crimes would bring in outside officials unsympathetic to the community, the antiviolence may be a means of achieving independence from such outside authority. The people are strongly conscious of the fact that their community is different from others in its peacefulness.

Zuni

The Zuni Indian reservation is located at the western edge of New Mexico on the western side of the Continental Divide. The basis of the Zuni economy consists of arts and crafts production, especially work with silver, raising livestock, work for wages, and agricultural production. Their traditional social structure was based on households dominated by women and a system of clans and priesthoods that provided the overall control of their society; political and social changes have modified these institutions over the past 50 years. As of February 1988, 8,299 Zunis lived on the reservation, though many also lived away from it. Several scholars have observed and discussed the Zuni antipathy to overt violence; however, vicious gossip (and sometimes physical violence) is also an aspect of pueblo life.[24]

429 Benedict, Ruth. *Patterns of Culture*. Boston: Houghton Mifflin, 1959.

As part of her analysis of the patterns of human culture, Benedict has a chapter describing the peaceful characteristics of the Zuni. An important aspect of Zuni culture is that they shun authority, leadership, and individual success--they strongly censor anyone who stands out above his peers. Necessary leadership positions in the kiva are forced on people by the others, and the leaders do not really exercise authority in the Western sense of the word. The Zuni belief focuses on their oneness with the universe rather than a dualistic view of existence: life and death are not opposed, but are rather part of the same creation. Their beliefs emphasize successful, pleasant relations with other people, including spouses, and since they do not place any particular emphasis on sex, they have no sense of guilt or sin. They do not place a high value on property, and they resolve conflicts in totally nonviolent ways.

430 Ferguson, T. J. and Wilfred Eriacho. "Ahayu:da: Zuni War Gods." *Native Peoples* 4(Fall 1990): 6-12.

In early times, according to Zuni mythology, before they were able to settle in their present community, they moved about, encountering and frequently fighting hostile peoples. During one period of warfare they needed new war chiefs so the Sun Father created Uyuyewi, Elder Brother, and Ma'a'sewi, Younger Brother, as Ahayu:da, or War Gods. These gods helped the Zuni people overcome their obstacles and settle in their present community, and they continue to protect them today. Although the wooden images of these gods are created out of inanimate objects by the religious leaders, the Zuni use vocabulary which describes them in human terms. Kept safely in proper Zuni shrines, with constant prayers and blessings by the religious leaders, they believe the powers of the gods are channeled into harmonious, productive, fertile, orderly ends, though the ones that have been stolen from them have caused a vast amount of destruction on earth. Since 1978 Zuni leaders have recovered 38 of their sacred War Gods from private collectors and museums, who owned and displayed them solely as valuable art objects and interesting pieces representing Pueblo culture.

431   Goldfrank, Esther S. "Socialization, Personality, and the Structure of Pueblo Society (with Particular Reference to Hopi and Zuni)." *American Anthropologist* 47(October/December 1945): 516-539.

While the Zuni deplore ambition, initiative, and the desire to be a leader, they admire generosity, a disposition to yield to others, emotional reserve, and personal restraint. In order to socialize their children in these characteristics, they treat infants with utmost permissiveness for their first few years: parents rarely punish, though they may scold and threaten. The infant gets hints of the adult world when, at times, tasty food morsels are suddenly withdrawn from their lips, teaching it that rewards are dependent on social conformity. When children reach three or four the socializing changes. In order to develop a fear of supernatural controls over human behavior, men dressed up as frightening gods enter the pueblo to interrogate little children. In one account, the masked demon thrust his knife menacingly at a three-year old boy while interrogating him, then turned on a girl of four. The old woman who had been sheltering her made her face the tormenter and answer his questions as well. The children become quite docile and conforming with this sort of upbringing.

432   Goldman, Irving. "The Zuni Indians of New Mexico." In *Cooperation and Competition among Primitive Peoples*, edited by Margaret Mead, 313-353. New York: McGraw-Hill, 1937.

The Zuni have a completely nonviolent, peaceful society according to this essay, in which the people gain great respect for sharing their food and other material goods. Aspects of their culture which the author examined include the Zuni cooperative system of labor; the absence of quarreling in their homes, which are completely controlled by the women; the fact that they place little value on material goods and attach no prestige to personal wealth; the absence of competition; and the way children are raised in a permissive environment, where shame is the major form of social control rather than scolding or punishment. Goldman does describe the Zuni tendency to form hostile political factions over various issues, and their habits of back-biting and malicious gossip about their neighbors. He speculates that this contradiction to their otherwise peaceful culture may be due to their chief form of social control--shame--which prompts people to avoid the criticism of others but which also fosters hypercritical attitudes toward the flaws of neighbors.

433   Li, An-che. "Zuni: Some Observations and Queries." *American Anthropologist* 39(Jan-March 1937): 62-76.

While the Zuni do not appear to seek to be leaders, those who naturally have ability will not shun leadership and those who do not will avoid it, since they will not want to look ridiculous. Adults all cooperate in rearing children; they will all correct any child's misbehavior, if necessary, only by a frown or brief gesture. Parents are not openly demonstrative toward children, who join the company of other children as soon as they can and only come back to their parents for food; the children, as a result, do not have the need to show off. When children do need to be reprimanded, it is done deliberately, without fuss. Husband and wife relations are based on the fact that the woman is not in any way ruled by the man. The man marries and moves into the woman's, or her mother's, home, and has to adjust to being a subordinate there. Unmarried brothers, sisters, and of course the woman's parents, all dominate, and the husband has to conceal his own desires in order to fit in with the family.

434   Osborne, A. Barry. "Insiders and Outsiders: Cultural Membership and the Micropolitics of Education among the Zuni." *Anthropology and Education Quarterly* 20(September 1989): 196-215.

An ethnographic study of cultural differences in Zuni primary schools revealed a variety of contrasts and power relationships between the Zuni and the Anglo teachers, such as the way the former didn't publicly reprimand the children, whom they encouraged to be more independent. The Zuni teachers sug-gested that the children would benefit from a curriculum that includes some transitional classrooms, but the Anglo teachers, the majority, closed ranks in opposition to any form of "special" treatment. A compromise was reached but tensions persisted. Meanwhile, if Anglos start asking questions about their culture, the Zuni teachers and aides begin conversing in their own language, pointedly excluding the Anglos present. The new Zuni school board which took office in 1980 made some significant changes in school practices which reflect their cultural sensitivities, but the Anglo teachers, misunderstanding their subtle importance, discounted them as minor. The Zuni have successfully protected their cultural heritage in these struggles with the outsiders; the Anglos might, in fact, benefit from greater exposure to their values, such as their peaceful relationship with the earth.

435   Pandey, Triloki Nath. "Images of Power in a Southwestern Pueblo." In *The Anthropology of Power: Ethnographic Studies from Asia, Oceania, and the New World*, edited by Raymond D. Fogelson and Richard N. Adams, 195-215. New York: Academic Press, 1977.

Traditionally, the Zuni were ruled by a theocracy which imposed a harmonious order fusing church and state into one society. Myth and ritual performance emphasized the importance of cooperation and forbade arrogance or strong emotions. However, frequent factional conflicts during the 20th century have been caused by uncertainties in the relative powers of the elected governor, the traditional priests, and U.S. government officials. The traditional Zuni priests--consisting of the sun priest, the priests of the four cardinal directions, and the bow priests--formerly selected qualified people to serve as officials, but after the Indian Reorganization Act of 1934 the governors were elected by popular vote. While there is ample historic record of quarreling among the priests, the major factional split in the pueblo developed early in the century between Catholic and Protestant groups. Since then internal conflicts have been exacerbated by the religious factions: the Zuni priests who supported one persuasion or the other, activist non-Indian priests, governors on one side or the other, and U.S. government officials who have taken sides in the different disputes.

436   Pandey, Triloki Nath. "Tribal Council Elections in a Southwestern Pueblo." *Ethnology: An International Journal of Cultural and Social Anthropology* 7(January 1968): 71-85.

Politics in Zuni have changed considerably during the past 60 years. Formerly the theocracy controlled the political system through the manipulations of the bow priests, but the power of the religious leaders has eroded considerably in favor of popular, democratic elections. Previously, everyone was reluctant to hold political office, and capable people were sought and pressed into service by the priests; now, candidates for leadership positions actively campaign for office. The election of 1963 for tribal leadership positions was conducted by a standing vote, but the election of 1965 was conducted by secret ballot, a change which produced much greater participation by pueblo members and strengthened the move toward democracy. While the candidates were supported by different factions, the political process demonstrated that the Zunis value leaders who are mature, have fluency in English, and are able to represent their interests effectively in dealings with the English-speaking Americans.

437   Smith, Watson and John M. Roberts. *Zuni Law: A Field of Values*. Cambridge, MA: Peabody Museum of American Archaeology and Ethnology, Harvard University, 1954.

Physical violence is rare in Zuni society, and when it does occur it is usually the result of alcohol consumption. Incidents were traditionally settled privately; the concept of "crime" is a recently introduced legalistic concept not in their language. The authors describe 81 cases brought before the Zuni Council since the late 19th century, which included two murders, a few rapes, and other types of violence. Personal animosities among the Zuni frequently resulted in verbal assaults such as arguments and slander. Council members often meet with the parties to a conflict before the trial begins to see if they can encourage a resolution, and if the hearing is necessary the judge seeks to resolve the matter through conciliation. After the parties have presented their arguments and the Council has announced its decision, the judge warns the guilty person that the penalty will be more severe the next time. He then delivers a lecture on the importance of friendly relations, harmony and good conduct. Most offenses are penalized by payments of property rather than corporal punishment; the Zuni believe that punishment is up to the gods.

438   Whiting, John W. M., et al. "The Learning of Values." In *People of Rimrock: A Study of Values in Five Cultures*, edited by Evon Z. Vogt and Ethel M. Albert, 83-125. Cambridge, MA:

Harvard University Press, 1967.

The Zuni teach their children nonaggressive values much more than the Mormons or Texans who live in nearby communities of western New Mexico. The Texan parents are quite tolerant of fighting among their children, intervening only if they get too carried away, and Mormon parents are nearly as permissive. In contrast, the Zuni actively discourage fighting among children. They explain to them the harm that comes to a family if relatives don't help one another, though if reasoning with the children doesn't work the parents may resort to physical punishment to try to make them stop fighting. They may even bring in a masked god--a bogeyman--who will threaten the children about their fighting. The authors believe that the Zuni began to promote harmony and aggression control about 1300 AD when they changed from nuclear housing units to compact, multi-family pueblos. Similarly, they argue, the Anglos adopted values such as independence, individualism, and aggressiveness when their ancestors moved to America from England and changed from the extended family units common in Elizabethan times to the nuclear family pattern of the frontier.

NOTES TO THE BIBLIOGRAPHY

1. The sources for the information found in each section introduction are the works cited in that section. When other works have been consulted, they will be cited.

2. *Yearbook of American and Canadian Churches, 1992* (Nashville: Abingdon Press, 1992); *The Brethren Encyclopedia*, edited by Donald F. Durnbaugh (Philadelphia: The Brethren Encyclopedia, Inc., 1983); Melton, J. Gordon. *The Encyclopedia of American Religions*, 3d edition (Detroit: Gale Research, 1989).

3. Mealing, F. Mark. "Doukhobors." In *Encyclopedia of World Cultures, Volume I, North America*, edited by Timothy O'Leary and David Levinson (Boston: G. K. Hall, 1991).

4. Melton, J. Gordon. *The Encyclopedia of American Religions*, 3d edition (Detroit: Gale Research, 1989); *Yearbook of American and Canadian Churches, 1992* (Nashville: Abingdon Press, 1992).

5. Banks, Marcus. "Jain." In *Encyclopedia of World Cultures, Volume III, South Asia*, edited by Paul Hockings (Boston: G. K. Hall, 1992).

6. *Illustrated Encyclopedia of Mankind, Volume 10* (New York: Marshall Cavendish, 1990).

7. DiMaggio, Jay. "Lepcha." In *Encyclopedia of World Cultures, Volume III, South Asia*, edited by Paul Hockings (Boston: G. K. Hall, 1992).

8. Morris, Brian. "Hill Pandaram." In *Encyclopedia of World Cultures, Volume III, South Asia*, edited by Paul Hockings (Boston: G. K. Hall, 1992).

9. *Illustrated Encyclopedia of Mankind, Volume 13* (New York: Marshall Cavendish, 1990); Matthews, Tracie. "A Reserve for Zaire's Ituri Forest," *Cultural Survival Quarterly* 17 (Spring 1993): 5-6.

10. *Mennonite Yearbook and Directory, 1990-91* (Scottdale, PA: Mennonite Publishing House, 1990); *The Mennonite Encyclopedia* (Hillsboro, KS: Mennonite Brethren Publishing House, 1955-1959).

11. Reid, Gerald F. "Montagnais-Naskapi." In *Encyclopedia of World Cultures, Volume I, North America*, edited by Timothy O'Leary and David Levinson (Boston: G. K. Hall, 1991).

12. Melton, J. Gordon. *The Encyclopedia of American Religions*, 3d edition (Detroit: Gale Research, 1989).

13. India. Office of the Registrar General. *Census of India, 1981*. (Delhi: Controller of Publications, 1983).

14. Melton, J. Gordon. *The Encyclopedia of American Religions*, 3d edition (Detroit: Gale Research, 1989).

15. "United Kingdom (Northern Ireland)." In *The Europa Yearbook, 1992* (London: Europa Publications, 1992); Great Britain. Central Statistical Office. *Annual Abstract of Statistics, 1992* (London: HMSO, 1992).

16. Lee, Richard Borshay. *The !Kung San: Men, Women, and Work in a Foraging Society* (Cambridge: Cambridge University Press, 1979) [147].

17. *Encyclopedia of World Cultures, Volume I, North America*, edited by Timothy O'Leary and David Levinson (Boston: G. K. Hall, 1991).

18. Steinbring, Jack H. "Saulteaux of Lake Winnipeg." In *Handbook of North American Indians, Volume 6, Subarctic* (Washington: Smithsonian Institution, 1981).

19. Dentan, Robert Knox. "Senoi." In *Encyclopedia of World Cultures, Volume V, East and Southeast Asia*, edited by Paul Hockings (Boston: G.K. Hall, 1993).

20. *The Statesman's Year-Book: Statistical and Historical Annual of the States of the World for the Year 1992-1993* (New York: St. Martin's, 1992).

21. "British Dependent Territories: St. Helena and Dependencies." In *The Europa Yearbook, 1992* (London: Europa Publications, 1992).

22. India. Office of the Registrar General. *Census of India, 1981*. (Delhi: Controller of Publications, 1983).

23. *Illustrated Encyclopedia of Mankind, Volume 15* (New York: Marshall Cavendish, 1990).

24. Frisbie, Theodore R. "Zuni." In *Encyclopedia of World Cultures, Volume I, North America*, edited by Timothy O'Leary and David Levinson (Boston: G. K. Hall, 1991).

INDEX

Numbers refer to entries rather than pages.

Quakers 308, 319
War and warfare
  Brethren 44
  Fipa 60
  Fore 61, 62, 65
  Ifaluk 78
  Jains 115
  !Kung 138
  Mennonites 188, 193, 200, 201,
    203, 204, 216, 228, 229, 236
  Moravians 246, 250
  Quakers 283, 297, 298, 308,
    312, 313, 322, 324, 325, 328,
    332, 333-336, 339
  Semai 381
  Zuni 430
  See also specific wars
War bonds 189, 219, 227
War Department, U.S. 42, 205
War Quakers 327
Ward, Barbara E. 389-392
Ward, Colleen A. 134
Warman, Saskatchewan 184
Warriors 61, 115, 116, 297, 336
Washington, George 218
Washington County, MD 218
Water-wheels 259, 261
Waura 413, 414
*Wayward Servants: The Two Worlds
  of the African Pygmies* 178
Wealth 313, 328
Weaning 92, 103, 423
Weapons, lack of 163
Weaver, J. Denny 239
Weber, Max 316
Weddle, Meredith Baldwin 334
Weinlick, John R. 251
Welfare support 105, 266
Wellenkamp, Jane C. 401-403
Wellenreuther, Hermann 335
West Branch, IA 296
Western Yearly Meeting 318
Westmoreland County, PA 295
White, Geoffrey 83

Whiting, John W. M. 438
Wichimai, Santus 78
Wiessner, Polly 157, 359
Wikan, Unni 27-30
Williams, Dorothy M. 336
Williams, Roger 339
Willis, Roy G. 1, 23, 48, 53, 56-60,
  280, 342, 377, 425
Wilson, E. Raymond 337
Wilson, Woodrow 204, 230, 338
Winkler, Eike-Meinrad 127
Witchcraft 108, 350, 413, 424
Witchcraft, fear of 30, 275
Withdrawal 396
Witte, William D. S. 338
Wolphat (Ifaluk god) 93
Woman the Gatherer 173
Womb 169
Women's rights 283
Women's roles 24, 58, 146, 196, 421
Women's status 122, 128, 146, 160,
  165
Woodburn, James 34, 45, 257, 273
Woodcock, George 55
Woodhouse, H. C. 360
Woolman, John 313, 330
Work 77, 266, 317, 365
World government 338
World War I
  Anabaptists 15
  Brethren 41, 42, 44
  Hutterites 75, 76
  Mennonites 192, 197, 199, 202-
    205, 209, 210, 219-221, 223,
    229, 230, 231, 236, 237
  Quakers 287, 307, 310, 338
World War II
  Brethren 44
  Hutterites 74
  Mennonites 179, 195, 201, 208,
    213-215, 219, 221, 223, 235,
    237
  Quakers 284, 296
Worrall, Arthur J. 339

ABOUT THE AUTHOR

BRUCE D. BONTA is a general reference librarian at the Pennsylvania State University Libraries who specializes in history and area studies.

He began his career at the Library of Congress in 1963 shortly before President Kennedy was killed. Three years later he retreated from Washington, D.C., to the serenity of rural Maine and the Colby College Library, but he moved on to Penn State in 1971 where he settled with his family on a peaceful, forested mountaintop.

He has served on various American Library Association committees and written articles on subjects such as reference service and CD-ROMs. He wrote several accounts of his experience in 1985 as an exchange librarian in Lima, Peru.

In the mid-1980s he became active in the International Federation of Library Associations and Institutions--his means of building peaceful international relations--and for two years he chaired the Section of Social Science Libraries of IFLA. He edited, with assistance from James G. Neal, *The Role of the American Academic Library in International Programs* (1992).